Britain

A Short History

Britain

A Short History

T.A. JENKINS

ONEWORLD

OXFORD

BRITAIN: A SHORT HISTORY

Oneworld Publications
(Sales and Editorial)
185 Banbury Road
Oxford OX2 7AR
England
http://www.oneworld-publications.com

ISBN 1–85168–266–X

Cover design by Design Deluxe
Typeset by LaserScript, Mitcham, UK
Printed and bound in Great Britain by Creative Print and Design

Cover photographs: City of London from Waterloo Bridge,
© Spectrum Colour Library.
Wiltshire, Stonehenge, © Pictures Colour Library.
Picture research by Image Select International.

Contents

Acknowledgements

I am very grateful to Dr Derek Plumb, who volunteered to read the whole of this work in draft form, to my colleague Dr Margaret Escott for offering advice on various points, and to an anonymous reader for some helpful comments. I would also like to thank the History of Parliament Trust for allowing the use of its computer facilities to type this book, and Great Eastern Railways for providing the conditions in which some of it was written.

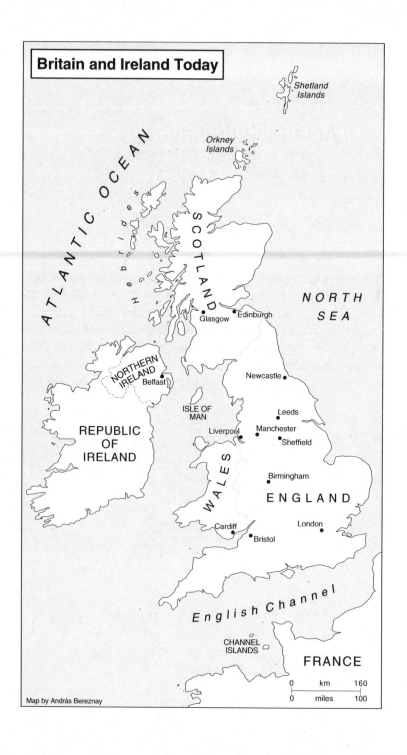

Britain and Ireland Today

Shetland
Islands

Orkney
Islands

ATLANTIC OCEAN

Hebrides

SCOTLAND

Glasgow Edinburgh

NORTH
SEA

NORTHERN
IRELAND

Belfast

Newcastle

ISLE OF
MAN

REPUBLIC
OF
IRELAND

Liverpool Manchester

Leeds

Sheffield

WALES

Birmingham

ENGLAND

Cardiff

London

Bristol

English Channel

CHANNEL
ISLANDS

FRANCE

| 0 | km | 160 |
| 0 | miles | 100 |

Map by András Bereznay

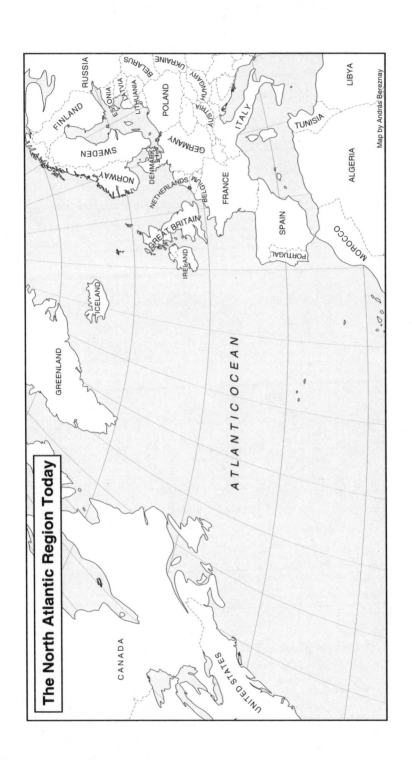

The North Atlantic Region Today

Map by András Bereznay

Introduction

The island nation of Great Britain has an exceptionally rich and fascinating history to relate. It embraces three distinct groups of people – the English, the Welsh and the Scots – with long histories of their own prior to their incorporation into a unified State. In the course of its near three-hundred-year existence, Britain has been transformed by the experience of industrialisation, which made it the first modern 'industrial nation' and, for a time in the nineteenth century, the 'workshop of the world'. It evolved a system of parliamentary government that was almost unique in the eighteenth century, and continues to enjoy a reputation for political stability and to stand out as a champion of Liberal values. It became the heart of the greatest empire of the modern era, covering one-fifth of the world's land surface in the early 1900s, and after its demise the links forged with peoples all over the globe still serve as powerful transmitters of the nation's culture and language. Britain also played a key role in the two world wars of the twentieth century, with profound consequences both for itself and for the rest of the world.

In view of Britain's remarkable past, readers may be surprised to find so many doubts currently being expressed about its future survival. The question of national identity has increasingly engaged the attention of British historians in recent years, precisely because it no longer seems possible to take for granted the existence of a clearly defined and widely shared sense of 'Britishness' among the inhabitants of this island. Since 1945, confidence in the country's ability to perform effectively on an international level, as a first-rate

1

economic and military power, has gradually drained away, and this has produced a corresponding loss of pride in British political institutions and cultural values. Fears of national debilitation and decay continue to grow, as sovereignty is surrendered to supra-national bodies including the European Union, while the spread of secessionist sentiment in Wales and Scotland threatens the internal cohesion of the British population. Only when the nation's future is challenged in such ways do people begin to ask fundamental questions about how it came into being in the first place, and how it has managed to survive for so long.

Examining the phenomenon of national identity is no straightforward matter, however, and some preliminary discussion is required at this point in order to clarify the assumptions underpinning this book. With a moment's thought, it ought to be apparent that an individual person is in fact a compound of many identities, which will vary in their relative importance according to context and personal temperament. Besides their needs and interests as individuals, most people belong to family units of one kind or another, and part of their identity is created by the ways in which they fit into that environment. For instance, they may be the eldest or youngest child, or an only child, and in mid-life they may find themselves in the position of being both parents and children simultaneously. At the same time, an individual's sense of self is partly shaped by an emotional attachment to the neighbourhood in which they live, and particularly where they grew up (perhaps a street, or just part of a street), and there may be rivalry and even hostility towards those residing in other neighbourhoods. On the other hand, all of those neighbourhoods may merge together, in a different context, as part of a district of a town or city, and this can find expression through loyalty to a school or support for a football team. Yet the whole population of a town may identify with one another when brought into contact with inhabitants from other towns (say, Manchester and Liver-pool). Even this distinction can be subsumed into a proud identification with the county in which all are located, in contrast to another county (Lancashire and Yorkshire being an obvious example), and in its turn county rivalries may be over-ridden by allegiance to a regional identity (North versus South). Most people will also think of themselves as English or Welsh or Scottish, as well as belonging to a greater British whole. All sorts of other identities have the potential to play a part in people's awareness of themselves and the way they connect with their fellow humans: whether it be common work experiences, shared leisure interests, affiliation to a particular religious denomination or ethnic origin. Looked at from this perspective, national identity must co-exist with a multitude of other social identities, and, depending on the precise circumstances, it is not always the most relevant or influential. Few people are likely to repudiate their national identity entirely, but this does not mean that it is necessarily uppermost in their minds every day.

Similarly, we need to consider the implication that 'class' identity, to which historians have often attached paramount significance, is itself just another possible form of social identity, and that it is likely to fluctuate in intensity according to time, place and circumstance. Indeed, one of the reasons for historians' heightened awareness of the importance of alternative identities is their loss of faith in 'class conflict' as the great dynamic force in human history. This development can be attributed to the collapse of Communism in Eastern Europe during the 1980s, and the wider discrediting of Marxist-inspired philosophies and methodologies at around the same time, which have produced something of an identity crisis among social historians themselves. The essential point to establish here is that most people, at any time in the past, probably had a fairly clear idea of where they stood in the social hierarchy, but it did not automatically follow that their actions were primarily determined by that belief. It is perfectly possible to possess a sense of class identity, among many other identities, without this inevitably being translated into forms of social or political antagonism towards other perceived classes. This observation seems especially pertinent in the case of a country whose people are usually considered to be obsessively status-conscious, and which is equally renowned for its relative political stability. As this book will seek to show, the organised expression of 'class' identities within the political system is largely a product of the late nineteenth and twentieth centuries, and even then it has seldom, if ever, operated in a very systematic fashion.

The difficulty at the present time is that an attempt to produce a general account of British history, encompassing all of the co-existing social identities mentioned above, will merely result in an incoherent and bewildering mass of local and personal particularisms. Many historians have therefore come to despair of the possibility of writing such a thing as the history of a nation. Yet the fact remains that Britain has an unusually clear objective existence: it is, after all, a single geographical unit, an island nation, and the consequent physical isolation has given its people an acute perception of the boundaries between themselves and others. The approach adopted in this book is to concentrate on those areas where a sense of common nationhood has been most clearly exhibited: namely, politics – the struggle for control of national institutions of government, and to regulate the relations between social groups working within national structures – and the attempts to define 'Britishness' by reference to other nations and peoples, which have sometimes led to military conflict and imperial expansion. Rather than writing a detailed narrative of events, the aim is to suggest connections between developments at the political level and various economic, social and cultural trends. Each chapter is designed to convey a sense of chronological progress, but at the same time it is organised around broad conceptual themes that will hopefully illuminate aspects of the nation's life. If this book at least succeeds in demonstrating the continued validity of the British nation as a subject for historical inquiry, it will have served a useful purpose.

Note: Ireland is the subject of a separate volume in this series and is therefore not dealt with here, except where it directly impinged upon events in Britain.

ONE

The Making of Great Britain

INTRODUCTION

Great Britain, as a single political entity, dates from 1 May 1707, when the Kingdoms of England and Scotland were formally combined by the Act of Union. This marked a new stage in the complex relationship between two nations, each having centuries of tradition behind it and a powerful sense of separate identity from the other. It is indicative of the balance of power in 1707, however, that Scotland's Parliament was the one to be dissolved, and thereafter Scottish representatives attended the Parliament in London instead. Wales, the other constituent part of Britain, had long before been absorbed into the English political system. For these reasons, it seems appropriate to begin this account of the creation of the British State by examining how England, clearly the dominant partner, evolved its own political structures and national culture, before considering why the English found it necessary to consolidate their links, first with the Welsh and later with the Scots. It must be emphasised that the purpose of this chapter is not simply to trace an 'inevitable' process of English expansion, culminating in the unification of all the peoples of the island of Britain, but to identify certain common historical threads that were, as it happened, woven together into a durable fabric.

THE KINGDOM OF ENGLAND

Between the first and the fifth centuries AD the southern portion of the island known to us as Britain formed an outlying province of the Roman Empire. Rome's authority over this remote corner of its vast dominions was seldom secure for long, though, and from the third century onwards the southern and eastern coasts of Britain were subjected to piratical raids by Germanic peoples from the northern seaboard of Europe, whom the Romans referred to by the generic name 'Saxons'. Early in the fifth century, Roman control finally collapsed, and the next two hundred years saw the gradual conquest and settlement of southern Britain by these Saxons. The migrants either subjugated or displaced westwards, into modern-day Cornwall, Wales and Cumbria, the Celtic 'Britons' who had occupied the land before and during the period of Roman rule. Among the Saxon settlers was a group who called themselves the *Engle* (or Angli to Roman writers), and for reasons that are obscure this particular name came to be used, first to describe the whole of the Saxon peoples and their language – English ('Englisc') – and, much later still, the geographical area they controlled – England ('Englaland'). From an initial cluster of small kingdoms, some of which later gave their names to counties such as Kent, Essex and Sussex, three powerful units emerged: Northumbria, Mercia and Wessex, and by the ninth century the latter had established itself as the dominant military force. Christianity, which reached England at the end of the sixth century, was firmly entrenched as the official religion of the English peoples by the time of Wessex's supremacy.[1]

While the royal house of Wessex eventually provided the first rulers of what can meaningfully be described as the 'Kingdom of England', this process was complicated by the appearance of new settlers originating from Scandinavia. During the course of the ninth century, the English peoples faced attacks of increasing intensity from Danish and Norwegian Vikings, who over-ran much of Northumbria and Mercia and came close to destroying Wessex. In the event, Alfred of Wessex (reigned 871–99) and his son Edward the Elder (reigned 899–924) retrieved their kingdom's position and steadily asserted their military power over the Viking settlers too, converting them to Christianity. Consequently,

Aethelstan (reigned 924–39) was described by contemporaries, with only slight exaggeration, as 'King of the English', and Edgar (reigned 959–75) further consolidated his control. Towards the end of his reign, in 973, Edgar underwent an elaborate coronation ceremony at Bath, where he was anointed and crowned by Archbishop Dunstan of Canterbury, and from this point a continuous history of the English coronation service can be traced. But the 'English' people whom Edgar claimed to govern were really an amalgam of two great waves of settlers, the Saxons and the Vikings, who had come from different places at different times and spoke different languages.

Dramatic changes in the ruling dynasty were a prominent feature of eleventh-century England. Renewed Viking attacks during the reign of Aethelred II ('the Unready') resulted in the Danish Prince, Cnut, securing the succession to the English throne in 1016. The English royal line did reappear in the person of Edward the Confessor (reigned 1042–66), but after his death the Crown was seized by William, Duke of Normandy ('the Conqueror'), the victor at the Battle of Hastings in October 1066.[2] Despite these political fluctuations, however, an underlying continuity is apparent in the structure of English government, as successive monarchs built on the work of their predecessors rather than demolishing the institutions they found in place. Cnut, for instance, consciously modelled his kingship on that of Edgar. After the Norman Conquest of 1066, as before, the Great Council brought together the most influential men in the land, lay and clerical, to consult with the King on important matters of policy and issue laws. Subsequent developments in the bureaucratic machinery meant that, by the early 1100s, the Exchequer had been established to audit the royal revenues from taxation. At the local level, the division of all except the northern part of England into shires, or counties, had been accomplished by the tenth century, and in each county the king's representative, the Sheriff, was responsible for collecting taxes and presiding over the shire court, where legal suits were heard. Later, in the twelfth century, judges appointed by the King were sent round the country to hear criminal cases in what came to be known as the Assize Courts. In the long term, then, there evolved in England a durable system for the administration of royal government and justice, which was characterised by a greater degree of centralised control than could be found elsewhere in Europe.[3]

If the Norman Conquest did nothing to retard the political development of the English Kingdom, it erected a major obstacle to the creation of a sense of cultural unity among the country's inhabitants. Whereas the King and most of his noblemen were French speakers, and still had considerable territorial possessions in France, the people over whom they ruled spoke a variety of English dialects and possibly, in some areas, the last vestiges of Danish and Norse. Only over the course of several generations were the English and Norman cultures assimilated, with inter-marriage probably playing a crucial part. The fact that during the reign of John (1199–1216) most of the French lands were lost may also have encouraged the King and nobility to identify more closely with their English power base. One telling sign of the intermixing of cultures that gradually took place is the increasing difficulty, by the thirteenth century, in ascertaining a person's origin from their Christian name: Saxon names like Alfred and Edward survived – Henry III, in 1239, even named his eldest son Edward – but Norman imports such as William, Robert and Geoffrey were common at all levels of society.

The presence of a formidable external foe did much to foster a sense of English national identity in opposition to it. English monarchs continued to dispute with their French counterparts over territorial claims in France, and this provoked a series of conflicts between 1337 and 1453 collectively known as the 'hundred years' war'. Ultimately, England's ambitions across the channel were thwarted, but not before some of the greatest victories in the nation's military history were achieved: Crécy (1346), Poitiers (1356) and Agincourt (1415). Moreover, such rivalry was no longer simply of a dynastic nature, for it aroused strong anti-French prejudices among the English people, becoming an expression of national consciousness. Edward III (reigned 1327–77), one of the more successful warrior Kings, was notable for the way he associated himself with the legend of King Arthur and the Knights of the Round Table, inspiring pride in the greatness of England's past and cloaking the monarchy in the virtue and mystique of the chivalric ideal.[4] It was also during this reign that St George was adopted as the nation's patron saint.

National sentiment was further manifested in the widespread adoption of English as the official language, in place of French. From 1362, for example, proceedings in the law courts were conducted in English; during the reign of Henry IV (1399–1413) English was spoken at the royal court, and Henry V (1413–22) was the first King to write in English. The language referred to here was a hybrid of Saxon English and Norman French, which, by the end of the fourteenth century, had evolved into a form that is just about recognisable to modern readers. In Geoffrey Chaucer (c. 1339–1400), England produced an author of exceptional dramatic skill whose works, most famously the incomplete *Canterbury Tales*, enhanced the prestige of the language in which he practised his art. Ballads, for singing, were also being composed in English by Chaucer's time, and the fifteenth century witnessed a burgeoning literature on political, historical, philosophical and theological subjects. One such work was Thomas Malory's English adaptation of the Arthurian legends, published in 1469, which served to elevate that fabled monarch to the status of a national folk hero.

The notion of an English monarchy and people bound together by a sense of common destiny was powerfully reinforced by the Reformation in the sixteenth century. Until the 1530s, England was a part of Christendom, meaning that the Church was subject to the authority of the Pope in Rome. But Henry VIII (reigned 1509–47), largely for personal reasons connected with his desire to divorce Katherine of Aragon and marry Anne Boleyn, broke with Rome and made himself the Supreme Head of the Church in England. English Kings, who had previously been addressed as 'your Grace', now became 'your Majesty', reflecting their claim to be exalted personages with no superior on earth, and subject only to God. Henry astutely exploited the violent antipathy towards foreigners which was by now a notorious facet of the English 'national character', in order to bolster his position in his dispute with the Pope and the other great Catholic powers in Europe, France and Spain. Like Edward III, he invoked the spirit of the Arthurian legends to retain the affection and respect of his subjects. The Reformation thus became a declaration of English national independence, and over the next few decades the English people embraced a Protestant theology which emphasised the right of each individual to interpret the scriptures – the only authentic voice of God – without interference from a humanly-appointed Pope.[5] As part of this process of conversion to Protestantism, an officially sanctioned English translation of the Bible was prepared by Miles Coverdale in 1535.

However, the Reformation was not a single event occurring in the 1530s. Following the premature death of Henry's only son, Edward VI (reigned 1547–53), the throne passed to Mary I, the daughter from Henry's first marriage, who had been brought up as a strict Catholic. She proceeded to launch a counter-Reformation, restoring England's links with Rome, and during her brief reign some three hundred Protestants, one-third of them clergymen, were burned as heretics. This helped to engender a ferocious hatred of Catholicism in the English mind, which equated that religion with tyranny and persecution. On Mary's death in 1558 she was succeeded by her Protestant sister Elizabeth I, the child of Henry's second marriage, and it was through her religious settlement in 1559 that England's Protestant identity was definitively established.

The response from Catholic Europe to Elizabeth's reassertion of her country's Protestantism profoundly influenced the development of the English national identity. In 1570 the Pope excommunicated Elizabeth, thus legitimising any attempt to overthrow her and restore England to the Catholic fold. For almost twenty years the nation lived under the shadow of military attack, while at the same time Catholic missionaries, including the Jesuits, sought to infiltrate the country. Elizabethan England was, in vital respects, an age of anxiety for the people. Finally, the Spanish King, Philip II, obtained the Pope's approval for his plan to send a vast naval force, or Armada, carrying an army with which to invade England. In June 1588 the 130-strong Spanish fleet set sail, and England, anticipating the 'Dunkirk spirit' of 1940, called upon numerous small vessels on the south coast to assist the regular navy. Fortunately for the English, an opportunity arose to strike against the Armada at Calais, where it had docked to pick up more troops, and further Spanish losses were suffered as the Armada tried to escape by navigating the heavy seas around Scotland and Ireland. The defeat of the Armada relieved England from any immediate danger of attack, but English support for the

Dutch Protestants in their revolt against Spanish domination ensured that hostilities with Spain continued until 1604. Protestantism had become a central part of the English psyche, helping the nation to define itself in relation to external threat from the great European powers, and promoting a heightened sense of unity of purpose. Queen Elizabeth's subjects were firmly persuaded of their difference from, and superiority to, the peoples of the European continent.

History – or, to be more accurate, mythology – is a vital tool for forging a national identity, and sixteenth-century England was notable for its people's eagerness to learn about their own past. There was a public appetite for books about English history, recent and distant, which were often given official encouragement, as in the case of John Camden's *Annals of the Reign of Queen Elizabeth*. One of the best-known works was the *Chronicles of England*, begun by Raphael Holinshed and completed in the 1580s by John Hooker and others. The *Chronicles* struck a patriotic and robustly Protestant tone, and provided source material for Elizabethan poets such as Edmund Spenser. Above all, they inspired the remarkable cycle of history plays by William Shakespeare who, in *Richard II* (1597), act II scene I, memorably expressed the proud insularity of an island nation:

> This royal throne of kings, this scepter'd isle,
> This earth of majesty, this seat of Mars,
> This other Eden, demi-paradise;
> This fortress, built by nature for herself,
> Against infection and the hand of war;
> This happy breed of men, this little world;
> This precious stone set in the silver sea,
> Which serves it in the office of a wall,
> Or as a moat defensive to a house,
> Against the envy of less happier lands;
> This blessed plot, this earth, this realm, this England,
> This nurse, this teeming womb of royal Kings,
> Fear'd by their breed, and famous by their birth ...

Shakespeare's plays were part of a much wider process of national self-discovery, involving, for example, antiquarian surveys of many English counties, and improvements in map-making which made possible the publication of Christopher Saxton's *Atlas of*

England (1574–9), complete with a frontispiece of the Queen sitting on her throne. The Elizabethans were thus equipped with a mental picture of their nation's geography that had not been available to earlier generations.[6]

If Protestantism was central to the English people's perception of what it was that made them English, the evolution of a form of limited monarchical government, in which a national Parliament had a part to play, was ultimately to be of no less significance. A crucial first stage in this process was the sealing of *Magna Carta* (Great Charter) by King John in June 1215. John's need to defuse aristocratic discontent with his rule, which had led to military disaster in France, compelled him not only to confirm publicly the rights and privileges claimed by the nobles, but also to guarantee the rights of the Church, the boroughs and the merchants, and to abolish many unpopular taxes. *Magna Carta*, which was regularly reissued by later monarchs, helped to substantiate the evolving doctrine, embodied in the writings of the lawyer Henry Bracton in the 1250s,[7] that there existed a fixed body of law which was ascertainable (because there were professional judges to interpret it), and that the King was obliged to rule in accordance with the law rather than acting in an arbitrary fashion.

Of course, laws themselves were still made by the King and those lay and church leaders whom he chose to summon to his Great Council, but profound long-term changes were taking place in this sphere as well. From the middle of the thirteenth century, for reasons that are somewhat unclear, the more important Council meetings were being described as 'Parliaments' (literally, where the King parlayed with the notables). A more novel and potent development was the fact that, in 1258 and 1264, elected representatives from the shires (knights of the shire) were invited to attend Parliament, and in 1265 representatives from the boroughs (burgesses) were added. At this stage, the knights and burgesses merely appeared before the Council to answer questions, and their involvement was in any case the exception rather than the rule. Nevertheless, the occasional participation of knights and burgesses at meetings of Parliament contributed to the emerging concept of a 'community of the realm'. In other words, the belief was gaining acceptance that the King required the assent of his people for important policy decisions and, in particular, for levying additional taxation. The frequent wars engaged in by Edward I and Edward III, and the consequent need to raise extra tax revenues, meant that these Kings often found it expedient to summon shire and borough representatives to Parliament. By the end of the fourteenth century, therefore, knights and burgesses were always present, around 250 in number, and they operated as a separate body from the Council – the House of Commons – and elected their own Speaker. Some one hundred peers and church leaders also met together in a separate chamber, the House of Lords, and though the Council continued to exist, a small nucleus of its members were effectively left with responsibility for transacting the day-to-day business of the King's government. During the fifteenth century, the Commons established its exclusive right to initiate the grant of new taxes, and such grants were often linked to the redress of specific grievances, while there were even times when the King was urged to change the councillors who advised him. After 1471, it was recognised that no law could be enacted without the Commons' consent.[8]

Sir John Fortescue, a distinguished lawyer whose publications (in Latin) in the 1470s included the *Governance of England* and *In praise of the laws of England*, expressed the kind of pride in the nation's political and legal institutions which was to become a recurring theme in the centuries that followed. According to Fortescue, the existence of a system in which the King was unable to alter the law or impose new taxes without Parliament's agreement, reflected the superiority of the English national character. The virtues of the English people, it was asserted, had enabled them to resist royal tyranny and secure equality before the law (for example, the right to trial by jury), making them and their institutions an object lesson for other nations.

Parliament, it should be stressed, remained an occasional feature of the political system, meeting only when it was summoned by the King. It is at least conceivable that, in different circumstances, the English Parliament might have been allowed to wither away: successive monarchs would have gladly seen this happen, and many of their subjects might not have regretted its demise, since Parliaments invariably meant taxation. But Parliament did survive, and its status was enormously enhanced by the Reformation in the 1530s. Henry VIII's decision to enlist public support for his policy, by using Acts of Parliament to legitimise his assertion of supremacy over the Church and the dissolution of the monasteries, had the effect of expanding Parliament's sphere of competence. The consequences started to become apparent during the reign of Elizabeth, when the Queen sometimes found herself in conflict with the House of Commons over the latter's claim to be allowed to discuss issues of its own choosing, rather than simply those referred to it by the monarch.

England's adherence to the Protestant faith, and its possession of one of the few Parliamentary assemblies with real influence, were seen to mark out its people as different from those of other nations. If all this seems distant and irrelevant today, it is worth bearing in mind that the English continue to celebrate bonfire night on 5 November. Without perhaps realising it, they are expressing a defiant pride in their religious and political identity, which had been challenged by Guido Fawkes and his fellow Catholic conspirators when they attempted to blow up Parliament in the Gunpowder Plot of 1605.[9]

ENGLAND, WALES AND SCOTLAND

The geographically logical expansion of the English Kingdom into one embracing the whole of the island of Britain was impeded for many centuries by the absence of any over-riding sense of cultural unity between the English, Welsh and Scottish peoples.[10] Not only were the Welsh and the Scots substantially different from the English in terms of ethnic origin; they also differed from each other, and they experienced quite separate historic relationships with the English kingdom. It is therefore necessary to summarise briefly the social and political development of Wales and Scotland and examine the nature of their respective connections with England.

In the case of Wales,[11] the Celtic inhabitants from pre-Roman times were untouched by the Saxon invasions of the fifth and sixth centuries, which did not reach beyond the river Severn. On the other hand, there was never a single kingdom of Wales, but rather a collection of smaller political units. This is hardly surprising given the formidable barriers to communication and logistical movements between the mountainous northern regions and the south. Whereas some of the southern Welsh kings proved amenable to English influence, giving their allegiance to powerful rulers such as Aethelstan and Edgar, the remoter Kingdoms of Gwynedd and Powys in the north were always much more hostile to England.

This pattern continued after the Norman Conquest of England, when castles were built in south Wales and the so-called Marcher Lordships created to maintain control along the length of the English–Welsh border. Wales, then, occupied an ambiguous position in relation to England, never enjoying complete independence yet never entirely under English domination. It was not until the 1280s that Edward I carried out a military conquest of north Wales, overthrowing the powerful Llywelyn ap Gruffydd, establishing new towns and castles and encouraging English settlers and merchants. In 1301 he proclaimed his eldest son Prince of Wales, a title customarily held by the heir to the English throne ever since. Even so, England's grip on Wales remained tenuous, and a number of native uprisings had to be quelled, most famously the one inspired by Owain Glyndwr in the early 1400s. The Marcher Lords, too, presented problems for English Kings, as the possessors of the borderlands tended to regard themselves as politically independent; their loyalty could never be taken for granted.

Wales was only fully integrated into English political, administrative and legal structures during the reign of Henry VIII. A series of measures enacted between 1536 and 1543 deprived the Marcher Lords of their franchises, abolished the Welsh legal code, substituting the English for it, and divided the whole of Wales into shires, each sending elected representatives to the Parliament in London. Local control in the shires was exercised by landowners, serving the King in the capacity of Justices of the Peace, who had responsibility for preserving law and order. (This model had been introduced to the English shires in the fourteenth century.) It was crucial for Henry to secure the enthusiastic participation of Welsh landowners in the new system of government, if its transplantation from England was to be successful. Fortunately, the King had the enormous advantage of being able to exploit the appeal of his own Welsh ancestry: his father, Henry VII, the founder of the Tudor royal dynasty, had been born in Wales and used that country as the springboard for his seizure of the English throne in 1485. By emphasising the Tudor monarchy's Welsh origins, it was possible to promote the belief that the Welsh people were merely coming into their rightful political inheritance rather than being conquered by the English. The Anglo-Welsh union occurred at the same time as the Reformation, and the deep roots laid down by the Protestant faith in Wales provided another important bond with the English.

Scotland differed fundamentally from Wales in that it had had a long history as an independent kingdom before its incorporation into the British State. The Scots, the tribe from whom the country derives its name, were Gaelic-speaking settlers from Ireland[12] who had established themselves in the Western Highlands before the end of the fifth century. In *c.*843 the Scots King, Kenneth MacAlpine, succeeded as ruler of the formidable Kingdom of the Picts, the people occupying the far northern lands, and formed what was known as 'Scotia', although at this stage it only covered part of the geographical area of modern Scotland. Malcolm II, in *c.*1018, seized control of Lothian, the south-eastern lowland region between the rivers Tweed and Forth; and when, in 1034, Duncan combined all of these lands with the south-western Kingdom of Strathclyde, inhabited by Celtic Britons, he ruled over a territory which roughly corresponded to the modern country. Like the English, the Scots in the ninth and tenth centuries were subject to attacks from Vikings, who infiltrated the north of the country, the Orkney and Shetland islands and the Hebrides, but by the eleventh century marriage connections had been established between the Scots and Viking rulers. The border with England remained a matter of dispute until the fifteenth century.[13]

An important division, similar to that in Wales, between the Highland and Lowland regions, was strikingly evident in Scotland. Apart from the obvious geographical reasons for this, it can also be explained by reference to the fact that Lothian had earlier belonged to the Saxon Kingdom of Northumbria, and its people were culturally closer to the English than to the Gaelic-Norse Highlanders. It was to the Lowlands that the centre of political gravity within the Scottish Kingdom shifted. English influences were reinforced by the marriage of Malcolm III (reigned 1058–93) to an English Princess, while David I (reigned 1124–53) was actually brought up at the English royal court and imported into Scotland the social, administrative and military systems with which he had grown familiar. He even brought with him some English families, such as the Bruces, to whom he gave lands. Scotland was therefore under the control of a ruling elite that was decidedly English in its cultural orientation, and Scottish Kings were faced with a number of rebellions by their own Highland subjects.

For all their similarities, political relations between Scottish and English monarchs were often tense and sometimes turbulent, as England threatened to encroach on Scotland's independence. Successive Scottish rulers, from David I onwards, were placed in an awkward position by virtue of the fact that they held lands in England granted to them by English Kings, for which they were expected to pay homage. This exposed them, by the thirteenth century, to claims that they likewise owed allegiance to the English King for their possession of Scotland itself. It is just conceivable that a union of the English and Scottish Crowns might have been achieved peaceably, following the treaty of 1290 by which Edward I's eldest son was betrothed to Scotland's child Queen, Margaret. Unfortunately, Margaret died soon afterwards, and Edward, who as we have seen had recently conquered north Wales, proceeded to assert his overlordship in Scotland by military force. Edward's action provoked fierce opposition among the Scots and inaugurated more than two centuries of intermittent warfare between the Kingdoms. The Lowland Scottish ruling elite was driven into identifying itself more closely with its own people, and what became known as the 'Auld Alliance' was formed with England's greatest enemy, France. England's army was humiliated by Robert Bruce's men at Bannockburn in 1314, but later warrior kings such as Edward III and Henry IV embarked on new campaigns to assert their claims over Scotland, perpetuating the tradition of Anglo-Scottish antagonism.

However, religious and dynastic forces worked to draw England and Scotland closer together towards the end of the sixteenth century. The Scottish people had had their own Reformation, and their Protestantism took a more radical form (known as Calvinism) than that in England. This at least created potential common ground between the two countries, and early in the reign of Elizabeth I England provided military support to help the Scots resist French pressure for the restoration of Catholicism.

More decisively, the fact that Elizabeth never married and therefore produced no heir meant the extinction of the Tudor line with her death in 1603. Consequently, the English throne passed to none other than the King of Scotland, James VI, who was descended from a daughter of Henry VII[14] and now became James I of England as well. In this way, the English and Scottish *Crowns* were united (a regnal union) under the royal house of Stuart, but the two countries remained politically independent, each with its own Parliament and legal system. Far from being the end of the story of Britain's evolution, another tumultuous century was to elapse before full Anglo-Scottish union was accomplished.

THE STUART DYNASTY AND THE UNION OF THE KINGDOMS

Two themes which have been identified already as central to an account of how the English nation-state developed, the influence of Protestantism and the role of Parliament, provide the keys to understanding the political and dynastic crises of the seventeenth and early eighteenth centuries. As we shall see, conflict between King and Parliament erupted into civil war in 1642, and ended in the execution of Charles I seven years later. The republican system of government that replaced the monarchy proved to be short-lived, and the Stuarts were restored to the throne in 1660; but the growing tension between James II, a Catholic, and his subjects, led to the 'Glorious Revolution' of 1688, when James fled the country. In the constitutional settlement that followed, a new relationship was established between Crown and Parliament, while the nation's Protestant identity was emphatically confirmed. Furthermore, the determination to preserve this new constitutional arrangement created the momentum for pushing through the complete union of England and Scotland in 1707.[15]

It is important to bear in mind that there was a general trend towards absolutist monarchical rule in seventeenth-century Europe, from which England was a notable exception. To later generations, this seemed to confirm the innate superiority of the English national character, which had ensured that the people repudiated the enemies of political liberty and the Protestant faith. Modern historical scholarship is more sceptical about such complacent and self-congratulatory assumptions, and it is now recognised that England could have gone down the path followed by most of Europe. The early Stuart monarchs, James I (1603–25) and Charles I (1625–49), were both adherents of the internationally fashionable doctrine of the divine right of Kings, which taught that subjects had no right to resist their rulers, whose authority was derived from God. Both Kings sought, as far as possible, to avoid summoning Parliaments, which they found troublesome and obstructive. What distinguished the English Parliament from other representative assemblies in Europe, and thus ensured English divergence from the absolutist norm, was the fact that it had previously succeeded in claiming exclusive control over grants of taxation, which severely restricted the monarch's freedom of action. Even this might not have been decisive had Henry VIII not squandered the wealth derived from the sale of monastic lands at the Reformation on costly European wars, preventing his successors from ever becoming entirely financially independent of Parliament. In the event, but partly fortuitously, the notion of a 'community of the realm' proved sufficiently deeply engrained for Parliament to serve as an effective focus for discontent with kingly misrule.

From 1629 until 1640 Charles I governed without Parliament. During this period, he levied new taxes without the necessary consent, stretched his powers over the law courts, and authorised arbitrary arrests and punishments. More alarming still, in the eyes of many of his subjects, the King and the Archbishop of Canterbury, William Laud, were suspected of being closet Catholics. Although this was not strictly true, Charles and Laud undoubtedly took a highly authoritarian view of the role of the bishops within the Church of England, and they favoured a greater emphasis on ceremonial ritual that resembled Catholic practice. The fact that Charles's French wife, Henrietta Maria, was a Catholic, and that certain members of the royal entourage shared her faith, also helped to fuel concerns that a sinister plot was being hatched to undermine the national religion, as part of a wider scheme to create a despotic Catholic state.

Within a generation, the house of Stuart had become utterly remote from its Scottish subjects, and it was ironic that events north of the border precipitated the crisis between the King and the English Parliament.[16] Charles's attempt to impose uniformity of religious worship on the Scottish Protestants (Presbyterians), by requiring the use of the English Book of Common Prayer, provoked a rebellion which he was unable to suppress. His initial use of Catholic soldiers from Ireland in an attempt to put down the revolt only aggravated matters by appearing to confirm that he was engaged in an anti-Protestant crusade. Finally, Charles was compelled to summon Parliament in order to obtain the additional resources necessary for him to reassert his authority over the Scots. Parliament, however, demanded concessions in return, including curbs on recent abuses of royal power and a more regular role for itself in the governing process. There was no intention, at this stage, of seeking to overthrow the monarchy, and a more shrewd and flexible king might yet have retrieved the situation without any fatal loss of prestige. As it was, Charles's obstinacy and palpable desire to put an early end to such a tiresome Parliament prompted more drastic demands for constitutional reform designed to exert closer control over the King's government. The country was plunged into a spiral of mutual distrust which resulted in the outbreak of civil war between the supporters of the King and those of Parliament in 1642.[17]

One particularly interesting aspect of the conflict between Crown and Parliament is the way that Charles's opponents were able to draw upon the idea of an 'ancient constitution', which seemed to provide intellectual legitimacy for what they were doing. In the account of English history put forward by the lawyer Sir Edward Coke, published in 1642 as the second part of his *Institutes of the Laws of England*, the nation's political and legal institutions were held to be part of its Saxon heritage. Coke believed that in distant times there had been a truly representative assembly, the Witan, the precursor of Parliament, and he even maintained that kings had been elected by it. The Norman conquerors of 1066 had sought to destroy this English political tradition, but happily *Magna Carta* had recovered the rights of free-born Englishmen. Of course, modern scholarship can easily expose the fallacious elements in Coke's interpretation of England's past, but the far more significant point is that many people in the seventeenth century accepted this account and consciously acted in accordance with it. Consequently, the Parliamentary critics of the Stuart regime saw themselves as being engaged in a struggle to *restore* England's political and legal institutions to their rightful condition, and they certainly did not consider their conduct to be 'revolutionary', in the modern sense of the term. Indeed, this distinctively 'English' view of the nature of the opposition to Charles I created a powerful current of radical political activity, which survived long into the nineteenth century. Radical constitutionalism was nostalgic, staunchly patriotic and even xenophobic in its attitudes.[18]

However, it was one thing to curb the excessive powers of a King and quite another to execute him, and the controversial outcome of the civil war served to elevate Charles to the status of a martyr in the minds of many people. The ensuing period of 'Commonwealth' rule, which was virtually a dictatorship wielded by Oliver Cromwell, lacked both the legitimacy of popular assent and the sanctity of hereditary right. After Cromwell's death in 1658 there was no one capable of filling the power vacuum, and the logical conclusion was the restoration of the Stuart monarchy under 'Charles the martyr's' eldest son, who had been living in exile. Unfortunately for the future stability of the country, the reaction in sentiment which brought Charles II to the throne in May 1660 also wiped away the legacies of the recent past, with the result that the new King exercised virtually all of the constitutional powers possessed by his father. Not only was Charles the head of State, the head of the Church and the head of the armed forces, there was still no effective provision for the regular summoning of Parliament. The potential therefore existed for future conflict whenever the Stuarts adopted a course of policy that disturbed the minds of their subjects.

The difficulties that did eventually arise centred mainly on the position of Charles's brother and heir, James, Duke of York.[19] James had secretly converted to the Catholic faith in 1669, and this became public knowledge four years later, shortly before his marriage to a Catholic princess, Mary of Modena. The anxieties stimulated by the prospect of a Catholic succession to the throne were manifested in the climate of hysteria at the time of the 'Popish Plot' of 1678, when there were fears of a Catholic conspiracy to assassinate the King. This prompted Parliament, during the 'Exclusion crisis' of 1679–81, to attempt to remove James from the royal succession, and the King's determination to resist such a move threatened to produce another military confrontation, until Parliament finally backed down.

Despite the misgivings about James, he duly succeeded his brother in 1685 as King James II. Initially, his position appeared to be reasonably secure, given that many of his subjects, especially those in the Church, were instinctively loyal to the lawful ruler, whatever his personal religious beliefs. He was therefore able to suppress, with comparative ease, an uprising in the West Country inspired by the Duke of Monmouth, an illegitimate (but Protestant) son of Charles II. However, early ominous signs of James's authoritarian approach to kingship included the suspension of the Habeas Corpus Act, which meant that people could be imprisoned without trial, his retention of the enlarged army raised to deal with the Monmouth rebellion, and a purge of the judiciary. Tension mounted as it became clear that James was bent on pursuing a policy of religious toleration aimed at assisting his fellow-Catholics (a small but significant minority within the English population). He unilaterally granted dispensation from the Acts of Parliament excluding Catholics from holding public office, and proceeded to appoint his co-religionists to senior posts in the government and the army, and as Justices of the Peace in the counties (purging many Protestants in the process). Steps were also taken to encourage Catholic schools, a Catholic press was allowed to operate, diplomatic relations were re-established with Rome, and Catholic Masters imposed on colleges at Oxford and Cambridge universities. Resistance to James's policy within the Church culminated in the temporary imprisonment of seven bishops in the Tower of London. In the meantime, vigorous action was taken by the King's agents to influence and re-model many constituencies prior to the Parliamentary elections expected to be held in 1688.

Whether James's objective was to reconvert England to Catholicism immediately or simply to secure equality for the Catholic section of the community in the short term, his heavy-handed methods merely confirmed the prejudices of his Protestant subjects against Catholic rule, which they equated with religious intolerance and political tyranny. The catalyst for the increasingly predictable challenge to James was provided by the birth of his son, in June 1688, which meant that England now had a Catholic male heir to the throne as well as a Catholic monarch. It was the need to discredit the legitimacy of this child that led to the circulation of a story that he had been smuggled into the Queen's bed in a warming pan. At the end of June, a number of prominent English noblemen issued an invitation to William of Orange, a Dutch Protestant Prince, to intervene and rescue the country from Catholic despotism. William's interest in England stemmed from the fact that he was married to Princess Mary, the eldest of James's two Protestant daughters from his first marriage to Anne Hyde (before his conversion to Catholicism). Mary's place at the head of the royal succession had been over-ridden by the birth of James's son. Consequently, on 5 November 1688, William landed at Torbay with a force of around twelve thousand men, and James, faced with numerous defections from his own army, panicked and fled the country. This came to be remembered as the 'Glorious Revolution', a bloodless coup engineered by members of the English ruling elite, which enabled the people to reaffirm their Protestant identity and their devotion to political freedom.

James's departure from the country greatly assisted the subsequent constitutional settlement. The convenient fiction that he had abdicated meant that when the English Parliament, in February 1689, offered the Crown to William and Mary as joint monarchs, the momentous implication that an elected assembly was taking upon itself the right to determine the royal succession could be avoided by those who were uncomfortable with such an idea. In August, Parliament also carried a 'Bill of Rights' (the Scottish Parliament carried a corresponding 'Claim of Right'), which further entrenched its position in the system of government. The monarch was obliged to rule in accordance with the laws laid down by Parliament, which he could not arbitrarily suspend in the way James had done, and he could not maintain a standing army in peacetime without Parliament's consent. It was also decreed that the monarch must not be a Catholic and must not marry a Catholic. Parliamentary elections were to be free from monarchical inter-ference, and Parliament was to meet 'frequently'. This last provision was underpinned by the refusal to grant the monarch the customary right to levy ordinary taxes for life, which ensured that it was necessary for Parliament to be summoned every year. A Triennial Act carried in 1694 actually stipulated that Parliamentary elections must be held every three years. In practice, the Revolution settlement secured the principle of 'Parliamentary government', which has survived to the present day. On the other hand, while it was accepted that English monarchs ruled in association with Parliament, their powers remained formidable as they exercised full control over appointments in central and local government, the Church hierarchy, the judiciary and the armed forces.

There was a wider, European dimension to William of Orange's involvement in English affairs in 1688, the consequences of which permanently sealed the link between Protestantism and England's sense of national purpose. William accepted the throne because he was anxious to draw England into a war designed to curb the ambitions of the French 'Sun King', Louis XIV. For many years, William's energies had been directed towards resisting French attempts to annex Dutch territory, and thanks to the Glorious Revolution he could now bring together the English and Dutch peoples in a crusade to defend European Protestantism from Catholic aggression. The fact that Louis was harbouring James II, whom he continued to recognise as the rightful King of England, provided an additional reason for the English people to bear the heavy expense of military campaigns that lasted for nine years, until the peace of Rijswick in 1697.

Still further measures proved necessary, however, in order to perpetuate England's Protestant regime. Queen Mary died in 1694 without producing an heir, and on William's death (which occurred in 1702) the throne was due to pass to Mary's sister Anne; but the death of Anne's only surviving child in 1700 made her the last of the Protestant Stuart line. These circumstances led to the passing of the Act of Settlement in 1701, by which Parliament fixed the succession to Anne on the royal house of Hanover, the Protestant descendants of a daughter of James I. Later that same year, when the exiled James II died in France, Louis XIV made the provocative gesture of recognising James's son as King James III. The resulting wave of patriotic anger in England facilitated the nation's entry into another European war for the purpose of combating an over-mighty French monarch. On this occasion, the conflict dragged on for eleven years, until 1713, although it was marked in its early stages by the Duke of Marlborough's brilliant victories at Blenheim (1704) and Ramillies (1706).

English pressure for full union with Scotland can also be explained in the context of anxiety for the security of the Hanoverian succession. The Scottish as well as the English Crown had been offered to William and Mary in 1689, but the new regime became increasingly unpopular in Scotland during the 1690s, one of the many reasons for this being the adverse economic effects of the Nine Years War. Mounting anti-English feeling climaxed in the Scottish Parliament's refusal to endorse the Act of Settlement, and to the passing of legislation in 1703–4 decreeing that on Anne's death the throne should pass to a Protestant 'of the royal line of Scotland' and that thenceforth Scotland would resume the right to make declarations of war and peace for itself.

The doubly worrying prospect for England, therefore, was that in the perhaps not too distant future James Edward Stuart ('James III') might be induced to embrace the Protestant faith in order to gain the succession to the Scottish Crown, after which Scotland would also be free to withdraw from the war which England was currently waging against Louis XIV. England's response was blunt, taking the form of an Aliens Act (1705) which stipulated that, unless the Scots accepted the Hanoverian succession, all property held in England by non-resident Scotsmen would be treated as alien property, and that embargoes would be placed on Scottish imports. Economic coercion thus obliged the Scots to enter into negotiations for a new political relationship with England, the outcome of which was the Act of Union. By the terms of the union, Scotland retained its distinctive religious, legal and educational structures, but its Parliament was dissolved and sixteen peers and forty-five MPs were sent to what was now the British Parliament in London, which met for the first time on 23 October 1707.

WHIGS AND TORIES

The enhanced status of Parliament in the late seventeenth century made possible a new political development that was to be of immense long-term significance, namely, the emergence of the Whig and Tory parties.[20] While the organisation and scope of these parties cannot remotely be compared to that of their strictly disciplined twentieth-century counterparts, their importance lies in the fact that the political leaders of the nation were coming, for the first time, to be associated with groupings rooted in Parliament itself, rather than being simply and exclusively the servants of the Crown. Eventually, as will be seen in later chapters, parliamentary parties became the essential foundation for governments, which needed their support in order to survive, and in this way the independent power of the Crown was effectively restricted. Another reason why the early Whig and Tory parties are of great interest is that their ideologies were shaped by the same dynastic and religious issues which have occupied so much of our attention in this chapter.

It was the Exclusion crisis of 1679–81 that prompted the appearance of two rival parties known by the abusive titles of Whig and Tory.[21] The Whigs, led by the Earl of Shaftesbury, were those who sought to exclude James, Duke of York, from the royal succession on the ground of his commitment to Catholicism. Following the collapse of the exclusionist campaign in Parliament, Shaftesbury was forced into exile where he died in 1683, but the Glorious Revolution five years later dramatically vindicated his stand against Stuart 'despotism'. Whig principles were given their most sophisticated exposition in the philosophical works of John Locke, a protégé of Shaftesbury's, whose *Two Treatises of Civil Government* were written during the Exclusion crisis but published only in 1689. Locke's basic argument was that the authority of royal government rested on a 'contract' between the King and his subjects, and that if the King broke this contract through misrule then his subjects were entitled to remove him. This idea seemed to become a practical reality in 1688–9, when James II was driven from the throne and Parliament offered it to William and Mary; and the subsequent Act of Settlement, which regulated the succession to Anne in favour of the Protestant Hanoverians, provided further confirmation that English monarchs owed their position to the consent of the English people as expressed through Parliament. In fact, Whig ideology was highly aristocratic in tone, maintaining as it did that the independence conferred by ownership of land afforded the only means of successfully resisting the power of Kings, and that the aristocracy were therefore the natural guardians of the liberty of the people. With regard to policy, Whig leaders of the 1690s and 1700s such as Somers, Wharton and Montague were committed to vigorously prosecuting the wars against France, engineering the union with Scotland, and ensuring the safety of the Hanoverian succession with which the future of Whiggism was inseparably linked.

Toryism was the creed of those who, while mostly of the Protestant faith themselves, were nevertheless unwilling to countenance the exclusion of the divinely-ordained heir to the throne – even if he was a Catholic convert. This reflected the persistent hold on many minds of the ideas of 'divine right' and 'non-resistance', associated with the early Stuart monarchs, which instructed that Kings were answerable to God alone and that their subjects had no right to oppose them in any way. A timely reiteration of these views was provided by the publication in 1680 of Sir Robert Filmer's *Patriarcha*, in which the relationship between the King and his subjects was likened to that between a father and his children: both were in accordance with the natural order of society intended by God. It is a tribute to James II's incompetence that during his short reign he managed to alienate so many people, Churchmen in particular, whose first thought was to obey him as the hereditary ruler possessing a heavenly sanction. The awful implications of the events of 1688–9 were masked, for such Tories, by the comforting fictions that James had abandoned his throne and that his son was illegitimate, which meant that Parliament was merely transferring royal power to the legitimate heiress, Mary, and her husband. The Tories were perfectly content with Anne as monarch after 1702, but the impending prospect of a Hanoverian dynasty, appointed by Parliament, placed great strain on their loyalties.

In terms of policy, the Tories of the 1690s and 1700s came increasingly to identify with a 'country' perspective shared by many of the landowners who filled the backbenches in the House of Commons. This 'country' mentality was suspicious of all government, because of its tendency to become corrupt, and especially critical of the heavy tax burden imposed by the prolonged military campaigns against France. The Tories were not opposed to the French wars in principle, but they favoured a 'blue water' strategy, relying on England's naval power, in the belief that this would be a far cheaper form of warfare than maintaining a large land army. Tories also condemned the Whigs for the latter's alleged religious indifference and sympathy towards the Protestant dissenting sects,[22] presenting themselves by contrast as the true friends of the Church of England. By 1710, war-weariness had combined with exaggerated fears about 'the Church in danger' to secure an overwhelming general election victory for the Tories.

During the last four years of Anne's reign, uncertainty surrounded the prospects of her designated successor. The Tory ministry headed by Robert Harley and Henry St John was suspected of being anti-Hanoverian in its intentions and eager to negotiate for a restoration of the male Stuart line in the person of 'James III'. Certainly, the haste with which ministers concluded peace with France, in the process abandoning Britain's continental allies including Hanover, was capable of being construed as an attempt to smooth the path for James, who, as a client of the French King, could hardly return to his home country while it was still at war with France. An irremovable obstacle to such a restoration remained, however, as James made it clear, in a secret communication with ministers at the beginning of 1714, that he was unwilling to renounce his Catholic faith. With the Whigs meanwhile stirring up public fears that the Protestant succession was in danger, and the Tories themselves deeply divided between pro- and anti-Hanoverians (and the undecided), the position of Tory ministers became completely untenable, not to say personally dangerous. The potential barriers to the Hanoverian succession had crumbled, and when Anne died on 1 August 1714 George, Elector of Hanover, was promptly proclaimed King George I of Great Britain.

Consolidating the Nation, 1714–1815

INTRODUCTION

The accession of the Elector of Hanover as King George I in 1714 marked less of an ending than the beginning of a new phase in the protracted story of how a sense of common nationhood developed in the hearts and minds of the British peoples. While it was true that Scotland had been politically united with England seven years earlier, no great cordiality existed in the relations between the two countries. Many Scots regarded the loss of their independent Parliament as a betrayal of national interests, and they feared that economic ruin might follow from unrestricted trade with their wealthier neighbour. Among the English people, for their part, hostility and contempt were commonly expressed towards the Scots, who found themselves depicted in print and in cartoons as beggars and cheats with all sorts of primitive habits. The passing of several decades would be required before the Act of Union was generally accepted as a mutually beneficial arrangement. At the same time, the legitimacy and permanency of the Hanoverian dynasty, and of the Whig governments associated with it, never went entirely unchallenged. It was from out of a painfully hesitant process of growth that a British national identity was eventually forged, and loyalty to the institutions of the British State secured, under the auspices of the Hanoverian Kings.

EARLY HANOVERIAN BRITAIN

For two generations the foundations supporting the Hanoverian regime failed to completely solidify, owing to the monarchy's inability to command the positive allegiance of its subjects by inspiring either enthusiasm, respect or affection. Neither George I nor George II was blessed with a charismatic personality, and both were widely perceived as alien figures. George I is usually only remembered as the King who could not speak English, which was certainly true when he ascended the throne, although there is evidence that he acquired some grasp of the language later on. His remoteness was perpetuated by his preference for the company of advisors and mistresses who had accompanied him from Hanover. George II had the advantage of fluency in English, and he was a more energetic ruler, but in many ways he was a less prepossessing individual than his father, being notorious for his brusque manner and irascible temper. The first two Georges showed little interest in domestic British affairs and were primarily concerned with foreign policy, reflecting their desire to protect the strategic interests of Hanover, where they still ruled. Indeed, George I regularly returned to his German homeland and actually died while he was abroad. This preoccupation with continental politics became a source of irritation for British politicians and the public, and there were recurring complaints that the nation's wealth was being tapped for the benefit of Hanover, while its own overseas interests were neglected. Nevertheless, as we shall see, these problems were ultimately outweighed by the single crucial fact that the Hanoverian presence offered a guarantee for the nation's Protestant identity.[1] At the very least, the German Georges were likely to be tolerated as a distinctly lesser evil than the alternative of a Stuart restoration.

The Whig monopoly of government, which lasted from 1714 until the late 1750s, was inescapably tied up with the survival of the unbeloved Hanoverian monarchy. In working to promote stability in the country, and so consolidate the new dynasty, the Whigs were also perpetuating their own power and registering the triumph of Protestant principles. As the immediate beneficiaries of the Hanoverian succession, which they had consistently supported before 1714, the Whigs seized every opportunity thereafter to tar their Tory opponents with the brush of disloyalty, confirming George I in his determination to exclude them from office. The Whig stranglehold on government extended all the way down to the local level, where the important offices of Lord Lieutenant and Justice of the Peace were purged of Tories. At the 1715 general election, the first since the advent of the Hanoverians, a Tory majority in the House of Commons of about 240 was converted into a Whig majority of 130, giving a considerable boost to the authority and credibility of the new regime.

Robert Walpole emerged as the dominant figure among the Whigs, after enhancing his reputation for sound financial administration during the South Sea Bubble crisis of 1720–1. This had resulted from extravagant speculation in the shares of the South Sea Company, which possessed privileged trading rights in Spanish America. When the bubble burst, panic set in and the shares plummeted in value, ruining many individuals; but Walpole managed to organise intervention by other financial institutions to stabilise the share price, while he arranged partial compensation for holders of government stock who had been persuaded to convert it into South Sea Company shares. Appointed First Lord of the Treasury in 1721, by way of reward, Walpole retained this post until 1742, becoming arguably the first true 'Prime Minister'.[2]

Walpole had a very clear understanding of his government's role in the quest for internal stability. His outlook was shaped by the experience of Britain's prolonged military engagements against Louis XIV's France between 1689 and 1713, and the tremendous burden this had placed on the country's financial resources. It was essential, in Walpole's view, that further expensive continental entanglements should be avoided, and the nation's wealth replenished through the expansion of trade. Thus, he relied on peaceful diplomacy whenever possible, cultivating a system of alliances with major European Powers which enabled Britain to enjoy the advantages of peace until near the end of his time in office. He simultaneously fostered industry and trade by removing export duties on over one hundred items and offering export bounties (effectively subsidies) for specific products such as silk cloth, while heavy import duties were imposed on foreign manufactured linen, paper and other goods in order to protect domestic producers. Peace and increasing prosperity – assisted by a fortuitous run of good harvests – meant that Walpole was able to lower the rate of land tax, which obviously delighted a Parliament full of landowners, and to reduce the National Debt. Sincerely committed, in his own pragmatic way, to the Whig principle of religious toleration, Walpole also sought to promote social tranquillity by carrying annual Indemnity Acts, from 1727 onwards, which relieved Protestant dissenters from the penalties otherwise applicable if they held any form of public office.

Although Walpole's position depended, ultimately, on the support of the King, who had appointed him and could dismiss him, his ministry could never have lasted as long as it did without the extraordinary personal authority he exercised over the House of Commons. He was not so much an eloquent as an able debater, capable of providing clear expositions of policy and inspiring confidence in his efficiency and sound judgement. Coming as he did from an old Norfolk landowning family, Walpole instinctively struck the right tone of frankness and earthiness required to win over fellow landed MPs of Whiggish or independent principles. But he was also ruthless and systematic in his use of the Crown patronage at his disposal – pensions, sinecures, appointments in the Church and the Army, and so forth – for the purpose of securing and rewarding loyalty to his government. By the 1740s, around one-third of MPs were 'placemen', holding offices of profit under the Crown, and many friends and relatives were being provided for too. Having once established a firm grip on the levers of power, Walpole could not very easily be dislodged so long as he retained the King's confidence. It took the expensive failure of a military campaign against Spain, sparked by the issue of British traders' access to colonial markets in Spanish America, which Walpole had reluctantly embarked upon in 1739, to undermine his parliamentary position and force his resignation three years later. Even so, after a brief period of instability, Walpole's legacy of one-party or 'oligarchical' rule passed to his protégés, Henry Pelham and the Duke of Newcastle, who kept the Walpolean system alive well into the 1750s.

It does not necessarily follow, however, that the Whigs' political supremacy was based on majority support in the country. 'Public opinion' in the eighteenth century is unfortunately beyond measurement, and even general election results tell us little, bearing in mind that no more than fifteen per cent of adult males (and no females at all) were eligible to vote. Furthermore, in 1716 the Whigs carried a Septennial Act, which meant that elections had to be held only every seven years instead of every three. The object of this measure was to help stabilise the new Hanoverian system by avoiding frequent election contests, and it worked only too well in stifling political activity in many constituencies, particularly because of the way it rendered contested elections prohibitively expensive (seven-year tenure made Parliamentary seats much more valuable for those who sought them). Consequently, only around one-fifth of seats were actually contested at a typical general election.[3]

Nor were Walpole's economic policies always universally popular. Reductions in the land tax undoubtedly suited a powerful vested interest which the government needed to conciliate, but they were achieved by shifting the burden of taxation on to the rest of society, through higher indirect taxes. Such manifest unfairness occasionally sparked off violent protests: there was serious rioting at Glasgow in 1725 against the introduction of a malt tax, and at Edinburgh in 1737 following the execution of a smuggler. In the most famous episode of all, Walpole's plan to impose an excise duty on tobacco and wine (1733) provoked bitter opposition and eventually had to be abandoned. The corruption underpinning the Whig oligarchy was another frequent target for criticism, being mockingly depicted for instance in John Gay's play, *The Beggar's Opera* (1728), which was banned by the authorities.

A more difficult question to judge is at what point, and to what extent, expressions of popular discontent with the actions of the Hanoverian-Whig State merged into outright repudiation of that regime. In other words, how many British citizens were 'Jacobite' sympathisers, wishing to see the throne restored to the descendants of the ousted Stuart King, James II, who were living in exile in France. This is a subject which has attracted considerable interest from historians in recent years.[4] It is evident from numerous rhymes and songs current at the time that not everyone after 1714 was able to come to terms with the existence of a royal family appointed by Parliament, and that there was a yearning for the return of a divinely-legitimated dynasty. One anonymous poem, dating from 1720, runs:

> Appear Oh James! approach thy native shore
> And to their antient State thy Realms restore
> When thou arrivest this nauseous tribe will fly
> Right shall revive and usurpation dye.

Such sentiments were naturally attractive to the small minority of British Catholics, who were heavily concentrated in the north-west of England; but many Protestant Tories, both in and out of Parliament, shared their 'divine right' instincts and were particularly fearful that the Whig oligarchy, with its tolerant attitude towards dissenters, might pursue policies hostile to the interests of the established Church. The battle cry of 'the Church in danger' thus inspired Jacobite-tinged riots in over twenty English towns on George I's coronation day, 20 October 1714, and there were further serious disturbances during the spring and summer of 1715 affecting major urban centres such as Oxford, Bristol and Norwich, as well as London itself. In the case of Scotland, enthusiasm for the Jacobite cause was connected with nationalist feeling, and it was fondly believed that a Stuart monarch would repeal the Act of Union and restore Scotland's Parliament.

Quite clearly, there was a diverse and potentially formidable constituency in the country, spanning the whole of the social spectrum, which was uncomfortable with the Hanoverian succession and not averse to the *idea* of a Stuart restoration. What is less certain is that these people were prepared to become actively and openly involved in a campaign to overthrow the existing regime. Few Tories in Parliament, for example, were avowedly Jacobites, and it seems unlikely that very many of them would have been willing to risk forfeiting their lives and property by joining in a conspiracy against the Hanoverians, even though they would have happily accepted the consequences of such a conspiracy had it proved successful. Furthermore, there was serious ambiguity about Tory support for Jacobitism, given that most Tories were ardent Protestants, and it was only possible for them to conceal this difficulty by embracing the deluded belief that the Stuarts would willingly renounce their Catholic faith once restored to the throne. In Scotland, where the religious dilemma was equally marked, support for Jacobitism eventually became confined largely to the turbulent Highland region. As for those who participated in the riots of 1714–15, or who indulged in shouting Jacobite slogans or displaying Jacobite symbols, as some continued to do even in the second half of the eighteenth century, such conduct may have amounted to little more than gestures of defiance against established authority, towards which they doubtless had a variety of grievances.

In the event, neither of the two serious Jacobite uprisings, in 1715–16 and 1745–6, was able to topple the Hanoverian regime. There would have been significant English backing for a movement on behalf of James Edward Stuart, the 'Old Pretender' (the warming-pan baby of 1688), in 1715, had the authorities not preempted this by arresting most of the leading conspirators. One of them, the Earl of Mar, managed to reach Scotland where he raised an army of at least twelve thousand men, but indecisive leadership meant that the military initiative was soon lost. Meantime, a separate revolt in the north-west of England led to the capture of Preston, before the Jacobites lamely capitulated to Hanoverian troops. The Old Pretender arrived in Scotland in December, barely in time to leave again with Mar in February 1716.

On the face of things, the campaign inspired by the unexpected appearance of the charismatic Charles Edward Stuart (Bonnie Prince Charlie), the 'Young Pretender', in the Scottish Highlands in 1745, seems more dramatic, but in fact it stood less chance of success once the authorities had regained their composure. Charles's Highland army of under five thousand men marched into England as far as Derby, before it retreated on discovering that there was little support for it among the English and that the hoped-for French invasion force was not going to materialise. At Culloden Moor near Inverness, in April 1746, the Jacobite army was slaughtered by Hanoverian troops (more than half of whom were Scotsmen) under the command of the King's son, the Duke of Cumberland, and Charles was forced to flee to the continent. The collapse of this uprising was followed by a systematic policy of destroying the distinctive culture of the Highland Scots, for example by ending the clan system, banning the wearing of kilts and replacing the Gaelic language with English.

WAR, COMMERCE, EMPIRE

By the 1750s Jacobitism was a spent force, posing no real threat to the security of Hanoverian Britain. There were solid negative reasons why the bulk of the population had proved unwilling, at critical moments, to risk their necks supporting a rival royal dynasty of dubious merit. But there were also positive, long-term influences tending to promote a collective sense of common purpose among the British people and to inspire feelings of loyalty towards the established regime. Most potent of all, in the middle of the eighteenth century, was the intoxicating mixture of commercial, military, imperial and religious motive-forces which stimulated the nation's historic antagonism towards France and Spain and ultimately defined Britain as the world's pre-eminent maritime power. The politician who offered the clearest vision of Britain's destiny, and supplied the means of fulfilling it, was William Pitt, later Earl of Chatham, a man who briefly achieved a uniquely commanding position in public life.

Britain's geographical position as an island nation on the north-western fringe of Europe, with no serious continental ambitions beyond the protection of Hanover, was ideally suited to the aggressive exploitation of opportunities for imperial and commercial expansion. Existing colonial possessions included the thirteen states on the eastern seaboard of America, and the Caribbean islands of Jamaica, Barbados and Bermuda, which were all acquired in the seventeenth century. They were highly valued for their trade with the mother country, supplying Britain with commodities such as tobacco, sugar and cotton, and providing markets for British exports in turn. In short, colonies meant trade and trade meant wealth and wealth meant power. This equation made a particularly forcible impact on eighteenth-century minds, for it was assumed that the quantity of international trade was fixed and that any increase in one country's total could only be achieved by seizing some of its rivals' share. The fact that Britain's main rivals, Spain and France, were both Catholic States, added a religious edge to the competition for supremacy, encouraging the belief that a struggle for trade and empire was also a struggle for national survival and the preservation of the nation's Protestant soul.[5] Naturally, the Royal Navy played a vital role in protecting British shipping routes, and the composition of the song 'Rule, Britannia' in the 1740s aptly reflected popular pride in the nation's maritime traditions.

The increasing friction with France in several imperial arenas – North America, the Caribbean, India and West Africa – provided the background to Britain's participation in the Seven Years War of 1756–63, when Pitt emerged as the most powerful figure in politics. Pitt, whose grandfather had made a fortune in India, was acutely conscious of the link between trade and national greatness, and he had a clear strategic plan for utilising the conflict in Europe to further Britain's global ambitions. While it was necessary to raise a substantial army to fight on the continent against France and its ally, Austria (twenty thousand British troops were engaged in Germany in 1760), and to assist her own allies, Russia and Prussia, with huge financial subsidies, the main thrust of Britain's military effort was directed towards asserting her supremacy on the high seas and launching attacks on French colonial settlements. After initial setbacks, which left the country vulnerable to invasion in 1756–7, the navy imposed a blockade on French ports, and the victories at Lagos and Quiberon Bay in 1759 secured British control both of the English Channel and the Atlantic. Pitt was determined, above all else, to destroy French influence in North America, where Britain's colonies were threatened with encirclement, and this was achieved through the capture of Louisiana in 1758 and of 'New France' (Canada) in 1759–60, the latter campaign being remembered for General Wolfe's heroic exploits and death at Quebec. Support was similarly forthcoming for the East India Company in its bid to establish British hegemony in India. Robert Clive's victory over a rebellious native prince at the battle of Plassey (1757), and his subsequent capture of Bengal, together with Eyre Coote's triumphs over the French at Wandewash (1760) and Pondicherry (1761), were enough to attain this objective. Other spoils of war included the Caribbean islands of Grenada and Dominica, and the Spanish colony of Florida.

Britain emerged from the Seven Years War as an outrageously successful global power. Pitt's eloquent, dramatic and almost messianic oratory carried Parliament and the country along with him in support of his ambitious policy. A vital display of public support came in 1757, when he was showered with testimonials and freedoms from eighteen towns and cities. His 'patriotism' received its greatest acclamation from within the ranks of the London business community, which obviously stood to benefit from colonial aggrandisement, and this was expressed in the favourable coverage provided by such newspapers as the *London*

Evening Post and the *Courier*. Pitt was in fact the first national politician to use 'public opinion' in order to strengthen his personal position within Parliament and the government.[6] He resigned in 1761 in protest at moves towards a peace settlement, and it is interesting to note that the alleged leniency of the terms finally extracted from France by the Treaty of Paris (1763) prompted vitriolic press attacks on the King's ministers by a Pitt supporter, John Wilkes, who was thereupon prosecuted by the authorities. The Wilkes affair became a long-running cause célèbre of the 1760s, raising as it did fundamental issues of personal liberty, even though Wilkes himself was clearly a self-serving scoundrel. Support for his cause was widely distributed through all levels of society in London, which highlights the 'patriotic' and xenophobic character of much eighteenth-century popular radicalism.[7]

From a broader perspective, the expansion of Britain's commercial empire in the mid-eighteenth century was significant for the way it helped to promote Scottish integration into the union with England. Access to the empire provided Scots with various opportunities for self-advancement, whether as merchants (Glasgow flourished from the 1740s onwards as a centre of the tobacco trade), as emigrants settling in the North American colonies, or as military and civilian employees in the colonial administrations, particularly in India. The Seven Years War saw, for the first time, massive recruitment into the armed forces from the Scottish Highlands, which was part of a deliberate policy of enlisting the Highlanders' martial traditions on behalf of the British State. In all these ways, the Scots gradually came to consider themselves as citizens of a British empire which was something more than simply an extension of *English* power.[8]

At an individual level, the evolution of a distinct sense of British identity can be most readily discerned in the case of members of the landowning elite. During the second half of the eighteenth century old barriers were being broken down and a socially and culturally homogeneous ruling class created which survived largely intact into the twentieth century.[9] The process of assimilation was aided by a number of trends: the way that many families from the Celtic periphery, desirous of recognition and advancement, were drawn into London's political and social life because of the opportunities it offered; the increasingly common practice for landowners from all parts of Britain to have their sons educated at the public schools and universities, where they absorbed common values and adopted modes of behaviour which further integrated them into the highest strata of society; and the effects of intermarriage between English, Welsh and Scottish families. Each of these trends interacted with and helped to reinforce the others. Thus, while Sir Watkin Williams Wynn, the third baronet, was a prominent Welsh Jacobite, his son, the fourth baronet, married an Englishwoman, and the fifth baronet was sent to Westminster School and Oxford University. Spectacular examples of landed families accumulating geographically diverse estates through marriage alliances include the Scottish Marquesses of Bute, who in three generations and four marriages added a hundred and sixteen thousand acres in England, Scotland and Wales, including the site of what became the Barry docks. Conversely, the Marquesses of Stafford, whose property was in the West Midlands, absorbed by marriage a vast eight hundred thousand-acre estate in northern Scotland, and their descendants became the Dukes of Sutherland. It did not necessarily follow that Celtic landowners abandoned their original heritage, but a sense of Britishness was superimposed which united them with their English counterparts. This was to have important consequences for the cohesion of the nation, especially after 1760 when a King ascended the throne who 'gloried in the name of Briton'.

GEORGE III: THE PATRIOT KING

George III was the first of the Hanoverian Kings to have been born in Britain, in 1738, and from the beginning of his long reign (1760–1820) he openly and proudly identified himself with the nation. In the course of time, much of the British public would come to accept him as the personal embodiment of national values and virtues. George's conception of his role as monarch was shaped by his tutor and mentor, Lord Bute, who instilled in him rather priggish notions of a strict adherence to public duty, coupled with personal piety and moral probity. Above all, Bute inspired George with the vision of a reign of virtue, in which the vice and corruption so endemic among politicians would be banished, factional party allegiances dissolved, and men of all political persuasions united in the service of the Crown, for the good of the country. This high-minded ideal of kingship drew upon the 'patriot' ideology espoused by critics of the Walpolean Whig oligarchy, whose cause had been opportunistically adopted by George's father, Frederick, Prince of Wales, before his premature death in 1751. When George succeeded his hated grandfather George II in 1760, therefore, he was resolved to fulfil what he took to be his father's dream, by presiding over an era of truth, harmony and beneficent government.[10]

In the short term, George undoubtedly achieved his ambition of smashing the old Whig–Tory party alignment, once he made it clear that the Whig monopoly of office was over and there was no longer any bar to the employment of talented Tories. The cost of this pursuit of a non-partisan system of government, however, was a decade of political chaos and instability, from which, ironically, the seeds were sown for the development of a new two-party alignment towards the end of the eighteenth century. Bute, whom the King initially pushed to the forefront, proved to be a disappointment, as he was temperamentally unsuited to the task of political leadership and soon resigned. Other short-lived ministries followed, including one headed by the great Earl of Chatham (formerly Pitt), but he was so riddled with gout and prone to mental depression as to be incapable of providing the national leadership which George was looking for. It was not until 1770 that the King at last found, in Lord North, a man who met his exacting criteria for the ideal Prime Minister: one who was upright and honourable yet good natured, with proven expertise in handling the national finances as Chancellor of the Exchequer, and popular and effective as a parliamentary manager. North quickly built a commanding position for himself, gathering a substantial parliamentary majority in support of his government.[11]

There appears to have been strong public backing for North's government when, in 1775, it embarked on a war with the North American colonists who were in revolt against British attempts to exercise powers of sovereignty over them. Unfortunately, from Britain's point of view, the country was militarily unprepared for such a conflict, and a fatal delay occurred in despatching troops which enabled the rebels to seize the initiative and overawe the loyalist minority in the colonies. Throughout the war, Britain was handicapped by the immense logistical problems of supplying and reinforcing troops operating across three thousand miles of ocean, and the army suffered serious depredations as a result of the colonists' use of guerrilla tactics. It is questionable whether Britain had the capability to impose its authority over its rebellious American subjects, but any possibility of success was removed by the entry into the war of France in 1778 and of Spain in 1779, both of whom were keen to extract revenge for the humiliations inflicted on them during the Seven Years War. Compelled to make defensive preparations against a possible invasion and to protect vital interests in the Mediterranean, the Caribbean and elsewhere, on top of campaigning on the North American mainland, Britain's resources were hopelessly overstretched and the outcome inevitable. At home, North's government faced mounting criticism, in and out of Parliament, because of its military failures and the high taxes and disruption of trade associated with it. Political support for the war effort steadily evaporated, and this situation was exploited by Whig oppositionists resentful of their exclusion from office since the 1760s and antagonistic towards the King. After General Cornwallis's surrender at Yorktown, in October 1781, Britain's will to carry on the fight was finally destroyed, and the independence of the 'United States of America' had to be recognised in the peace treaty of Versailles (1783).[12]

The loss of the American colonies was a devastating blow to British pride, and many people feared that the country might never recover its economic strength and international prestige. It was also a personal defeat for George III, who wanted to fight on at all costs. North had already resigned in 1782, completely demoralised, and domestic politics was plunged into a period of crisis until the King installed William Pitt the Younger, Chatham's twenty-four-year-old son, as Prime Minister in December 1783. The circumstances of Pitt's appointment were controversial, as the King exercised his prerogative power to dismiss an administration dominated by his Whig enemies, who had earlier forced their way into office against his wishes because they commanded a majority in the House of Commons.[13] Indeed, George was obliged to go further and allow an early general election to be held so that Pitt could strengthen his parliamentary position. On the other hand, it should be added that the election results in 1784 in the larger constituencies, where 'public opinion' counted for something, suggest that there was considerable backing for the King's action in asserting his customary right to choose his own ministers.

In building what proved to be a stable and durable government, Pitt presided over an extraordinarily rapid revival of national confidence and prosperity. Cold and aloof in his personal manner, yet rigorously dedicated to the pursuit of the public good, Pitt's chief contribution lay in his ability to inspire faith in the soundness of the national finances, which were left in disarray at the end of the American war. Administrative structures were overhauled, so that revenue collection became more efficient, a single consolidated fund replaced 103 separate revenue accounts, departmental expenditure was subject to auditing, competitive tendering for government contracts was introduced, economies were achieved by abolishing superfluous posts, high taxes on commodities such as tea and tobacco were reduced to discourage smuggling, and the budget deficit and the burden of the National Debt gradually diminished. Luckily for Pitt, the country benefited from a decade of peace, and it was particularly reassuring to find that trade with the USA was soon buoyant.

A grave new threat faced the country in 1793, however, when war again broke out with France. This differed from previous conflicts, in that following the revolution of 1789–92 France had declared itself a republic, executed its King and many members of the aristocracy, and sought to spread its revolutionary principles to the rest of Europe. Traditional French impulses for territorial aggrandisement, always infused with nationalist fervour, had acquired a dangerous ideological edge. Furthermore, the war proved to be an unusually prolonged affair, lasting, with one short break in 1802–3, until 1815, and for long periods France achieved military dominion over much of the continent. Unprecedented strains were placed both on the British economy and the people. Whereas annual government expenditure averaged £16 million in the peacetime years 1786–90, by 1811–15 the figure had reached £97.5 million. There were desperate moments, in 1797 and 1805, when Britain was totally isolated and its independent existence threatened by imminent French invasion, until the naval victories at Camperdown and Trafalgar respectively eased the pressure.

In the later stages of the conflict the French Emperor, Napoleon Buonaparte, pursued an alternative strategy of economic warfare, attempting to block British trade with Europe. This succeeded in inflicting severe hardship, causing as it did both unemployment and inflation, and these effects were exacerbated in the bleak years of 1811–12 by bad harvests. Nevertheless, it can be argued that on balance the experience of war, and the struggle for national survival, served to reinforce the British people's sense of unity under their Hanoverian King.[14]

It is true, as we shall see in chapter 3, that some in Britain were inspired by French revolutionary ideas, but recent historical scholarship has placed greater emphasis on manifestations of popular loyalism.[15] The early 1790s saw 'Church and King' riots in towns such as Birmingham and Manchester, which were directed at those suspected of sympathising with subversive foreign doctrines. Once the war had started, the British people as a whole, far from seeing the French as liberators, evidently regarded them as aggressors and tyrants. Indeed, the authorities found it necessary to mobilise the country's manpower resources on a much larger scale than in previous wars, as this was the only way of matching the 'people's armies' of France. Consequently, by 1809 at least ten per cent of the adult male population was enlisted in the regular armed forces, and another ten per cent were serving in local militia or volunteer units. Evidence from the militia returns gathered in 1798 and 1803 shows that substantial proportions of adult males, especially in the towns, had declared their willingness to join home defence units in the event of a French invasion. The decision taken in 1804 to distribute some two hundred thousand guns among the civilian population was a remarkable sign of the extent to which the country's governors were obliged to enter into a contract of trust with those whom they governed.

For members of the ruling elite, the opportunity to serve the nation in a patriotic cause, by supplying military leadership, helped to enhance their prestige and encourage a more favourable estimate of their social worth. In 1806, for example, around forty per cent of the country's naval officers came from landed families, while one-fifth of MPs were regular army officers and many more served in the local militia. At the same time, Pitt, who worked and drank himself into a premature grave through his single-minded commitment to the war effort, established a tradition of administrative professionalism which he passed on to disciples such as Spencer Perceval, Lord Liverpool and George Canning. The Pittites' detached, high-minded pursuit of what they took to be the 'national interest', rather than the selfish interests of sectional groups and classes, marked them out as the prime exponents of a distinctively British set of political values. Of course, the ideological dimension to the war meant that the Pittites were also defending an aristocracy-dominated status quo from the contagion of French democratic ideas. The rights of property were accordingly upheld (subject to an income tax imposed in 1799), and law and order maintained, with temporary coercive legislation considered justifiable to stamp out 'subversive' radical activity. Pitt and his followers thus laid the foundations for a new 'Toryism', which was to be the dominant political force until 1830, virtually monopolising the government of the country. Intellectual strength was drawn from the philosopher-politician Edmund Burke, whose *Reflections on the Revolution in France* (1790) had warned of the folly of sweeping away ancient social and political institutions, which he believed could only lead to instability and violence. Burke's argument for moderate, gradual change, cautiously adapting institutions whose very survival demonstrated their usefulness to the nation, was the main source of inspiration behind nineteenth-century Conservative ideology.

The most treasured institution of all was the monarchy, which, during the latter part of George III's reign, commanded something approaching the level of respect and affection which he had always desired for it. Since the 1780s, there had been unmistakable signs of a shift in public attitudes towards the King: the custom of playing 'God Save the King' before the start of theatre performances was established at this time; his portrayal in cartoons as a villain or tyrant gave way to a more flattering view of him as the personification of the nation and the national spirit – a John Bull or St George figure; and mythological stories were frequently told of how he travelled among his people incognito. George's obvious honesty, devotion to duty, personal respectability, frugality and love of domestic life all helped to shape this favourable perception of him, and they were reinforced by sympathy for his suffering as a result of periodic attacks of mental illness (which may have been symptomatic of an organic disease, porphyria). Patriotic responses to the French war accelerated this trend towards revering the monarch as a symbol of national unity and resolve. Thus, a crowd of two hundred thousand people watched the royal procession to St Paul's Cathedral in 1797 to give thanks for recent naval victories, and in 1809 jubilee celebrations were organised in 650 separate locations, including Liverpool, where a statue of the King was erected, and Birmingham, where the hero of Trafalgar, Lord Nelson, was similarly honoured.

Tragically for the King, by the time the Duke of Wellington triumphed over Napoleon at the battle of Waterloo in 1815, he was no longer able to appreciate the nation's achievement, having sunk into a permanent state of insanity, blindness and deafness. His eldest son had been appointed as Prince Regent, to rule on his behalf, in 1811. Public warmth was nevertheless memorably displayed when the old King finally died in January 1820, with London shops closing as a gesture of respect, and the poor wearing marks of mourning. The contrast with the indifferent reaction to the deaths of the first two Hanoverian Kings is a good indication of how firmly entrenched the dynasty now was, and temporary spells of unpopularity during subsequent reigns never came near to undermining its position.

As for the nation itself, Britain in 1815 was in the unaccustomed position of being able to exercise considerable influence in the councils of Europe, owing to its heavy commitment of manpower as well as money to the military crusade against Napoleonic France. At the Congress of Vienna, where the post-war map of Europe was drawn, Britain enjoyed equal status with the major continental States, Austria, Prussia and Russia, and worked to create a balance of power intended to preserve the future peace. The war had also provided fresh opportunities for the familiar pursuit of colonial acquisitions, and Britain's maritime supremacy enabled the strategically valuable islands of Malta and Heligoland, along with Trinidad, Tobago and other Caribbean islands, to be added to the nation's already extensive overseas territories. One effect of the conflict, indeed, had been to cripple the overseas trade of Britain's main continental rivals, France and Spain.

In one other respect, too, the war occasioned an extension of British political authority, but with altogether more ambiguous consequences. Ireland was finally incorporated into what became the 'United Kingdom', by the Act of Union of 1800, and thereafter it sent representatives to sit in the Parliament at Westminster. This assumption of formal control over a people who for centuries had been subject to British interference and direction was motivated by security considerations, as it was feared that the hostile Catholic majority in Ireland might offer their country as a platform for a French attack on Britain. Unsurprisingly, given this context of mutual hatred and suspicion, Catholic Ireland proved resistant to the process that had drawn Protestant Wales and Scotland into an English-dominated political system in earlier centuries. Instead, the relationship between the two islands was to be a constant source of friction and recrimination throughout the nineteenth century and beyond.

THE STATE OF THE NATION

After a lengthy period when historical writing on eighteenth-century Britain was in a rather moribund state, the 1980s saw the publication of a number of challenging reinterpretations which have greatly enlivened debate on the subject. Despite the fundamental contradictions between these competing accounts, none of which presents an entirely convincing picture by itself, each has important things to tell us about the Hanoverian age. Their apparent incompatibility merely highlights the diversity and complexity of a society at any given moment, and the danger of relying on a single analytical tool to encompass and explain the attitudes and experiences of a whole people.

Certainly the most controversial perspective is that offered by Jonathan Clark, who argues that England (he does not mention Scotland) ought properly to be considered as an *ancien régime* State, similar to continental nations like France.[16] Clark is dismissive of the conventional view that English society differed fundamentally from others in Europe, maintaining that it too was essentially static and hierarchical, dominated as it was by the triple pillars of monarchy, aristocracy and Church. He points to evidence for the continuing belief in the divine right of Kings, and for the repudiation of the Whig doctrine that Parliament could legitimately settle the succession to the throne, in the way that it had presumed to do in 1689 and 1701. Clark places particular emphasis on the role of the Church of England which, through its alliance with the political regime, underpinned what he describes as a 'confessional State'.

After all, the Church and its communicants enjoyed a privileged status in various respects. Only Anglicans, in theory at least, possessed full rights of citizenship, entitling them to hold public office and serve in the higher ranks of the armed forces. The Church also occupied a prominent position in parish life and in the education system at all levels (entrance to Oxford and Cambridge Universities was restricted to Anglicans). According to Clark, the ministration and teaching of the Church provided a robust moral code which reached down to the lowest strata of society, acting as a powerful force for discipline and cohesion.

These claims have aroused some strong scholarly feelings,[17] and there are many obvious flaws in Clark's argument, but this is not to say that his thesis is without value. It is clearly true that belief in divine right theory was not extinguished by the Glorious Revolution of 1688–9, and that it survived at least until the middle of the eighteenth century, finding an intellectual home at Oxford University and helping to sustain the Jacobite case. But Clark's insistence that such ideas remained at the forefront of political thinking until the 1820s seems strained and eccentric, and relies on a very narrow range of evidence. In reality, while eighteenth-century monarchs undoubtedly exercised important constitutional powers, including the appointment and dismissal of ministers, they were always obliged to operate within a framework created by the permanent existence of Parliament, which represented a triumph for the principles behind the Glorious Revolution. This also distinguished England from the major European States, where there had been a long-term trend towards the centralisation of power in the hands of monarchs and the decline of representative assemblies.

As for the Church, its alleged social omnipotence is difficult to square with the problem that, owing to the unequal distribution of resources, it was manifestly failing to meet the spiritual needs of large sections of the population. In 1780, less than forty per cent of English parishes actually had a resident clergymen, and this was one reason why the Church's role was being usurped by the dramatic expansion of other Protestant denominations. From the 1740s onwards the most dynamic religious force was the Methodist movement, founded by John Wesley, which sought to reach out to people in distant areas poorly served by the established Church, such as the north-east and south-west of England and much of Wales. At their emotionally charged, open-air mass meetings, Methodist preachers spread the evangelical message that *all* souls, however humble, could find salvation through faith in Jesus. Later in the century, two of the older dissenting bodies, the Baptists and the Independents, were revitalised by evangelical fervour and experienced a rapid growth in membership.[18] Quite apart from all this, we must be careful not to exaggerate the extent to which Anglicans really possessed a monopoly of the trappings of citizenship. Since 1689 the law had tolerated other forms of religious worship (hardly consistent with the idea of an Anglican confessional State), and Walpole's Indemnity Acts made it possible for dissenters to circumvent the bar to their holding public office. Furthermore, there is the irony that while a strident Protestantism shaped the outward manifestation of the 'national character', it did so by promoting a sense of pride in the superiority and distinctness of the English to other peoples. Most contemporaries would have been utterly aghast at Clark's assertion that they were living under a continental-style *ancien régime*.

One aspect of Clark's argument, however, concerning the continued social ascendancy of the aristocracy, has been endorsed by scholars who would not necessarily agree with the rest of his *ancien régime* thesis. John Cannon's study of the peerage[19] has questioned the notion, popular at the time as well as with many historians since, that Britain benefited from having an 'open elite' to which successful businessmen and others with newly-created wealth were able to gain admission. Eighteenth-century Britain's relative stability, compared to many European States, has often been attributed to this process of upward social movement, which supposedly prevented the development of antagonism between the elite and the 'middling orders' by introducing new blood into the elite.[20] However, Cannon demonstrates that only about ten per cent of peerages awarded in this period went to people without previous aristocratic connections, leading him to conclude that the elite largely retained its exclusivity. He goes further, maintaining that aristocratic families were even *strengthening* their grip on the levers of political and social power, since they supplied much of the personnel for central government, the diplomatic service, the judiciary, and the upper echelons of the Church and the armed forces, while the shared experience of education at the public schools and universities reinforced their sense of group solidarity. For instance, of the sixty-five individuals who sat in the Cabinet at some stage between 1782 and 1820, forty-three were peers and fourteen were sons of peers. By 1800 English peers (who sat in the House of Lords by hereditary right) also controlled the election of over two hundred members of the House of Commons, double the figure of a century earlier, thanks to their ownership of landed property. The idea of an 'open elite' emerges from Cannon's research, therefore, as little more than a complacent myth.

Much of what Cannon has to say about the tentacles of aristocratic power is undoubtedly correct, but his specific denial of the existence of an 'open elite' can be criticised on the ground that it is based on far too narrow a definition of what constituted the elite. He focuses solely on the English peers, of whom there were just 271 in 1800, but this is to ignore the point that the peerage was the apex· of a considerably larger social elite characterised by its ownership of land. In 1760 there were approximately seven hundred baronets and knights (who did not sit in the House of Lords) and far larger numbers of untitled 'gentry'. A better appreciation of the situation can be gained from the fact that in 1780 some twelve to thirteen thousand families, titled and untitled, owned half of the land in England. And it was precisely at the lower levels of landed society that recruitment from the 'middling orders' tended to occur, as a minority of businessmen and professional people used their wealth to acquire an estate and so gain a vital first step on the ladder of social respectability. Several generations might pass before the process was complete, in which time connections with the existing aristocracy were likely to be made, thus explaining Cannon's findings. It is arguable that, contrary to Cannon's view, there was a wider landowning elite whose composition was sufficiently fluid to prevent the existence of a privileged minority of peers, at the very top of the ladder, from becoming intolerable to the rest of society.

Another stimulating contribution to recent historical debate has suggested that, while Britain was definitely not an autocratic State like its *ancien régime* neighbours, given the accepted role of Parliament in the system of government, the country nevertheless acquired certain features normally associated with the continental autocracies. John Brewer has described Britain as a 'fiscal-military State', which, by effectively harnessing its resources, was able to claim a place alongside the major European powers.[21] Contrary to the widely-held belief that the British people enjoyed the blessings of light-handed government and low taxation, Brewer shows that the nation's frequent involvement in major international conflicts – in 1689–97, 1702–13, 1740–8, 1756–63, 1775–83 and 1793–1815 – necessitated the development of a formidable State apparatus. The raising of taxation was of course vital, and this task was performed by a comparatively efficient and uncorrupt bureaucracy, and involved a growing legion of local revenue officials who gathered the land tax and customs and excise duties. Of even greater importance was the evolution of new financial institutions and practices which enabled the State to pay for its military campaigns increasingly through long-term loans. The Bank of England, founded in 1694, raised public loans for the government, and Parliament guaranteed the interest payments on them from tax revenues. In this way, governments were able to obtain money reliably and cheaply, without recourse to ruinous levels of taxation. Nevertheless, the National Debt rose from £14.7 million in 1697 to £243 million in 1784, and by the latter date the per capita tax burden imposed by central government was heavier than in France (although this does not take account of feudal dues, for which many French people were also liable). Incidentally, the fact that many thousands of people had money invested in government stock created a powerful interest group desirous of maintaining political stability.

While there is much to commend Brewer's thesis, it does require some qualification. Compared to the European autocracies, Britain still possessed a small land army and was therefore incapable of intervening on the continent without allies. The armies that it did raise always contained a high proportion of foreign mercenaries. Even in the supreme military effort to defeat Napoleon, the decisive part was played by the mass armies of Russia, Prussia and Austria, before the battle of Waterloo. Britain's chief asset was its highly professional navy, which protected the country from invasion and made possible the expansion of its commercial empire. Furthermore, while Britain was clearly capable of mobilising its resources for war to an impressive degree, this did impose serious strains on the country, and it is significant that the armed forces were always drastically cut back as soon as peace was restored. Brewer is right to emphasise the strength of the British State, but we should not suppose from this that the country was a vast military machine.

To the extent that Britain was a well-organised 'fiscal-military State', this reflected its ability to tap into the new sources of wealth being created by its flourishing commercial and financial sectors. This in turn raises the question of what impact the resulting expansion of the 'middling orders' of society had on the nation as a whole. No precise data exists, but contemporary estimates in the 1750s indicated that about one-fifth of families had annual incomes of £50 or more, and another one-fifth had between £40 and £50. Since £40 was roughly double the level needed for basic subsistence, it appears that a significant portion of the population was living in reasonable comfort. Paul Langford has argued that the economic interests and cultural and political values of these 'polite and commercial people', as he calls them, became ever more central to the way Hanoverian Britain was run. Their aspirations and concerns, Langford insists, exerted a profound influence on standards of public behaviour.[22]

Such a perspective is totally at odds, of course, with Clark's belief in a hierarchical *ancien régime*, and it also substantially modifies Cannon's claims for aristocratic domination. In Langford's view, parliamentary business was preoccupied with the need to represent local interests in regard to the passing of legislation. MPs spent far more time sitting on committees dealing with parochial matters such as land enclosures, roads and water supplies, than they did in debating great national issues. The landowning elite might have been formally in control, occupying as they did many of the places in Parliament and the government, but there was no question of them exploiting this position simply to pursue their own ends. Frank O'Gorman's work on the electoral system substantiates Langford's argument, as he finds that while voters were often deferential towards those who ruled over them, the relationship between electors and elected was a reciprocal one, involving rights and obligations on both sides.[23] Again, the fact that the landed elite filled so many of the seats in the House of Commons did not mean that the opinions and wishes of their constituents could be ignored.

That it can be possible for historians to present such dramatically conflicting accounts of the nature of eighteenth-century Britain testifies to the rich ambiguity of its political and social structures. Britain was a nation in which the monarch still exercised considerable power, but subject to the constraints imposed by the obligation to work through Parliament, while the rights of all subjects (to trial by jury, for example) were guaranteed by the rule of law. The landowning elite similarly retained great power and influence, notably in Parliament, but it could not afford to disregard the views of other sections of society. The Church of England enjoyed many privileges attaching to its status as the official Church, but in practice its position was being undermined by the growth of rival Protestant denominations, and probably also by mounting religious indifference. Britain prospered thanks to the expansion of commerce, but it relied heavily on the military arm of the State to protect and procure its overseas markets. Ultimately, the existing social and political framework proved to be sufficiently flexible, yet resilient enough, to withstand the military, economic and ideological pressures emanating from the French Revolution.[24] How the nation survived the effects of internal economic and social change, and the rise of new political methods and ideologies, will be considered in the next chapter.

THREE

The Early Industrial
Age, 1750–1832

INTRODUCTION

If Britain, at the end of the Napoleonic wars in 1815, was indisputably a great international power, widely admired (and self-admiring) for its traditions of parliamentary government and political liberty, it was also rapidly emerging as the dominant economic force in Europe. A long-term process of economic growth and development was taking place, with roots stretching far back into the eighteenth century and even earlier, and its climax would not be reached until the second half of the nineteenth century. By that time, Britain was the most highly industrialised and urbanised nation in history, and its social character had been irreversibly altered.

The term 'Industrial Revolution' is still commonly used to describe this phenomenon, although its validity has been called into question by specialist scholars.[1] In fact, the concept of an Industrial Revolution did not exist in Britain before the 1880s, and it is therefore always important to bear in mind that no one, during the period covered in this chapter, actually thought of what was happening to their country in quite the terms with which we are so familiar. Another reason for caution about using such a grandiose phrase is that the word 'revolution' hardly seems appropriate for what was a gradual and cumulative process of change. Nor did Britain experience a simple transition from being an agrarian to an industrial nation. By around 1720, for instance, London had displaced Amsterdam as the commercial and financial capital of Europe, and, as we saw in the last chapter, an overseas trading empire was being built up throughout the eighteenth century. These and other sectors continued to be vitally important to the nation's economy. What really has to be described, then, is a complex picture of expansion and diversification, one aspect of which was the addition of a thick industrial layer to an already comparatively well-developed economy.

Any account of Britain's economic transformation is inevitably going to be hampered by the absence of adequate and reliable statistical data on such matters as growth rates of National Income, output levels in specific industries, the value of imports and exports, and workers' living standards. No amount of mathematical ingenuity on the part of economic historians can ever remedy this fundamental defect. To attempt to provide a definitive evaluation of the various components in Britain's economic equation would therefore be quite futile. Instead, the first section of this chapter will confine itself to the less ambitious task of identifying these components, and considering their general effects on the country and the ways in which they interacted. Perhaps it was not inevitable that they should have become connected and produced the results that they did, but these economic components were nevertheless inextricably linked at this time.

ECONOMIC AND SOCIAL CHANGE

In the specific case of Britain, economic growth derived much of its momentum from the effects of a population explosion. No national census was carried out during the eighteenth century, but scattered evidence from local counts suggests that, whereas numbers were fairly static up to about 1750, they began to increase thereafter. It is believed that the British population in 1750 stood at around 7.5 million. The first national census, in 1801, arrived at a figure of 10.69 million, and by 1831 this had increased to 16.37 million. Indeed, the British population expanded at a rate in excess of ten per cent per decade throughout the nineteenth century, so that in 1901 it totalled 37 million. Scholarly debate continues over the causes of this spectacular increase, but one major influence was surely a fall in the death rate resulting from the disappearance, probably for biological reasons, of that great scourge of Europe since the fourteenth century, the bubonic plague or 'black death'. Rapid population growth, after all, was not unique to Britain, and occurred in many other parts of Europe, including Ireland, which did not experience industrialisation. Other possible contributors to a lowering of the death rate were the declining incidence of smallpox, due to the spread of vaccination from the 1760s, of typhus ('gaol fever') thanks to the wider use of washable cotton fabrics, and of malaria ('ague') owing to the drainage of low-lying areas of land. At the same time, there is strong evidence to indicate that birth rates were rising, particularly among the urban population, as greater employment opportunities enabled people to marry at an earlier age, thus lengthening women's effective period of fertility. Once the birth rate had started to rise it became self-perpetuating, as ever-larger proportions of the population were of child-bearing age: in 1821 over sixty per cent of the British people were aged under thirty. To a very qualified extent, therefore, it is true to say that industrialisation in Britain helped to create its own workforce.[2]

Had circumstances been different, a substantial rise in the number of Britons might easily have led to famine and mass-starvation – a calamity not unknown in other countries at this time. The fact that such a disaster was avoided is a tribute to the improvements that had been made in methods of agricultural production since the seventeenth century. These improvements included the adoption of new crop rotations to maximise the yield from the soil, the expansion of 'mixed farming' (where some arable crops were used to feed livestock, which in turn supplied manure to fertilise the soil for more arable crops), the application of scientific breeding methods to increase the size of livestock, and the trend towards larger-sized farms geared to producing surpluses for sale at market, in place of small-scale subsistence farming. Prior to 1750, the ironic effect of greater efficiency in agricultural production was to depress the price of cereal crops, but thereafter, rising demand for foodstuffs created by population growth brought higher prices and prosperity for farmers. Far from being incompatible, agricultural and industrial growth in Britain went together: a flourishing agricultural sector helped to create the conditions in which industry could develop.[3]

Advances in agricultural production meant that an expanding population could be supported, even though increasing proportions of it were engaged in industrial and other non-agrarian occupations. It is estimated that by 1801 only thirty-six per cent of the workforce was employed in agriculture, compared with twenty-nine per cent in industry and mining and eleven per cent in trade and transport.[4] As these figures might imply, there had been significant industrial activity even before 1750, but this was subsequently conducted on a vastly greater scale and often in new locations. Woollen textile production, for example, had previously been concentrated in the towns and villages of East Anglia and the West Country, but during the eighteenth century these areas were overtaken by the West Riding of Yorkshire and Lanarkshire, and eventually they went into decline. Meantime, in Lancashire, cotton textile manufacturing rapidly emerged as a dynamic new sector, employing three hundred thousand people by 1835. Deposits of coal and iron ore made South Wales, Staffordshire, Yorkshire, the north-east of England and the Clyde Valley in Scotland, important centres of iron and steel production, while the last two of these regions were also noted for shipbuilding. Numerous metalworking trades grew up in Sheffield and Birmingham and their vicinities, while Staffordshire established itself as the heart of pottery-making.

There was also a slow but unmistakable trend towards the concentration of production in factories rather than small workshops or people's homes, although the pace of change varied from industry to industry. It occurred much earlier in cotton than in woollen production, while in the hosiery and boot- and shoe-making districts of the East Midlands it did not become widespread until late in the nineteenth century. Associated with the rise of the factory was the introduction of new machinery with enormously enhanced capacity, including the celebrated spinning looms of the cotton industry. The progressive application of steam power to work such machines, from the 1780s onwards, became the defining characteristic of British industrialisation.

Sustainable population growth generated a thriving home market for the output of these new industries. This was particularly so because growing proportions of the non-agrarian workforce were living in urban settlements and required the provision of a wide range of goods and services. By 1801 the population of London exceeded one million, around ten per cent of the British total, and industrial towns like Birmingham, Sheffield, Manchester, Leeds and Glasgow, as well as older centres like Bristol, Liverpool and Norwich, had more than fifty thousand residents. Basic items of clothing, footwear, furnishings and domestic ware were naturally in heavy demand, while enterprising businessmen such as the pottery manufacturer Josiah Wedgwood deliberately targeted the more affluent consumers. The success of Thomas Chippendale's designs, published in his *Gentlemen's and Cabinet Maker's Directory* (1754) and copied by many regional furniture-makers, likewise testified to the growing disposable wealth of the nation.[5] Rising internal demand, as an accompaniment to population growth, was crucially important for the industrialisation process, but there was another side to this particular coin. The application of new technology, which brought improved efficiency of production, helped to make many manufactured items considerably cheaper, opening up a wider market among poorer consumers previously unable to purchase such things.

Overseas trade provided a valuable supplement to the domestic market for British manufacturers. Exports accounted for perhaps one-third of total industrial output in 1800, and the textile and iron sectors were particularly dependent on custom from abroad. During the course of the eighteenth century there was a shift in emphasis away from markets in Europe towards greater trade with the Americas, the Caribbean, Asia and West Africa. These areas in turn supplied British consumers with tea, coffee, sugar, tobacco, rice, silks, spices and so on, while industry gained essential raw materials such as cotton and dyes. Where Britain exercised imperial control, profits could also be made by re-exporting colonial produce to European countries, which were prohibited from trading directly with the colonies. The shipping industry was similarly boosted by its exclusive rights to the colonial carrying trade. In London and other major ports, banking and insurance services developed to help facilitate overseas trade. Until 1807, slaves formed an integral but increasingly controversial part of Britain's international trading system: acquired on the West African coast in exchange for manufactured goods, they were shipped across the Atlantic, sold to pay for produce which could be brought back to Britain, and then put to work on the sugar and cotton plantations.

The transformation of Britain into the world's premier industrial nation could not have occurred without major improvements to its transport infrastructure. Turnpike trusts – in effect, public toll roads – were growing in number throughout the eighteenth century, and created a network of better-constructed and better-maintained roads covering some twenty-five thousand miles by 1830. From the 1760s onwards, developments in canal construction led to an expansion of water-borne traffic, and by the 1820s around four thousand miles of canals linked the country's navigable rivers, opening up the industrial heartlands to the major urban centres and ports. Canals were the real arteries of early industrial Britain, until the advent of railways in the 1830s and 1840s provided a more rapid means of communication between different parts of the country.

Banking facilities were another vital prop for industry, although the leading role here was played not by the big London houses, whose operations were geared towards financing international trade and making loans to governments, but by the provincial, or so-called 'country', banks. There were only a dozen or so country banks in 1750, but this figure rose to about a hundred in 1775 and six hundred in 1815. One such institution was Lloyds of Birmingham, which went on to join the ranks of the London houses. Not only did the country banks handle deposits, transfer funds across the country and provide businessmen with short-term credit (capital investment was less common), but they issued their own banknotes which helped to lubricate the wheels of their local economies.

Long-term economic development over the course of the eighteenth and nineteenth centuries further consolidated Britain as a national entity by creating a more fully-integrated economic structure. Far from meaning that Britain became a more homogeneous nation, however, economic integration encouraged the various regions to specialise in producing those commodities in which they possessed the greatest comparative advantage, allowing them to develop distinctive characteristics. Improved transport communications and sophisticated trading and banking networks made it possible for one area to concentrate on, say, textile manufacturing, secure in the knowledge that demand for its output existed beyond its immediate vicinity, and that supplies of other industrial goods and foodstuffs could readily be obtained from outside. Regional economic specialisation, in other words, rested on an enhanced degree of interdependence between the regions, and thus brought the country closer together. Britain enjoyed the immense advantage, after the Act of Union in 1707, of being a single, large free-trading area, unlike many parts of Europe, which were politically fragmented into small States with customs barriers. Economic success stimulated national awareness in another way, fuelling the already legendary prejudice against foreigners by reinforcing the belief in the superior character of the British island race. In particular, the work ethic and spirit of enterprise found among the British people were often attributed to their Protestant culture, and unfavourable contrasts were drawn with 'backward' Catholic countries like Spain and Ireland.

With regard to the social consequences of economic change, the overall effect was to add to the rich complexity of a multi-layered structure. It is customary to associate economic growth and urbanisation with the rise of the 'middling orders' or the 'middling sort' (to use contemporary terminology), those involved in running industrial, commercial and financial operations, along with members of professions like the law and medicine. This is an entirely valid perspective, and the political significance of the 'middling orders' will become clear later in this chapter. But it is also important to emphasise that economic expansion brought new prosperity to many members of the older, landowning elite. Not only did they benefit from rising rental incomes, thanks to improvements in agricultural production and the buoyant price of foodstuffs, they were frequently involved in related business activities as well. Those fortunate enough to have coal or other mineral deposits under their land, such as Lord Fitzwilliam in Yorkshire and Lord Durham in the north-east, were enormously enriched as a result. Landowners also invested in turnpikes and canals (and, later on, railways), because of the advantages they brought in terms of transporting their own produce and minerals. Happiest of all were those families, including the Grosvenors (later Dukes of Westminster) and Russells (Dukes of Bedford), who owned land on which urban development was taking place, and who consequently found their rental incomes soaring.[6] The reality of industrial Britain, therefore, was that the landed interest fully shared in the gains accruing from economic growth: the burgeoning wealth of the 'middling orders' did not automatically mean the demise of the landowning elite.

For the 'lower orders' of society, the picture is far more ambiguous and controversial. Remarkable though it was that the economy proved capable of supporting such a rapidly rising population, it is by no means certain that the labouring classes in general experienced significant improvements in their living standards until the 1820s and possibly later. If it is true that labourers were attracted to the industrial towns by the wider employment opportunities and higher wages on offer, compared to what they could expect in agriculture, this advantage has to be offset by a number of unquantifiable considerations. For instance, industrial production was prone to cyclical fluctuations in demand, which meant chronic insecurity and occasional periods of mass unemployment for the workforce; there was the problem of adjusting to the disciplined working environment of factories, which was suited to the rhythm of the machine rather than the human being; and there were often extremely long hours of work (twelve to fourteen hours a day, six days a week, was not unknown), as well as unhealthy and dangerous conditions. A large proportion of the workforce in textile factories and coal mines consisted of women and children, and it was not until the 1830s and 1840s that effective legislation was carried to regulate their employment.

To keep matters in perspective, it must be remembered that the unrelenting grimness of life in the factories and mines typified the experience of only a fraction of the labouring population, many more of whom were employed in a diversity of occupations including agriculture, fishing, construction work, transport services, all kinds of crafts, and domestic service. Much industrial production at the beginning of the nineteenth century was still carried out in workshops or in the home, where entire families worked on raw materials supplied by middlemen who then collected the finished product and organised its distribution. Factories were an important new feature of the landscape of early industrial Britain, but this period did not witness anything like the creation of a uniform, factory-based 'proletariat'. Whatever their form of employment, though, labouring families often found themselves in overcrowded and insanitary towns which had grown up without much thought for the environmental consequences. This was the area where real improvement was longest delayed, despite various pieces of public-health legislation enacted from the 1840s onwards, and a scandalously high rate of infant mortality (over one hundred and fifty per thousand births) persisted as late as the 1890s. Recent research has even indicated that, among the poorer social groups, people born after the 1830s were smaller in height than those of previous generations, a downward trend that continued until the 1860s. It may well be the case, therefore, that poor nutrition and deteriorating environmental conditions long continued to outweigh any improvements in monetary incomes.[7]

CONSTITUTIONAL DEVELOPMENTS

The purpose of the next two sections of this chapter is to examine the changes taking place in the political system over roughly the same time-span as the economic and social trends just described. Important developments can be identified both in political institutions and in the way in which politics was conducted. As with the economy, there was no sudden 'revolution' in British politics, but rather a gradual process of evolution involving the acquisition of new characteristics. Nor was it the case that a direct causal relationship existed between economic and social change, on the one hand, and political change, on the other, although there undoubtedly was a continuous interaction between these different spheres of human activity.

During the eighteenth and early nineteenth centuries, the British constitution assumed a form that, in many of its essentials, is recognisable to modern eyes.[8] Above all, we can identify the emergence of the Cabinet, as a co-ordinating body consisting of senior government ministers, and of the office of Prime Minister. The absence of any written constitution, and the consequent tendency for new practices to be recognised as established conventions only very slowly, means that we cannot pinpoint precise dates for the appearance of these practices. Technically, throughout this period, all ministers were appointed by the monarch and were accountable to him or her, and the monarch also presided over the Privy Council, which consisted of ministers and other eminent lay and clerical advisors. In practice, however, the Privy Council played an increasingly honorary role, and from the 1690s a small inner group of leading ministers took to meeting together – originally in the monarch's presence but after 1714 independently – in what came to be known as the 'Cabinet Council'. For various reasons, including the early Hanoverian Kings' preoccupation with German affairs, the monopoly of office enjoyed by the Whigs, and the growing scale and complexity of government business, the monarchy became distanced from the everyday conduct of affairs and reliant on the advice of the Cabinet before exercising its prerogative powers. Very gradually, this pattern was reinforced by the principle of Cabinet solidarity, or 'collective responsibility', which decreed that individual ministers must adhere to the line of policy agreed with their Cabinet colleagues and not formulate policy personally with the monarch.

Associated with the rise of Cabinet government was the tendency for one minister to achieve a position of pre-eminence, becoming 'primus inter pares' (first among equals) and the Cabinet's chief representative in its dealings with the monarch. Certain ministers in Queen Anne's reign, notably Sidney Godolphin and Robert Harley, briefly achieved a position resembling that of a Prime Minister, but it is from the time of Sir Robert Walpole, First Lord of the Treasury from 1721 until 1742, that the continuous history of the office is usually dated. It subsequently became the norm for the post of First Lord of the Treasury to be connected with the premiership (as it is today), although not all of Walpole's successors exercised the same degree of personal authority. As the Prime Minister's position became openly recognised and accepted, he also acquired greater say in who his Cabinet colleagues should be, with the result that by the time of Lord Liverpool (1812–27) he was effectively choosing the rest of the government. Apart from his ascendancy in the Cabinet, the Prime Minister derived independent power from his leadership role in Parliament, which had secured for itself a permanent place in the constitutional set-up since 1688, meeting every year. The monarch's need for someone capable of building and managing a parliamentary majority, with which to transact government business, made an efficient Prime Minister an indispensable asset.

Parliament, rather than the royal court, was now the crucial arena for political debate and conflict, and the idea accordingly gained acceptance that politicians excluded from office might legitimately form themselves into an organised group, or party, for the explicit purpose of opposing the King's ministers and seeking to take their place. There was nothing new, of course, about parliamentary opposition to governments and their policies, but it was only towards the end of the eighteenth century that politicians found it possible to engage in *systematic* opposition without this being construed as disreputable or even treasonable behaviour. A wide gulf separated the early Hanoverian period, when the Tories were permanently excluded from office because of their suspected leanings towards Jacobitism, and the later decades of the century when this threat to the ruling dynasty had disappeared. The concept of systematic opposition to the government is particularly associated with the Whig leaders, Lord Rockingham (1765–82) and Charles James Fox (1782–1806), who not only sought to attack ministers whenever possible but also insisted that they would only take office en bloc, as a party, and not allow themselves to be recruited individually. Powerful intellectual justification for this stance was supplied by Rockingham's protégé, the philosopher-politician Edmund Burke, whose pamphlet, *Thoughts on the Causes of the Present Discontents* (1770), defined party as an honourable body of men joined together in the pursuit of shared principles (whether it was always like this is another matter). Consequently, by the beginning of the nineteenth century, it was considered both necessary and *desirable* that there should be a loyal opposition to act as a check on ministers. In the 1820s the term 'His Majesty's Opposition' was coined and quickly entered into the political vocabulary.

What these developments were ultimately leading towards was a system of parliamentary politics in which two parties, based on government and opposition, dominated the scene. It is true, as we saw in chapter one, that Whig and Tory parties had come into being late in the seventeenth century, and their philosophies and traditions were continually adapted and refined during the century that followed.[9] However, there was no simple linear progression in terms of party organisation, and it remained the case that large numbers of MPs were uncommitted to either side, regarding themselves as 'independents'. This situation only really seems to have altered after the end of the Napoleonic wars in 1815, when the ideological conflict between a Tory government and a Whig opposition (discussed in the next section) absorbed the vast majority of backbenchers, at least to the extent that they voted consistently with one side or the other on major issues.

The wider significance of this trend towards something resembling a competitive 'two-party system' was that it encouraged both government and opposition to engage with various political movements manifesting themselves outside Parliament. Politicians, before the end of the eighteenth century, were aware of the dangers, and the potential, of what they themselves called 'public opinion', and this term was often used virtually synonymously with another, which made its appearance in the 1790s, namely 'the middle classes'.[10] We shall now consider some of the ways in which this mysterious force was making its presence felt and contributing to the growth of a *national* political culture.

AN EXPANDING POLITICAL CULTURE

An impression still commonly persists that the system for electing Members of Parliament was entirely divorced from considerations of political principle, because the behaviour of the few who were allowed to vote was determined by the twin influences of bribery and intimidation. Admittedly, there is a good deal of truth in this view of things: in 1831 the total electorate was less than half a million, all of them males; many boroughs were absurdly small and property owners were effectively able to nominate the MPs; where there was an electorate to be influenced, monetary rewards and lavish hospitality were often regarded as a normal part of a candidate's expenditure; and votes were cast in public, with no ballot box, making the task of bribery or coercion so much easier.

All the same, signs of a vibrant political culture can be detected in a substantial minority of constituencies. Frank O'Gorman's study of the period 1734 to 1832 shows that 124 of the 215 English and Welsh boroughs remained completely dormant, but in the other ninety-one there were at least some signs of life for at least some of the time. In around sixty of these active constituencies, including Canterbury, Exeter, Norwich, Preston and Shrewsbury, national issues helped to shape local political conflict, which increasingly mirrored the rivalry between the Whig and Tory parties in Parliament. The fact that there was no uniform voting qualification for boroughs (it varied from one place to another) goes far towards explaining this situation, because in constituencies with a relatively generous franchise the electorate was far too large to be controlled by a patron. Westminster, for instance, had seventeen thousand voters by 1830, the City of London twelve thousand, Bristol seven thousand, and Liverpool, Leicester and Nottingham about five thousand each. As for the counties, landowners were usually able to maintain control, but the relatively low forty-shilling freehold qualification for voting meant that there were large electorates of farmers whose interests had to be taken into account. Thus, even within the 'unreformed' electoral system there were significant representative elements.[11]

If the 'unreformed' system was capable, to some degree, of reflecting popular feeling, a more potent and persistent force for articulating public opinion existed in the form of the newspaper and periodical press, which enjoyed sustained expansion both in numbers and total sales. By 1750 it seems that there were already about a dozen newspapers published in London (not all of them dailies) and over thirty provincial titles, and periodicals such as the *Spectator, Examiner, Tatler* and *Gentleman's Magazine* were well established. According to recent research, London had fifty-five newspaper titles in 1830, the rest of England and Wales 158, and Scotland thirty-seven. The most successful London paper at this date was *The Times* (founded in 1785), with daily sales approaching ten thousand; its main rivals were the *Morning Herald* and the *Morning Chronicle*. Of the provincials, a few of the more weighty titles like the *Leeds Mercury* and the *Manchester Guardian* were achieving daily sales of three to four thousand. Such figures would have to be multiplied several-fold, though, in order to gain an accurate impression of these newspapers' effective readership, as they often circulated in coffee houses and taverns, where they might also be read aloud for the benefit of the illiterate. Government and opposition parties both attempted, with limited success, to influence press reporting by offering subsidies and other financial inducements to proprietors and editors, but most found it more profitable to operate on an independent commercial basis, which meant representing the public mood of the moment. The significance of the press was that it contributed to the growth of a national rather than a purely local political culture. For instance, provincial newspapers placed great emphasis on reporting proceedings in Parliament (the legality of which was established in 1771), helping to bring national issues regularly into the consciousness of people living far from London.[12]

The most powerful expression of what may broadly be termed 'middle class' political consciousness came through the humanitarian campaign for the abolition of slavery and the slave trade. This movement, which originated in the 1780s, attracted support from a wide spectrum of society, including affluent businessmen and professionals, as well as borderline groups like shopkeepers and skilled artisans. There was a strong religious impulse behind the agitation, provided most famously by the Clapham sect, a group of Anglican evangelicals. One of them, William Wilberforce, the son of a Hull merchant, acted as the parliamentary spokesman for the cause. The anti-slavery campaign is of great importance for the way it pioneered a number of techniques for bringing pressure to bear on governments and MPs, which were subsequently adopted by many other organisations. Petitions were drawn up and presented to Parliament (510 of them in 1792), marches were held, voters canvassed, pledges demanded from candidates at election time and unwelcome publicity given to MPs who voted the wrong way. Full use was made of newspapers as a weapon in the struggle, and some were even founded specifically to promote the anti-slavery case. After Britain's involvement in the slave trade was outlawed in 1807, a temporary lull in activity followed until the 1820s, when new networks of hundreds of local groups emerged to press for the emancipation of slaves already in the colonies. One interesting feature of this later campaign was the appearance of separate women's organisations, which pitched their arguments in ways that were particularly relevant to women, emphasising for example the disruptive effect of slavery on Negro family life and encouraging shoppers to boycott slave-grown sugar. It was primarily as a result of this accumulated external pressure that Parliament finally abolished slavery in the British Empire in 1833.[13]

Whereas the anti-slavery campaign directed its efforts towards securing a specific change in public policy, other movements active around the same time were demanding fundamental reforms in the system of government itself. One notable example is the agitation for 'economical reform', by which was meant reductions in government expenditure and an easing of the burden of taxation. It was a commonplace criticism of eighteenth-century governments that they were extravagant and corrupt, buying political support and providing for friends and relatives by wasting public money on pensions and sinecures (salaried posts with no duties attached to them), and tolerating various forms of financial malpractice at all levels of the administrative structure. If the government was also perceived to be inefficient and incompetent, as was the case in the late-1770s when it became clear that Britain was losing the war to retain the American colonies, the public mood could turn very ugly. In December 1779 the Revd Christopher Wyvil summoned a meeting in Yorkshire to protest at profligate government expenditure and excessive taxation, and in the early months of 1780 his movement spread around the country, with petitions to Parliament being organised in twenty-six counties and twelve large towns. Significantly, Lord Rockingham and the opposition Whigs took up the issue in Parliament, and their short-lived ministry of 1782 enacted the first instalments of economical reform, including the abolition of 134 posts and some pensions, and legislation to bar holders of government contracts from sitting in Parliament. More remarkably still, this work was carried further by the Whigs' opponents, as the governments of Pitt and Liverpool took responsibility for additional measures aimed at streamlining and purifying their administrations. This was a good sign of how conscious all politicians had become of the need to satisfy public expectations. Whereas in the 1780s some 180 MPs held salaried offices, by the 1820s this figure had dropped to between sixty and seventy, most of whom were genuinely government ministers. Economical reform served as a vehicle by which Pitt and his Tory successors tried to cultivate a reputation for probity and frugality, and thereby demonstrate to the country the traditional ruling elite's continued fitness to govern. Notwithstanding these efforts, there was still intense pressure in the 1820s for further government economies, stimulated by sensational publications such as John Wade's *Black Book* (1820 and later editions), which highlighted certain grotesque cases of greed and nepotism. Consequently, the Whig governments of the 1830s felt obliged to search for more economies, achieving substantial cuts in the pension bill.[14]

For Wyvil and his friends in the 1780s, economic reform was not enough by itself, as they believed that the only sure way of combating 'corruption' was by reforming the system for electing MPs – 'parliamentary reform'. The abolition of small boroughs and the transfer of their seats to the counties, along with a return to triennial (three-yearly) elections, were deemed essential if MPs were to be rendered accountable to their constituents and not seduced by the temptations of government patronage. However, some campaigners for economical reform, mainly based in London, were prepared to go much further, advocating universal manhood suffrage, annual elections, voting by secret ballot and equal-sized constituencies. This was the programme of John Cartwright's Society for Constitutional Information, founded in 1780, which was inspired by the principles of equality embodied in the American colonists' struggle for independence. In 1810, the case for democracy was endorsed by the philosopher Jeremy Bentham, whose 'scientific' analysis of human nature, and application of the utilitarian doctrine of 'the greatest happiness of the greatest number', led him to conclude that only a political system in which all were represented could accurately reflect the interests of the whole community. Bentham and his disciples, known as the 'philosophic radicals', were to exercise considerable influence over reformist thinking for the next few decades.[15]

Enthusiasm in the country for some kind of parliamentary reform tended to wax and wane depending on the state of the economy, but a major intellectual stimulus to democratic radicalism was provided by the French Revolution – in its early stages, at least, before it descended into violence. Around eighty reform associations are known to have existed at some time or other in the 1790s, most conspicuously the London Corresponding Society (so called because it aimed to liaise with provincial societies by means of correspondence), which had perhaps eight hundred active and five thousand occasional members. Scotland had its own Convention of the Friends of the People. These organisations seem to have stimulated political awareness at lower levels of the social strata than had previously been the case, although it should be noted that the sorts of people involved were usually craftsmen, small traders and artisans, rather than unskilled labourers. Thomas Paine's *The Rights of Man* (1791) was an influential text, basing the case for rational reform on the idea of 'natural rights'. In other words, Paine believed that all men were born equal, and that social injustice therefore stemmed from inequalities produced by man-made laws and institutions, which could be rectified through universal manhood suffrage. Other radical perspectives were equally important, however, including that of Cartwright and Sir Francis Burdett, who rejected the idea of 'natural rights' and adhered to the mythical notion of an 'ancient constitution', dating back to medieval times, which had to be restored in order to secure popular rights. Their brand of 'radical constitutionalism' was intensely patriotic and loyal to the Crown, in contrast to Paine's republicanism.[16]

The outbreak of war with France in 1793, and the accompanying din of patriotic fervour, gave Pitt's government justification for carrying emergency legislation designed to stamp out 'subversive' radical activity, but it never completely disappeared. Indeed, it resurfaced in a more aggressive form, under a new generation of leaders such as William Cobbett and Henry 'Orator' Hunt, during the traumatic period of economic adjustment following the end of the war in 1815. It was at this stage that elements within the factory workforce were drawn into the agitation, suggesting that in certain specific circumstances the potential now existed for limited displays of 'working-class' political consciousness, expressing antagonism towards both employers and a 'corrupt' government (they wanted less government and less taxation, not more).[17] When a mass demonstration in favour of reform, attended by some sixty thousand people, was held at St Peter's Field, Manchester, in August 1819, the local magistrates panicked and ordered the use of the mounted yeomanry, which led to the deaths of eleven people and the injury of hundreds more – an event remembered with bitter irony as the 'Peterloo Massacre'. Lord Liverpool's government reacted with the 'Six Acts', temporary measures to suppress further agitation. They were intended to reassure 'respectable' public opinion, which was becoming alarmed by the scale of the unrest.[18] This was effective enough in the short term, as the economy revived and agitation subsided in the 1820s, but a decade later the forces gathering behind the cause of moderate parliamentary reform proved to be much more formidable.

THE REFORM ACT OF 1832

In June 1832 Parliament carried legislation to reform the system of electing MPs to the House of Commons. Through the total or partial abolition of small English boroughs, whose existence had long been condemned by advocates of reform, 144 seats were made available for redistribution. Sixty-two of these were allocated to provide additional representation for the counties, while sixty-four were used to create new borough constituencies, notably for industrial towns in the Midlands and north of England such as Birmingham, Manchester, Sheffield and Leeds (the remaining seats were given to Wales, Scotland and Ireland). At the same time, a standard voting qualification was introduced for the boroughs, where adult males occupying (not necessarily owning) property with a rental value of £10 per annum were allowed to vote. The effect of the Great Reform Act, as it came to be known, was to increase the size of the electorate in England and Wales from approximately four hundred and thirty-five thousand to six hundred and fifty-six thousand, or, to put it another way, from one adult male in seven to one in five. Scotland was covered by a separate Reform Act and the voting qualification there remained more restrictive, but even so the Scottish electorate expanded from a tiny four thousand five hundred to about sixty-five thousand.[19]

Arguably the most impressive feature of reform in 1832 was less the provisions of the Act itself and more the fact that it was passed without the violent overthrow of existing political institutions. Parliament voted to reform itself. How this was achieved, and what the consequences of the Reform Act were, provide the subjects for the remainder of this chapter, but they can only properly be considered in the light of our preceding discussion of economic, social and political changes. As we have seen, economic and social developments were spread over a long period of time and were not the product of a sudden 'Industrial Revolution'. Furthermore, Britain, unlike most other European States, already possessed an independently functioning Parliament before 1832, which was to some degree sensitive to public opinion, and the reform question itself had been debated on and off for several decades before decisive action was taken. The key to understanding how events unfolded, therefore, lies in the interaction between parliamentary politics and extra-parliamentary pressure.

At the parliamentary level, the trend after 1815 was towards a more all-embracing two-party alignment. The heirs of Pitt the Younger, men such as Spencer Perceval, Lord Liverpool, George Canning and the Duke of Wellington, were of a generation whose political identity had been shaped by the experience of a prolonged and anxious war for national survival. There was a powerful ideological dimension to this struggle, for in resisting the contagion of French revolutionary ideas the 'Pittites' took their stand on the resolute defence of the existing social order, based on the principles of monarchy, aristocracy, religion and property. Many 'independent' MPs naturally rallied to the King's government in wartime, and their attachment was subsequently confirmed by the uncompromising response to the post-war agitation for reform. Consequently, these MPs tended to side with ministers because of the general political principles which they espoused, and not simply because they were the King's ministers. For their part, ministers like Liverpool, while still regarding themselves as servants of the King, did not feel the same sense of personal reverence for the selfish and extravagant George IV as they had for his father, George III, and this aided the almost imperceptible process by which they assumed a new role as leaders of a 'Tory party' in Parliament. On one issue, however, a serious division of opinion existed within the Tory ranks, which ultimately brought their political domination to an end. In 1829 Wellington's government, fearing the loss of authority over Ireland, which had been brought into union with Britain in 1800, reluctantly granted 'Catholic Emancipation', thus enabling Catholics (eighty per cent of the Irish population) to hold public office. This pragmatic decision was denounced by the so-called 'ultra Tories' as a betrayal of British Protestant principles, and their alienation played a crucial part in the government's downfall in November 1830.

Wellington was replaced as Prime Minister by the Whig leader, Earl Grey, whose party had achieved an impressive recovery in parliamentary numbers and in political confidence since 1815. Once the war against France was over, and internal problems dominated public affairs, the Whigs' earlier 'unpatriotic' fatalism about the possibility of defeating Napoleon, and their carping criticism of the military campaigns, were quickly forgotten. Among the younger Whigs, such as Lord John Russell, there was enthusiasm for the idea of parliamentary reform as a means of breaking the Tory monopoly of government. This represented a significant refinement of Whig ideology, which had historically rested on opposition to 'tyrannical' kingship but now focused increasingly on the menacing behaviour of Tory ministers, whose repressive measures to combat the post-war reform agitation were seen as a threat to popular liberties. Convinced that their Tory opponents were abusing the powers entrusted to them, the Whigs presented reform as the only way of rescuing the existing system of government from its own shortcomings. To this end, the Whigs sought to invoke the support of what they liked to term the 'sober', 'respectable' middling classes, people with a natural interest in the preservation of social order, whose incorporation into the constitutional framework would bring to it greater strength and stability.

The events at Westminster culminating in the formation of Grey's ministry coincided with a revival of agitation in the country for reform. As in the past, the effects of a temporary economic depression helped to sharpen the edge of public dissatisfaction with the nation's bizarre and illogical arrangements for electing its parliamentary representatives. The novel aspect to the reform movement of the early 1830s was the breadth of its social support: 'Political Unions' emerged in many towns, and they succeeded in combining members of the middling and lower classes in a common cause. One explanation for this phenomenon is that as the new industrial towns continued to grow in size, so too did their sense of civic identity and the belief that they required separate representation in Parliament with which to further their distinct interests. It was no longer considered sufficient for the relevant county member to look after the affairs of a large industrial town.

Parliamentary reform also became an umbrella movement, drawing in groups such as the anti-slavery campaigners, who realised that they could best secure their specific objectives by first helping to make the House of Commons more responsive to the electorate's views. For all these reasons, the reform movement acquired a degree of 'respectability' which had been absent in the immediate post-war period, a fact that was reflected in the approval expressed by influential newspapers like *The Times* and the *Leeds Mercury*. Vital credibility was thus given to the Whig argument that it was essential to absorb the middling classes into the parliamentary system in order to protect it against a more dangerous, democratic attack.

It is now possible to show how a reform bill could be carried by the very institution that was being reformed. Grey and the Whigs came into office in 1830 committed to introducing a bill sufficiently comprehensive to satisfy public opinion, and in the inflamed circumstances of the time this meant a more drastic measure than had been contemplated while they were in opposition. However, the Whigs' first bill was defeated in the House of Commons, where they lacked a reliable majority, and it was found necessary to make a direct appeal to the country through a general election in the spring of 1831. Remarkably, such was the strength of feeling in favour of reform, the Whigs were able to obtain a sweeping endorsement for their measure from the 'unreformed' electorate, proving how open it potentially always was. The Whigs were assisted by their ability to pose as loyal servants of the King, William IV, who had accepted the need to settle the reform question. Armed with their new majority in the Commons, the Whigs' second bill was carried easily, only to be rejected by the hereditary chamber, the House of Lords, in October 1831. This action provoked violent demonstrations in towns including Bristol, Coventry and Nottingham (not the work of Political Unions), and the dangerous situation that was developing bolstered the Whigs in their determination to force a resolution of the issue. Introducing their third bill, only to see it blocked once again by the Lords, ministers were driven to the ultimate step of extracting a pledge from an alarmed and unhappy King that he would, if required, swamp the hostile majority in the upper House by creating large numbers of new peers favourable to reform. Once it was known that this pledge had been given, the opposition peers backed down and allowed the reform bill to pass, rendering the threatened creation of peers unnecessary.

From the foregoing account of the economic, social and political changes occurring after about 1750, and how they fed into the reform crisis of the early 1830s, it is also possible to make sense of important features of Britain after the Reform Act, which might otherwise seem surprising.[20] Above all, it must be emphasised that what happened in 1832 was no simple story of the displacement of an old, landed ruling elite, by a rising 'middle class'. While the Whigs undoubtedly recognised the power of the burgeoning middle ranks of society, and wished to convert this into a bulwark of the constitution, they had no intention of conceding control of the levers of government. For Whigs like Grey and Russell, the landed aristocracy were still the natural champions of popular rights and liberties, and they regarded the Reform Act as a 'final' measure designed to bring Parliament and the nation back into harmony. In fact, Grey's Cabinet of 1830, which proceeded to introduce the reform bill, was overwhelmingly aristocratic in its composition, as nine of the thirteen members were peers, one was the heir to a peerage, another was an Irish peer, and of the remaining two, both of whom were landowners, one was a baronet (the hereditary order of knighthood). More remarkably still, when Russell formed his second ministry in 1865, the Cabinet of fourteen still included eight peers and two landowning baronets. Similarly with the House of Commons, there was no dramatic change in its personnel after 1832, and those with aristocratic and landed connections were far more likely to gain election than men from business or other backgrounds. In the Parliament of 1841–7, for example, at least seventy-one per cent of MPs belonged to aristocratic or landed gentry families, whereas only twenty-two per cent had active and substantial business interests. This situation can be attributed in part to the lack of rigour in the reform settlement of 1832, which aimed to remove the worst abuses of the system of parliamentary representation but not to put a uniform structure in its place, so that the balance was still heavily weighted towards the counties and small boroughs with electorates of a few hundred, where traditional forms of control continued to be exercised.

Significant changes were, nevertheless, taking place in the balance of power *within* the constitutional structure, aided by the effects of the Reform Act. Politicians found themselves increasingly obliged to cultivate the electorate's support, and this accelerated the pre-existing trend towards a two-party alignment both in the constituencies, where some form of organisation was often necessary, and in Parliament. As the parties strived to define themselves in the public's eye, the labels 'Liberal' and 'Conservative' came into fashion, largely superseding 'Whig' and 'Tory'. This was part of the process by which Parliament's ascendancy over the Crown was firmly established. Prime Ministers found that their principal requirement was for reliable support from a parliamentary party, and that mere possession of royal favour was no longer enough to carry on a government. During the long reign of Queen Victoria, beginning in 1837, the implications of a party-based political system were fully worked out, and the monarchy responded by consciously adopting a neutral position, raising itself above the party fray. The events of 1832 also registered the psychological triumph of the elected House of Commons over the hereditary House of Lords, and thereafter peers had to be more circumspect in how they used their powers – although theoretically they were unchanged. In both these ways, Britain's hereditary institutions were forced to adapt to an altered environment, accepting greater constraints on their constitutional role relative to the representative chamber.

The achievements and limitations of the Great Reform Act exemplify the multi-dimensional character of early industrial Britain. In a country where the elements of both continuity and change were so powerful, the outcome of events in the early 1830s was always likely to be determined by the interplay between these elements rather than by the outright victory of one over the other. The co-existence of old and new is indeed one of the recurring themes of British history. No complete 'bourgeois' revolution, either political or cultural, accompanied the industrialisation process.[21] As Britain entered into its greatest period of international distinction, as the foremost industrial nation, the legacy from its past would continue to exercise a restraining influence on its social and political development.

FOUR

Britain Pre-eminent, 1832–75

INTRODUCTION

The decades following the passage of the Great Reform Act saw further developments that decisively shaped the character of the nation. Continued economic expansion and diversification meant that by the 1850s Britain enjoyed the reputation of being the 'workshop of the world'. As the first truly industrial nation, Britain held a commanding lead in areas of production like textiles, iron and steel, and shipbuilding, and it is estimated that in 1850 Britain accounted for approximately forty per cent of total world output of traded manufactured goods, while about twenty-five per cent of all world trade passed through British ports. At the same time, population growth proceeded at a rapid rate, with numbers rising from over sixteen million in 1831 to nearly twenty-one million in 1851 and over twenty-six million by 1871. The movement of people away from the countryside and into towns and cities was equally relentless, and the census of 1861 showed that the urban population had finally overtaken the rural population.

Such dramatic long-term changes in the economic and social life of the people were not without their own problems of dislocation and insecurity. For instance, the trend towards factory-based production in textiles and other industries gradually destroyed the livelihoods of groups of 'outworkers' labouring in their own homes in industrial villages. Even in the newer industrial centres, regular employment could never be taken for granted, because production went through cycles of boom and bust. A lethal combination of industrial depression and high bread prices, owing to the effect of adverse weather conditions on successive harvests, resulted in mass unemployment and appalling distress for large sections of the workforce between 1837 and 1843. In overall terms, the economy was less unstable after mid-century, and a dramatic boom took place in 1868–73; but there were still sharp, if temporary, downward fluctuations, notably in 1858–9 and 1865–6. This was certainly not the easy 'golden age' that it was subsequently made out to be by late-Victorian businessmen anxious about the effects of growing foreign competition, but modest improvements in wage rates did occur in many occupations, and, perhaps more importantly, economic maturity created greater opportunities for people to move into better-paid forms of employment.[1]

Politically speaking, the most serious challenges to established authority materialised during the acutely depressed years of the late 1830s and early 1840s. The best-known example is Chartism, a disparate and diverse phenomenon united around the demand for adult manhood suffrage and other reforms such as the secret ballot for elections and annually-elected parliaments, which were intended to make the nation's leaders accountable to the people. Feargus O'Connor, a flamboyant, blustering Irish landowner, whose newspaper the *Northern Star* was the main Chartist organ, came nearer than anyone to providing national leadership for the movement. Some two million signatures were obtained for the petitions presented to Parliament in 1839 and 1842, and a final petition was organised in 1848. In terms of social background, Chartist leaders tended to be lawyers or journalists, while the rank and file were typically craftsmen, artisans and 'outworkers' living in small industrial communities facing extinction, rather than the inhabitants of very large towns, factory workers or agricultural labourers. Both in its demands and its sources of support, Chartism arguably represented an extension of older radical reforming traditions (see chapter 3), not the beginnings of a 'modern' political movement drawing on a fully developed sense of 'working-class' consciousness. There was some violence associated with the Chartist agitation, but the government was able to deal with this by deploying troops where necessary and arresting the ring-leaders. In 1848 one hundred thousand citizens were enrolled as special constables to help deter the Chartist demonstrators from marching on Parliament. Chartism ultimately suffered from the lack of any clear strategy for enforcing its demands, given working men's limited voting power within the existing parliamentary system and the general reluctance to advocate the violent overthrow of that system. Consequently, the movement always relied on severe economic hardship to stimulate interest in its political programme.[2]

The political elite at Westminster was evidently more alarmed by the activities of another pressure group, the Manchester-based Anti-Corn Law League, founded in 1839. Richard Cobden and John Bright, the League's most prominent spokesmen, expressed open antagonism towards a system of government dominated by landowners, who were allegedly abusing their power in order to protect their own economic interests. The target in Cobden and Bright's sights, the Corn Laws, was a set of tariff barriers designed to shut out imports of foreign grain and so maintain high prices for British farmers (which in turn meant that landowners could keep their rents high). With its emotionally charged cry of 'cheap bread', the League was asserting the superior claims of urban consumers, and of the industrialists who paid their wages, over the interests of the agrarian sector. In addition to its use of conventional pressure-group techniques, the fact that the League commanded substantial support from the 'middle classes', particularly businessmen, meant that it wielded significant influence within the electoral structure created in 1832, even fielding its own candidates in some constituencies.[3]

Despite these obvious signs of tension, the central theme of this chapter is the way in which the old ruling elite managed to preserve its power substantially intact, by being seen to embrace 'progressive' change and by capitalising on the widespread sense of pride in the nation's achievements. As part of this process, the Liberal and Conservative parties emerged in succession to the Whigs and Tories, and we shall see how the Liberals became the dominant force in government, embodying values with which much of the nation felt able to identify.

PROSPERITY AND PROGRESS

It is one of the great ironies of political history that some of the vital foundations for what became the Victorian Liberal ascendancy were laid by Sir Robert Peel, the leader of their Conservative opponents. The widespread adoption of the name 'Conservative' as a party label occurred in the 1830s, after the Reform Act, and it provided a means of redefining the Tory political tradition in the context of the new electoral structure, which they had tried to prevent. In the Tamworth Manifesto, an address to his constituents in 1834, Peel sought to reassure the public that he was not at the head of a reactionary party, bent on overturning the Reform Act, and that indeed he was anxious to act in accordance with the spirit of the times by giving an impartial consideration to reasonable demands for reform in various areas of policy. His aim was to broaden the base of his party's support in the constituencies, by attracting the urban middle classes empowered in 1832. Electoral gains made in the second half of the 1830s, though concentrated in the counties and smaller boroughs, did suggest that his strategy was achieving some degree of success. Peel's own family background is relevant here, for while he was educated at Oxford University in preparation for a political career, his father had been a successful Lancashire textile manufacturer who purchased a nine-thousand-acre estate in Staffordshire and secured a baronetcy, both of which Peel inherited in 1830. Peel therefore felt himself to be a part of the traditional ruling elite, and believed that the landed aristocracy were the natural leaders of the country, but he also saw that the best way of preserving its power was by avowedly serving the interests of all sections of society, especially the business community from which his family had sprung. His austere manner and intellectual arrogance tended to conceal the essentially conciliatory nature of his political strategy.[4]

When Peel became Prime Minister, after the Conservatives' general election victory in 1841, he was faced with the problem of how to combat the prolonged economic depression, which had, among other things, spawned the Chartist and Anti-Corn Law League agitations. The decline in the volume of trade had also affected government revenue, which was mainly derived from import duties, and as a result there had been a series of budget deficits since 1837. Peel's response to this situation, in the budget of 1842, was to introduce an income tax of 7*d*. (3*p*.) in the pound on those earning more than £150 per annum (considerably above the average income at that time), and to devote the surplus revenue this generated to cutting import duties on foodstuffs and raw materials for industry. The object was to stimulate production and consumption, by making Britain a cheaper place in which to work and live. This 'free trade' approach, which had a long intellectual pedigree,[5] appeared to be remarkably successful, so much so that by 1845 buoyant revenue from the expansion of trade allowed Peel to make further cuts in import duties, and to abolish 430 of them altogether, including the duty on raw cotton for the textile industry. Firmly convinced that the continual rise of population made it imperative for Britain to import foodstuffs freely, Peel went further with his dramatic decision to repeal the Corn Laws in 1846. It was only possible for him to carry this measure with help from the opposition leader, Lord John Russell, as two-thirds of his own party rebelled against what they considered to be a betrayal of the landed interest and a shameful surrender to the demands of the Anti-Corn Law League. Outraged Conservative MPs proceeded to drive Peel from office, even though this paved the way for the formation of a Russell government instead.

From Peel's perspective, the repeal of the Corn Laws represented a pre-emptive strike against class agitators aiming to stir up popular resentment towards the landed elite. By promoting a timely settlement of the issue, he believed that he was shielding the nation from possible social convulsion in the future. In fact, the British political establishment was able to enjoy the best of both worlds for the next thirty years. On the one hand, credit could be claimed for having abandoned agricultural protection, but, on the other, agriculture flourished without the Corn Laws thanks to continued population growth and the absence of large supplies of cheap foreign grain. Corn Law repeal thus proved to be a supremely symbolic gesture, doing nothing to harm the funda-mental interests of landed society yet removing a potential source of popular discontent. The deep impression made by Peel's free-trade measures was revealed by the extraordinary display of public grief at the time of his sudden death, following a riding accident, in

1850. Black-bordered newspaper columns, cartoons, ballads and cheap biographies, all sentimentally proclaimed the wise statesman who had defied the vested interests in his own party, delivered untaxed food to the tables of the poor and brought prosperity to the whole nation. Statues were erected in many towns, paid for by penny subscriptions raised among thousands of ordinary people. Even the Conservative party, which had denounced Peel as a traitor in 1846, accepted soon after his death that free trade was politically irreversible. By this time, however, Peel's legacy had been claimed by the Liberals as part of their heritage, and for the next generation it was they who were regarded as the authentic exponents of 'progressive' ideas.

On the morning of the day Peel suffered his fatal accident, he had attended a meeting of the organising committee for an international exhibition of arts and manufactures to be held in London. The resulting 'Great Exhibition', which opened in Hyde Park on 1 May 1851, would have been remarkable if only for the building constructed to house it. This was the so-called 'Crystal Palace', a huge prefabricated structure of iron girders, containing nearly one million square feet of glass, which measured 1,848 feet (about 600 metres) in length, 408 feet (about 130 metres) in width and up to 108 feet (about 34 metres) in height (it covered the trees already on the site). Exhibits were sent from forty countries and included machinery, manufactured products, craft work and specimens of raw materials, along with curiosities such as a doctor's walking stick equipped with test tubes and an enema kit, and a mechanically tilting bed designed to give its occupant an abrupt alarm call.

Two points of general interest can be made about the Great Exhibition. First, it escaped no one's attention that the project was a vast advertisement for the host country's economic supremacy: nearly half of the exhibits came from Britain or its colonies, and they won most of the prizes, sweeping the board in the machinery category, for instance. As a reassuring symbol of Britain's standing in the world, the Exhibition triumphantly vindicated the country's recently adopted free-trade principles, firmly fixing in peoples' minds the simple equation between free trade and prosperity, and making it the sacred cow of public policy for the remainder of the century.[6]

Second, the Exhibition belied the dire predictions of some pundits by proving to be an impeccably orderly event. Over six million visits were paid to the Crystal Palace during the 140 days that it was open, with people travelling from all over the country to see it, some on special excursions organised by Thomas Cook; yet there were no serious disturbances (very wisely, only soft drinks were on sale, supplied by Messrs Schweppe). Coming only three years after revolutionary outbreaks had swept across much of Europe, the conduct of the crowds seemed to confirm the prevailing optimism about the nation's progress, in moral as well as material terms. Statistical proof of all this, if needed, was supplied by the revised edition of G.R. Porter's *The Progress of the Nation* (1851), which greeted the 'general prosperity' accompanying free trade and declared that the country had 'made the greatest advances in civilisation that can be found recorded in the annals of mankind'.

Predictably enough, Britain's position as the world leader in trade and industry for the next generation was interpreted as a reflection of the superior virtues of the national character, but even such complacent arrogance as this was frequently wrapped up in pious expressions of faith in the universally beneficial influence of unfettered commercial intercourse. All nations, it was said, stood to gain from the apparently limitless expansion of the international economy, and it was hoped that this would inaugurate an era of peace and harmony in which economic interdependence would make wars a thing of the past. Material progress was thus seen as an engine for the spread of civilisation, and the temptation could not always be resisted to liken the British to God's chosen people.[7]

The railway network, which made possible Thomas Cook's popular excursions to the Crystal Palace, became the other great symbol of progress in Victorian Britain, epitomising the age of steam power. Beginning in earnest with the opening of the Liverpool to Manchester line in 1830, there followed a series of investment booms in railway construction, most spectacularly in the late 1840s and the early 1860s. By 1850, 6,084 miles of track had already been laid down, and this increased to 9,069 miles in 1860 and 14,510 miles in 1875. At the time of the Great Exhibition, the main arterial routes had either been established or were about to be completed, linking London with all the major provincial centres, including Bristol, Birmingham, Manchester, Liverpool, Newcastle, Glasgow and Edinburgh. Few towns of any importance lacked a railway station by 1875. The number of passengers carried rose from 54.4 million in 1850 to 490.1 million in 1875, while freight carriage increased from 88.4 million tons in 1860 to 196.2 million tons in 1875. The railway system, combined with the telegraph network which ran alongside its lines (making it possible for the first time to send messages instantly from one part of the country to another), enormously accelerated internal communications, drawing the British people closer together in time and space, and helping to erode regional barriers. Cheaper transportation of bulky commodities such as coal, and speedier movement of perishable foodstuffs such as meat, milk and vegetables, crucially facilitated the ongoing process of urbanisa-tion. Railways likewise sustained the phenomenon of suburbani-sation, whereby the more affluent classes chose to live away from the city centres and commute to their workplace.

Pride in Britain's achievements as a nation was strongly expressed in the political sphere, where the absence in 1848 of any revolutionary outbreak remotely comparable to those else-where in Europe was accepted as proof of the inherent stability of British institutions and of the national temperament. By a happy coincidence, 1848 saw the publication of the first two volumes of the *History of England* by the Whig politician Thomas Babington Macaulay, which provided an eloquent account of how the Glorious Revolution of 1688 had saved the country from Stuart tyranny and secured the blessings of parliamentary government and individual liberty. Indeed, Macaulay asserted in his preface that the 160 years since the Glorious Revolution were 'eminently the history of physical, of moral, and of intellectual improvement'. A long tradition of evolutionary adaptation had ensured that essential measures such as the Great Reform Act were implemen-ted without destroying the foundations of the political system. Britain, as Macaulay observed in a public address in Edinburgh (he was a Scotsman) in 1852, did not have a perfect government, but it was 'a good government ... its faults admitted of peaceable and legal remedies ... [and] it had never inflexibly opposed just demands'. There was no need for revolutions or violence when reforms could be obtained 'by the mere force of reason and public opinion'. Macaulay's triumphant version of British history was a best-seller, and his 'Whig interpretation' remained influential well into the twentieth century, notably through the works of his great-nephew, G.M. (George Macaulay) Trevelyan.[8]

THE AGE OF EQUIPOISE

The view that Britain, by the time of the Great Exhibition, had overcome the worst of the traumas of industrial transformation, and achieved a temporary state of balance in its political and social relations, was expressed by W.L. Burn in his book, *The Age of Equipoise*, published in 1964. Burn's argument rested partly on the observation that the tensions of the 1830s and 1840s had been defused, thanks chiefly to Peel's free-trade settlement, and that there followed a period in which the interests of land and industry apparently reached a point of equilibrium (or stalemate), from which neither side could expect to prevail over the other. He also stressed the importance of what he termed 'social disciplines', the unwritten rules of public behaviour, which he believed exercised a far more profound influence on popular attitudes than any formal restrictions imposed by the law.

Indeed, the 1850s witnessed the highest point of the evangelical wave that had swept over most strata of society since the late eighteenth century, injecting an urgent sense of Christian consciousness into public life, effecting a reformation in manners and fuelling the moral campaign against slavery. Proclamations of national days of fasting, humiliation and prayer were issued in 1854 and 1855, when Britain was at war with Russia, and in 1857 after a native uprising in India, and there was mounting pressure for legislation to compel a stricter observance of the Sabbath. A 'census' of attendance at religious services in England and Wales, conducted on 30 March 1851, revealed that out of a total population of around 18 million some 10.2 million had been to a church or chapel. Impressive as this may seem today, the revelation that perhaps 5.25 million people, most of whom were thought to be from the poorer classes in large towns, had failed to participate in formal worship without good reason, was cause for consider-able alarm and prompted all of the religious denominations to redouble their efforts to bring Christianity to the urban masses.

The Church of England, in particular, strove hard to retrieve the position it had allowed to slip away, and 1,727 new churches were built and 7,144 old ones restored between 1840 and 1876. Ultimately, this campaign to 're-christianise' the nation failed to halt the long-term trend towards the secularisation of society, but it nevertheless exerted a profound influence on public attitudes in the mid-Victorian years.[9] Partly for this reason, the prevailing belief in progress in all its forms was tightly bound up with anxiety to achieve and maintain 'respectability' in the eyes of one's neighbours, and this impulse survived for several generations despite the decline of formal religious observance. To modern minds, the depressingly stultifying moral atmosphere that was often created merely bred hypocrisy, but it may also be the case that such a climate fostered the solidity of a society experiencing rapid and potentially disorientating change.

One obvious reason why the mid-nineteenth century has been characterised as an age of equipoise is that the traditional landowning elite continued to predominate in Parliament and in government, ironically benefiting from the sacrifice of the Corn Laws in 1846, which had helped to restore its credibility as custodians of the 'national interest'. Thus, the forces of continuity were as much in evidence as the forces of change. Perhaps the best way of illustrating the concentrated economic power of landed proprietors is by reference to the findings of the 'New Domesday Survey', conducted in 1873, which revealed that four-fifths of the land in the United Kingdom was owned by less than seven thousand persons. More strikingly still, twenty-four per cent of land in England and Wales was owned by just 363 individuals (including 186 peers and 58 baronets) in estates of ten thousand acres or more, while a further seventeen per cent of land was held by a thousand individuals in estates of between three and ten thousand acres.[10]

The formal sources of power, which sustained the authority of the landed elite, were underpinned by claims to enhanced moral virtue. In this respect, the lead came from the very top, as Queen Victoria and Prince Albert sought to restore the monarchy's reputation to the level attained in the age of George III, from which it had slipped during the reign of his extravagant, dissolute and unpopular son, George IV. Albert's influence was crucial; he recognised that the royal family needed to present itself as a model of devotion to public duty, and as the exemplar of blissful domestic life (there were nine children), in order to satisfy the expectations of public opinion. Among members of the wider elite, the revival of religious feeling meant that there was less tolerance of the rakish, reckless behaviour openly exhibited by their ancestors, and they adopted a more earnest, serious approach to their public responsibilities, as they endeavoured to prove their worthiness to retain their privileged status.

Hippolyte Taine, a French radical who visited Britain in the 1860s, was impressed by the good breeding and broad-mindedness of the 'gentleman' of independent fortune, and it seemed to him that the country owed its famed political stability to the existence of an hereditary ruling class, rooted in the land, which produced a steady supply of 'capable governors'. Taine thought that the public-school education received by sons of elite families, with its emphasis on Christian character-formation rather than purely academic achievement, offered a valuable training in citizenship, inculcating values of leadership and service. Many pupils went on, of course, to hold responsible positions in government, the civil service, the Church, the armed forces and the colonial administration.[11]

It certainly seemed true, as Taine discovered when he visited Manchester, that there was little prospect of a systematic challenge by the business community to the hereditary wielders of political power, and little desire that it should even be attempted. The repeal of the Corn Laws represented a triumph for 'middle-class' policy rather than for the advancement of middle-class personnel in government, as they saw their principles being absorbed by the political Establishment. Once the Corn Law irritant was removed, campaigners like Cobden and Bright experienced frustration in their efforts to find a new issue on which to focus a continued assault on what they bitterly called 'feudalism'.[12] The uncomfortable fact was, as they were forced to admit, that many Anti-Corn Law League supporters aspired to genteel status for themselves and their families, and it continued to be common practice for successful businessmen, especially the very wealthy, to purchase landed estates as the first step on the road to social acceptance. Approximately one-half of those men leaving property worth

£500,000 or more at their death, had bought at least two thousand acres of land. The public schools, which greatly expanded in number with the opening of some fifty new institutions between 1840 and 1900 to supplement the nine traditional schools, also played a part in fusing old and new wealth, although this was more likely to occur with the offspring of fathers engaged in commerce and finance than those from backgrounds in manufacturing.[13]

There is ample evidence as well to support the view that the cult of respectability pervaded the thinking of large sections of the 'working classes', for whom 'self-improvement' became a watchword. Naturally enough, the material gains and spirit of buoyant optimism that were increasingly apparent from mid-century onwards did much to encourage contemporary celebrations of the independent achievement of individuals. Samuel Smiles, a radical journalist, encapsulated this mood in his best-selling book, *Self Help* (1859), and in subsequent re-workings of the theme such as *Thrift* (1875), along with heroic biographies of self-made men like the railway engineer, George Stephenson. Smiles's works are only the best-remembered specimens of a whole genre of improving literature. His basic message was that all individuals were capable of raising themselves up the social ladder through hard work, learning, honesty, self-reliance, frugality and sobriety – personal virtues that could never be legislated for.

In practical terms, the desire for self-improvement was manifested in thriving institutions such as Sunday Schools, which originated as far back as the 1780s and catered for two million children by 1851, and which were often staffed and managed by working people themselves. Post Office Savings Banks, set up in 1861, had one million depositors a decade later, and they seem to have been particularly popular among female domestic servants saving for the future when they hoped to have their own households. Friendly Societies, offering insurance cover against sickness, had 1.5 million members in 1850 and 2.2 million in 1880 (around thirty per cent of adult males), while at a more modest level, burial societies paid the cost of that most essential of all trappings of respectability, a proper funeral, for the majority of adult males. Trade union membership in this period extended to less than ten per cent of the workforce, mostly skilled labourers, but these organisations too performed many of the functions of benefit societies. Thomas Wright, an engineer very much in the Smilesean mode, who published a book entitled *Our New Masters* (1873), confirmed just how status-conscious working people were, and how misleading it was to talk of 'working men' as a single homogeneous body. On the contrary, he maintained, there was 'an educated and really intelligent section, and an uneducated and ignorant section ... a trade unionist, and a non-trade unionist section; a sober, steady, saving section, and a drunken, unsteady, thriftless section'. Consequently, 'between the artisan and the unskilled labourer a gulf is fixed', creating considerable 'antagon-ism of feeling', and this was mirrored in the way that 'artisans' wives hold the wives of labourers to be of a lower social grade, and very often will either not "neighbour" with them at all, or else only in a patronising way'. In many communities, a prerequisite of respectability by this time was that married women should not go out to work, since their responsibilities were seen to lie in taking care of the home, bringing up their children (often enforcing very strict standards of behaviour), and keeping the front doorstep well scrubbed.[14]

It would be a great mistake to suppose that popular aspirations to 'respectability' were simply a phenomenon of the post-1850 period, associated with improvements in economic conditions, or that this marked an abrupt departure from an earlier commitment to militant agitation against the established order. Thomas Sotheron, a Conservative MP who was present in London during the festivities for Queen Victoria's coronation, in June 1838, recorded in his diary how struck he was by the 'good behaviour, even courteous demeanour of the countless crowds', observing that there was 'no drunkenness, no brawling' and that this made him feel 'proud of my countrymen'.[15] The quest for self-improvement indeed formed an integral part of much Chartist thinking, and leaders such as William Lovett and Henry Vincent desired political rights for working men precisely because this was an essential precondition for elevating their character. There was a socialist strand within Chartism, represented by Bronterre O'Brien and a few others, but it is doubtful whether the millions of signatories to the Chartist petitions shared in these beliefs. On the contrary, there was instinctive hostility to State interference in people's lives, which was entirely in keeping with the radical reforming tradition stretching back over several decades. Far from seeking to control the State in order to effect a transformation of society, most Chartist supporters probably wanted to use the vote in order to liberate themselves from a State that they considered to be corrupt and oppressive, and certainly not a benevolent agency. While Chartism did not achieve its immediate political objectives, the free-trade measures of the 1840s onwards went a long way towards satisfying its supporters' underlying economic concerns. This helped to ensure that Chartism never provided the organisational foundations for a new, industrial-working-class movement.[16]

LIBERAL BRITAIN

In the spring of 1853 a by-election took place to fill the vacant seat for the borough of Taunton, in Somerset. The victorious candidate was Sir John Ramsden, a young landowning baronet from Yorkshire, whose electoral address contained the confident declaration that 'in avowing myself an advocate of Liberal Principles, it is unnecessary that I should offer any vindication of those Principles beyond the facts which are known and felt by us all'. According to Ramsden, the application of Liberal principles in recent decades had led to many great achievements, including:

> the removal of Religious disabilities ... an extension of Political Privileges, and the establishment of Free Trade. The happy results of this policy are now seen in our National Freedom, in our commercial greatness, and in the loyalty of our People – in the stability of our Institutions, and in the tranquillity and contentment which pervades all parts of our Dominions, while the other Governments of Europe are insecure or disturbed.
>
> These, Gentlemen, are the results of PROGRESS, and as a Progressive Policy has borne such good fruits in the past, so it is to a Progressive Policy that we must look for security in the future.
>
> Much has been achieved of late years by the joint action of the Legislature and Public Opinion. Much however still remains to be done.[17]

Such optimism proved to be well justified, given the Liberals' impressive record as a party of government. This can be expressed by the simple facts that in the period between the Corn Law crisis of 1846 and the general election of 1874 the Conservatives *never* had a majority in the House of Commons, and that the brief spells when they were in office amounted to a little over four-and-a-half years.

It was only around the time of the Corn Law crisis that the party label 'Liberal' came to be widely adopted, and even then it never entirely obscured the reality that the Liberal party was an amalgam of several distinct political traditions. To put it another way, Liberalism was an umbrella movement, sheltering certain common principles, which brought together politicians from diverse backgrounds holding differing opinions on many issues. At the heart of all Liberal governments were the Whigs, who continued to supply most of the Cabinet personnel, possessing as they did a strong sense of public duty and the belief that the landowning elite were the natural leaders of the country. Lord John Russell, Prime Minister from 1846 until 1852, was the proud representative of a tradition of aristocratic reformism which had not stopped with the passing of the Reform Act in 1832, but had been renewed through such measures as the abolition of slavery in the colonies (1833), reforms to streamline the Church of Ireland (1833), the introduction of State grants for elementary education (1833), the creation of a proper system of elective local government for municipal corporations (1835) and legislation allowing dissenters to marry in their own chapels (1836). The basic principles of political and religious liberty informed most of the Whig reforms. One of their more controversial pieces of legislation, the Poor Law Amendment Act (1834), fitted into the same pattern, in that the responsible local officials, the Poor Law Guardians, were subject to election by the ratepayers. The requirement for those applying for poor relief to enter a workhouse, and face conditions less attractive than those available outside, was designed to encourage mobility of labour and discourage irresponsible procreation. It represented an attempt to address contemporary fears, which eventually proved to be unfounded, of an impending social catastrophe arising from chronic over-population.

In 1846, support from Russell and his colleagues was crucial in enabling Peel to repeal the Corn Laws, and thereafter the Liberals appropriated the free-trade cause (commercial liberty) for themselves. The administrative leadership of the Whigs was gradually reinforced during the 1850s by the adhesion of a number of Peel's protégés, most of whom were similarly drawn from the landed aristocracy. Commitment to free-trade was the single great common denominator between the Whigs and the 'Peelites', and also between them and another parliamentary grouping, the radicals, who included in their ranks the heroes of the Anti-Corn Law League campaign, Cobden and Bright. Radicals were critical of the aristocracy's continued dominance of the political Establishment in its widest sense – the government, the civil service, the armed forces and the Church of England – and they purported to be truer representatives of 'the people', although they themselves were usually businessmen or lawyers, not working men. In practice, however, the radicals were neither strong enough nor sufficiently united among themselves to present a serious challenge to aristocratic rule, and they usually sought to work with the Whigs and Peelites as far as they could. Russell and later Liberal Premiers managed to recruit a few radical representatives to their governments, and by 1868 the process of Liberal integration had gone so far that even Bright agreed to serve in the Cabinet.[18]

The diversity of the Liberal party in Parliament was undoubtedly an occasional source of weakness, as in 1852, 1858 and 1866, when internal fissures presented the Conservatives with opportunities to form temporary minority governments. Nevertheless, it can be argued that on balance the Liberals' ability to span a very wide spectrum of opinion was a considerable advantage to them. This point becomes more compelling when we consider what the Liberal party represented in the country as a whole. Liberalism was a socially transcendent creed, embracing a significant portion of the aristocracy and landed gentry, as well as large numbers of factory owners, merchants, bankers, newspaper proprietors, lawyers, shopkeepers, craftsmen and artisans in the urban areas. In the matter of religious affiliation, the Liberals included Anglicans, dissenters and Jews (and, more uneasily, Irish Catholics), united in the pursuit of religious liberty. Electorally speaking, the Liberals enjoyed their greatest preponderance in the larger borough constituencies, but they held their own in the more numerous small boroughs with a few hundred voters, and they regularly won a substantial minority of county seats too. In geographical terms, they were capable of securing a majority of the seats in England, but their numbers were augmented by the overwhelming majorities routinely obtained in Scotland and by the increasingly dominant position achieved in Wales by the 1860s. In both of these countries, Protestant dissent played a vital part in shaping popular attitudes, which made it possible for the Scots and Welsh to relate to a wider Liberal movement espousing many issues of vital concern to them. For all sorts of reasons, then, the Liberal party performed a valuable integrative function, successfully combining traditional elements with newer, more dynamic forces in British society, and channelling them into a progressive political movement which expressed the dominant cultural attitudes of the age: economic progress through free trade; evolutionary constitutional growth; purity and efficiency in administration, and self-improvement of the individual.

Protecting and extending the free-trade principles laid down as the basis of government policy in the 1840s provided Liberals of all shades with a shared sense of purpose. Free trade also fitted into a more general approach to policy, which stressed the virtues of minimal interference by central government in people's lives. National progress, it was believed, could best be achieved by liberating individuals and allowing the free market to flourish, and good government therefore consisted of economical government which kept the tax burden as low as possible and refrained from distorting the operations of the market by meddlesome regulations or tariffs. John Stuart Mill's *On Liberty* (1859), the classic text of Victorian Liberalism, argued that the individual should be free to do anything which did not harm others, since individual behaviour and individual thought were the essential preconditions for personal growth.[19] In practice, however, this did not mean that Liberal governments adhered to a strictly laissez-faire (leave alone) approach in every case. Education, as Mill recognised, played a crucial part in the development of the individual, and it was therefore considered legitimate for State funds to be used to subsidise those voluntary agencies (principally the Church and other religious bodies), which were striving to provide elementary schooling for the masses. In 1870 a Liberal government went further, setting up locally-elected boards to supply additional school places where the voluntary sector was failing to do so, and ten years later elementary education up to the age of twelve was finally made compulsory. Local initiatives, locally financed, were always considered superior to centralised dictation, and another field in which Liberal governments were keen to stimulate activity was public health, beginning with the Act of 1848 requiring the creation of boards of health in certain urban areas. Intervention by central government itself was also permissible when it was designed to protect the interests of those deemed incapable of protecting themselves, and from the 1830s onwards legislation was passed regulating the employment of women and children in factories and mines. By the 1870s a fairly effective system of inspection was in place to ensure that the law was properly enforced. Indirectly, many of these measures could not help but affect the conditions in which adult males laboured. While laissez-faire was theoretically the preferred rule for Liberal governments, the complex realities of life in a rapidly changing society meant that numerous exceptions had to be made to that rule.

Two leaders stand out as the greatest practical exponents of Victorian Liberalism, although their personalities were remarkably dissimilar. Lord Palmerston, who served as Foreign Secretary in every Whig government between 1830 and 1851, was over seventy years of age when he became Prime Minister in 1855, yet he retained this office, with a brief interruption in 1858–9, until his death in 1865. William Ewart Gladstone, after two distinguished spells as Chancellor of the Exchequer (1852–5, 1859–66), assumed the premiership for the first time in 1868, and held it on three subsequent occasions before his retirement in 1894, when he was in his mid-eighties. In their different ways, Palmerston and Gladstone skilfully exploited the rich veins of Liberal sentiment and political support which they found in the country.

As Foreign Secretary, Palmerston had carefully cultivated a reputation for 'patriotism' through his trenchant assertion of British interests abroad in certain well-publicised cases. Most notorious of all was the 'Don Pacifico' affair of 1850, when warships were sent to bombard Athens in support of a merchant, claiming to be a British citizen, who had a grievance against the Greek government. Palmerston's conduct of foreign policy went beyond the aggressive pursuit of national interests, however, for he liked to depict Britain as 'the champion of justice and right' in the world, applying the 'weight of her moral sanction' on behalf of foreign peoples struggling to secure the same freedoms as the British had long enjoyed. The targets of his attacks were continental 'tyrants' like the Tsar of Russia and the Emperor of Austria, who were guilty of oppressing their ethnically diverse subjects and denying them the right to national self-determination. Palmerston's ostentatious display of sympathy for the Hungarian nationalists in 1849, for instance, went down well with British public opinion, and even commanded the support of many radicals in and out of Parliament. It was conveniently overlooked that Britain, for all its economic might, lacked the large standing army with which to deal by itself on equal terms with the continental Powers and make its opinion count.

Popular enthusiasm was again aroused in 1854 when Britain and France went to war in the Crimean peninsula to defend the Turkish Empire in south-eastern Europe from Russian encroachment. The Crimean campaign is usually remembered for the disastrous charge of the light brigade, at the battle of Balaclava, but greater contemporary outrage was provoked by the subsequent evidence of bureaucratic mismanagement of the military expedition. As a result, many British soldiers were forced to spend the winter of 1854–5 in the Crimea without adequate clothing, shelter or medical facilities – in this last respect, the arrival of Florence Nightingale helped to improve matters. So serious was the undermining of public trust in the competence of the political Establishment, that Lord Aberdeen's government was brought down in January 1855 by a vote of censure in the House of Commons. However, this crisis enabled Palmerston, who happened to be Home Secretary at the time and therefore less directly implicated in the whole fiasco, to come to the forefront as the man best qualified to head a new government and win the war. The satisfactory conclusion of hostilities in March 1856 after the Paris peace negotiations, which substantially maintained Turkey's territorial integrity and kept Russia out of the Eastern Mediterranean (from where it was feared she might threaten vital routes to India), reinforced Palmerston's image as a successful national leader.

One interesting and quite novel aspect of Palmerston's political style was his willingness to reach out beyond Westminster and address public audiences in the provincial towns and cities. In

1856, after the Crimean war was over, he visited Liverpool, Salford and Manchester, delivering the message that Britain could look forward to further 'progressive improvement' in its social and political institutions, under the leadership of a responsible, enlightened aristocracy. A recurring theme in his speeches was the blessing bestowed by the nation's growing material prosperity, and the scope for individual self-improvement within a flexible, hierarchical social structure. Moreover, he maintained that the superiority of Britain's internal organisation made it an object lesson to the rest of the world. Palmerston's appeal seems to have been particularly strong among the business community, which appreciated his determination to promote Britain's commercial interests abroad (demonstrated by the China wars of 1857–60, fought to secure British traders' access to Chinese markets) while providing a stable political environment at home.[20]

It was entirely appropriate, given the nature of the Liberal party, that the cause that did more than anything else to promote Liberal unity was the Italian movement for national independence ('Risorgimento') in 1859–60. Liberal sympathy for the Italian struggle to throw off Austrian domination proved to be politically beneficial for Palmerston who, having been forced to resign in 1858 following a backbench revolt,[21] was able to recover his position in June 1859. Italy provided a valuable bond of sentiment for Liberals at the celebrated meeting of the parliamentary party at Willis's rooms, in London, on 6 June. A few days later Palmerston formed a more comprehensive Liberal government than had been previously possible, permanently fusing the Whig and Peelite ministerial traditions, and bringing two prominent radicals, Charles Villiers and Thomas Milner Gibson, into his Cabinet. Subsequent fears of a French plan to invade Britain also worked to Palmerston's advantage, underlining the apparent indispensability of his strong leadership. Public opinion was duly satisfied by the expenditure of £9 million on useless coastal fortifications, and by the formation of a volunteer rifle movement for home defence. Jocular and self-confident, Palmerston's robust, no-nonsense style helped him to remain in office until his death, two days before his eighty-first birthday, in October 1865.

During the first half of the 1860s, the man who emerged as Palmerston's likeliest long-term successor was his Chancellor of the Exchequer, Gladstone. Originally one of Peel's young Conservative protégés, Gladstone had hesitantly moved towards the Liberal side in the years following the Corn Law crisis. His family background was similar to that of his political mentor, as Gladstone's father, like Peel's, was a successful northern business-man (a Liverpool merchant) who had acquired land and social respectability, and sent his son to a public school and Oxford University with a view to a political career. As a minister in Peel's government Gladstone imbibed the doctrines of free trade, and after Peel's death he came to be recognised as the foremost expert on financial and commercial policy. His ambition was to implement more fully the principles laid down by his master, and he did this in his budgets by making further reductions in import duties and abolishing many of them altogether. Gladstone's greatest triumphs were achieved in the budgets of 1860 and 1861, which, like Peel's first budget of 1842, appeared to have an almost magical effect in stimulating the economy. By 1865, trade and government revenue were so buoyant that Gladstone managed to reduce the rate of income tax to 4*d*. (less than 2*p*.) in the pound, and he hoped that through reductions in military expenditure he might yet fulfil his dream of abolishing this form of taxation altogether.

The success of Gladstone's policies, and the consequent public acclamation he received, brought about a remarkable transfor-mation in his political persona. Hitherto regarded as a formidable parliamentarian, he emerged in the early 1860s as a charismatic popular orator as well, addressing audiences in urban centres such as Newcastle, Manchester, Bradford and Middlesbrough. In this way, he built up a diverse personal constituency in the country, combining enlightened landed aristocrats and urban businessmen with radical plebeian reformers. The last of these groups included many former Chartists, who by the 1860s had been absorbed into grass-roots Liberalism. Gladstone's increas-ingly favourable estimate of the worthiness of working men translated into his famous House of Commons speech of 1864 advocating an extension of the franchise to incorporate the 'respectable' elements from the lower orders into the parliamen-tary system. The powerful sense of religious imperative, which he brought to everything he did, also had a widespread emotional appeal, particularly to Protestant dissenters. For Gladstone, the Liberal party was not merely a vehicle for improving people's lives in secular, material terms, but an agent for promoting the moral welfare of the nation. Individual liberty, he believed, was a gift from God, and an essential precondition for social progress. What Gladstone offered was a crusading, visionary style of leadership, which he endeavoured to use as a means of channelling the moral energies of the people and directing them towards some noble cause defined by himself.[22]

At certain stages in his career, the great issue on which Gladstone focused public attention was the plight of Ireland and the need for Britain to deliver 'justice' to the Irish people. This provided an effective rallying cry for Liberals during the general election campaign of 1868, and when Gladstone subsequently became Prime Minister he devoted much of his time to tackling the 'Irish question'. In 1869, the Anglican Church of Ireland, an anomaly in an overwhelmingly Catholic country, was disestablished, and the following year a Land Act offered Irish tenant farmers improved conditions of tenure. Both measures, Gladstone was convinced, would help to reconcile Ireland to the union with Britain.

His first ministry of 1868–74 was notable for its reforming endeavours in many other areas, as it confronted tricky issues that the more moderate Palmerston had been content to leave dormant. Entrance to the civil service became more meritocratic, through the use of competitive examinations in place of patronage; the practice of purchasing commissions in the army was ended; religious tests for college fellowships at Oxford and Cambridge universities were abolished, opening them up to dissenters; the judiciary was overhauled, with the creation of a single High Court of Justice; the secret ballot was introduced for parliamentary elections, in a bid to combat the bribing and intimidation of voters; and the Education Act, mentioned earlier, extended the provision of elementary schooling. With the exception of the Grey and Melbourne administrations of the 1830s, no other nineteenth-century government achieved so much in the field of domestic reform, and the period between 1868 and 1874 can reasonably be described as the climactic years of Victorian Liberalism.

CONSERVATIVE REHABILITATION

The Conservative schism occasioned by the Corn Law crisis of 1846 drove the party into the political wilderness for a generation. Narrowly identified with the agricultural interest, and having limited electoral appeal in the major urban constituencies, the Conservatives also lacked credibility as a viable alternative to the Liberal administrations. Most of their weightiest figures and brightest young talents, after all, had followed Peel out of the party and gravitated towards the Liberal side. The task of gradually restoring Conservative fortunes fell to an unlikely duo. In the House of Lords, the party was led by the fourteenth Earl of Derby, one of the wealthiest landowners in the country and therefore ideally suited for his role; but in the House of Commons, the shortage of debating talent meant that the Conservatives became heavily dependent on a man whom many considered to be an unprincipled adventurer. Benjamin Disraeli, who was born a Jew but converted to Christianity while still a child, had made a reputation of sorts as a society poseur and novelist, before he seized the opportunity to establish himself as the spokesman of backbench landed Conservatism in 1846 by launching a series of brutal character attacks on Peel. Profoundly distrusted, none the less, by rank-and-file Conservatives, he was tolerated because the party needed him and because Derby was always the unquestioned overall leader.[23]

Despite their opposition to Peel's policy of ending agricultural protection in 1846, the logic of the political situation dictated that within a few years Derby and Disraeli would be compelled to draw their party away from the idea of restoring tariffs and force it to come to terms with free-trade commercial principles. Any attempt to reintroduce the Corn Laws risked causing serious political and social upheaval in the country, possibly reigniting the Anti-Corn Law League and Chartist challenges. In any case, the Conservatives lacked the parliamentary numbers required to carry such a reactionary policy, and if they wished to recruit more support their best chance lay in winning over wavering moderate Liberals uncomfortably allied with the radicals. For this strategy to succeed, of course, it was essential that the Conservatives embraced free trade and occupied a more central position in politics. Accordingly, when internal Liberal quarrelling paved the way for Derby to form his first brief minority government in 1852, it was officially acknowledged that Peel's free-trade settlement was sacrosanct. Indeed, during Derby's second minority government of 1858–9, Disraeli, as Chancellor of the Exchequer, showed himself to be positively 'Gladstonian' in his determination to curb expenditure and reduce taxes. This government was also responsible for carrying a number of useful reforms, such as the Government of India Act, a Public Health Act, and a measure relating to Scottish universities, all adopted in the spirit of what Derby termed 'Conservative progress'. By the end of the 1850s, then, the Conservatives could plausibly present themselves as a party at least moderately attuned to the prevailing Liberal values of the age.

Derby's appointment as Prime Minister for the third time, in 1866, was followed by dramatic evidence that the Conservatives were even prepared, in certain circumstances, to outbid the Liberals in the competition for popularity and power. With their opponents in a state of disarray, after failing to unite behind a very modest instalment of parliamentary reform proposed by Russell,[24] the Conservatives proceeded to enact a far more radical measure of their own. The second Reform Act of 1867 extended the franchise to adult male householders in the boroughs and to occupiers of property valued at £12 per annum in the counties. Its effect was to increase the electorate in England and Wales from about 1.1 million to nearly 2 million (roughly one in three adult males). A separate measure was carried for Scotland, applying stricter qualifying conditions, but even so the Scottish electorate was more than doubled to approximately 235,000. Disraeli subsequently claimed that the Reform Act testified to Conservative confidence in the loyalty and good sense of the people, who he argued were deeply attached to the Crown, the Church and other traditional institutions of State. Whatever truth there may have been in this version of Conservative motives, the simpler reality was that a party that had been in a perpetual parliamentary minority for over twenty years had little to lose from a bold throw of the electoral dice.

In the event, it was the Liberals who immediately profited from the second Reform Act, reuniting under Gladstone's leadership and achieving a resounding 110-seat majority at the 1868 general election. And yet, by the early 1870s, Disraeli, now the overall Conservative leader in succession to Derby, was able to capitalise on growing disenchantment with Gladstone's ministry, skilfully cultivating an image of the Conservatives as the more truly 'national party' representative of all classes in society. This was possible because a number of the reforms carried by Gladstone and his colleagues alienated sections of their own support. For instance, the Education Act was denounced by militant dissenters connected with the National Education League, who wanted to destroy the Church of England's dominant role in the education system, while the restrictions on public houses contained in the cautious Licensing Act of 1872 angered the powerful temperance lobby which wanted a much more drastic measure. The spectacle of Liberal ministers coming under intense radical pressure on these and other fronts alarmed many moderate voters, and it was to them that Disraeli was appealing in his famous public speeches at Manchester and the Crystal Palace, in 1872, where he emphasised the allegedly 'destructive' tendencies within Liberalism. The Irish Church and Land Acts were depicted as dangerous precedents likely to lead in future to attacks on institutions and property rights in Britain. At the same time, Disraeli's accusation that Gladstone was weakly allowing British interests abroad to be negated was part of a strategy designed to claim for the Conservative party the Palmerstonian mantle of 'patriotism'. The public reaction in favour of Disraeli and the Conservatives culminated in the party's remarkable general election victory in 1874, when significant inroads were made into the Liberals' urban strongholds. Most impressive of all was the way that the Conservatives entrenched themselves in London and the surrounding 'home' counties, demonstrating the party's growing popularity among the expanding legions of suburban, 'middle-class' voters.

Ironically, Disraeli, the man who had done so much to destroy Peel's leadership in 1846, eventually fulfilled Peel's great aim of constructing a Conservative party capable of embracing the interests of both urban and rural property owners. Political conditions in the 1870s, it must be said, were far more auspicious for such an undertaking, given the unsettling activity of Gladstone's ministry and the signs of alienation from Liberalism on the part of important sections of the expanding 'middle classes'. But the Conservatives' potential as a party embodying 'national' ideals was not fully realised until some years after Disraeli's death (1881), when the issue of empire finally shattered the Victorian Liberal hegemony.

FIVE

Imperial Heyday, 1875–1914

INTRODUCTION

From the 1870s onwards Britain found itself in an increasingly competitive international environment in which many comfortable attitudes and assumptions from the recent past were becoming ever less valid. The leading role in world trade, achieved by virtue of the fact that Britain was the first nation to experience industrialisation on a massive scale, was steadily eroded as other countries with superior natural resources and larger populations, notably the USA and Germany, underwent rapid economic development. Contemporary anxieties about the country's future status were mirrored in the sphere of domestic politics, where there was a gradual shift of power away from the traditional landowning elite towards the forces of 'democracy', and signs that the parties were being obliged to re-define themselves in relation to the question of 'class'. In terms of foreign policy, the insular, freelance approach favoured by Palmerston, of lecturing the Great Powers while avoiding any long-term commitments to them, was an unacceptably hazardous strategy in a Europe dominated, at the turn of the twentieth century, by two suspicious and potentially hostile camps. This period also witnessed a new phase of British imperial expansion, involving extensive acquisitions in Africa, the Far East and the Pacific, which was largely a by-product of the rivalry between European States. Imperial ideology gained an inspirational hold over the national consciousness, providing new ways for the British people to understand themselves and their place in the world order.

WINDS OF CHANGE

It must be emphasised that Britain's experience was that of *relative*, not absolute economic decline. In other words, the economy continued to grow and the nation was becoming wealthier, but the economies of Germany and other industrialising rivals were expanding at a faster rate and they were therefore taking a larger slice of world trade. For instance, Britain's share of total world exports of manufactured goods slipped from around forty-five per cent to twenty-nine per cent between 1875 and 1913. And yet the value of all exported goods produced in this country, adjusted to take account of changes in the value of money (inflation or deflation), rose in the same period from £223.5 million to £525.2 million. Similarly, it is estimated that the National Income grew from £912 million (£27.8 per person) in 1875 to £2,021 million (£44.3 per person) in 1913.[1] The long-term weakness of the economy lay in its heavy dependence on a few basic sectors such as textiles, coal, iron and steel, and shipbuilding, and its failure to keep up with the competition in newer industries such as chemicals, machine tools and electrical engineering. Consequently, Britain relied increasingly on sales of its traditional products to less developed parts of the world, and by 1913 nearly one-half of exports went to Africa, Asia and South America. On the other hand, the service sector was expanding and generating more 'white-collar' employment for clerks and other occupational groups, and the city of London stood supreme as the world's supplier of financial services. The country also reaped the benefit in this period of its accumulated overseas investments, which totalled £4 billion in 1913 and yielded an annual return of £200 million.

The greatest casualty of intensified foreign competition was agriculture, which suffered after the mid-1870s from a flood of cheap grain from the USA. Prices were accordingly forced down and farmers' incomes followed suit, with the predominantly cereal-growing counties in the south and east of England becoming depressed as a result. Matters were less serious in other parts of the country where livestock or dairy farming was widespread. In any case, developments that spelt gloom for many farmers, and for landowners whose incomes from agricultural rents dropped, were rather good news for urban consumers. Bread prices were nearly halved between 1875 and 1900, as were those of fresh meat, thanks to new sources of foreign supply and the introduction of refrigerated cargo ships. Many other items, including tea and sugar, also became cheaper, and the overall effect was that average *real* wages (measured by what money could buy) rose by about one-third in the final quarter of the nineteenth century.[2] Improving living standards were substantially reinforced by another trend, the fashion for smaller families, which meant that between the 1870s and the 1900s the average number of children born to each marriage fell from just under six to just over three. The growing prosperity of large sections of the population sustained the rise of a mass-consumption society, characterised, among other things, by the appearance of chain stores, processed foods, cheap newspapers (including the *Daily Mail*, *Daily Express* and *Daily Mirror*), and new visual forms of advertising.

Indeed, it was during this period that Britain fully assumed the physical and psychological characteristics of a 'modern', urbanised society. At a time when the overall population continued to rise rapidly – from just over twenty-six million in 1871 to over forty million in 1911 – the agricultural depression brought about depopulation in some rural counties, and the accelerated migration of workers away from the countryside intensified the well-established trend towards urban expansion. The resulting building boom of the late nineteenth century was in evidence in all of the industrial regions, but it was spectacularly apparent in the suburban areas surrounding the major towns and cities, including London's 'home counties' of Surrey, Hertfordshire, Middlesex, Essex and Kent. By 1911 approximately seventy-five per cent of the British people were town dwellers, and forty per cent lived in the largest urban centres with over a hundred thousand inhabitants each. Generations now grew up who had mostly been born in towns, and whose mental outlook had been shaped by the experiences of urban living. The greater concentration of numbers in certain geographical locations also exacerbated, and made more clearly visible, social problems associated with over-crowding and poor sanitary facilities in the slum districts.

With the agricultural depression making land less attractive as an economic asset, some smaller proprietors decided to sell up altogether, while the great magnates tended to dispose of parts of their estates and invest the proceeds in stocks and shares. In this way, landowners were slowly merged into a new and socially more diverse elite of moneyed wealth, although the process was not complete until the 1920s.[3] Before then, a parallel development effected a substantial transfer of political power away from the old landed elite and in favour of the mass of the people. The second Reform Act of 1867 had already enfranchised heads of households in English and Welsh boroughs, and the third Act of 1884 extended this principle to boroughs and counties throughout Britain, so that around sixty per cent of adult males now had the right to vote. An accompanying Redistribution Act in 1885 swept away 138 seats from small boroughs and gave many of them to London and the industrialised areas in the Midlands and the north, creating a more equitable spread of parliamentary representation in accordance with population levels.

In the new political world thus created, it was essential for the Liberal and Conservative parties to find suitable ways of addressing the interests of the enlarged electorate and of trying to manipulate it. Formal party organisation became more important in the constituencies, and regular platform speaking and canvassing was the unavoidable lot of even ordinary MPs. New issues entered into the realm of public debate, including some that raised the whole question of the appropriate functions of the State. For a small minority, mainly intellectuals and some trade unionists, socialism offered an all-encompassing creed, pointing towards the inevitability of class conflict between the forces of capital and labour. These ideas received closer attention during the 1880s and 1890s as part of a wider appraisal of the needs and expectations of ordinary people, stimulated by the violent demonstrations by unemployed workers in London, in 1886 and 1887, the female match-makers' strike in 1888, the London dockers' strike of the following year, and similar episodes. Around the turn of the century, politicians of all shades of opinion were obliged to rethink their attitudes towards the poor when the alarming surveys, conducted by Charles Booth in the East End of London and Seebohm Rowntree in York, showed that poverty affected thirty per cent of the population and was the result primarily of sickness, irregular employment and old age, rather than of individual failings.

In the realm of foreign affairs, the long-term diplomatic consequences of German unification in 1871 compelled Britain to redefine the nature of its relationship with the rest of Europe.[4] By 1894, fear of German expansionary ambitions had led France and Russia to form a military alliance, and, while their combined naval strength initially seemed to present the main challenge to Britain's supremacy on the high seas, within a few years Germany's programme of naval armament clearly posed a more direct threat. Through the ententes reached with France and Russia, in 1904 and 1907 respectively, Britain therefore sought to achieve a better understanding with these powers as a basis for future co-operation. No binding military commitments were entered into, but the sense of obligation to assist in curbing the aggression of Germany and its ally, Austria, resulted in British intervention in a major European conflict in 1914.

Another prominent feature of the growing international rivalry in the final decades of the nineteenth century was the impulse to carve out exclusive spheres of imperial control in more distant parts of the globe. It is estimated that between 1874 and 1902 around 4.75 million square miles of territory was added to the nation's existing colonial possessions, much of it in Africa.[5] In some cases, Britain's reasons for acting were plain enough: Egypt was occupied in order to protect the interests of British investors and secure the trade route via the Suez Canal to India, the jewel in the Imperial crown; South Africa was also strategically important for control of the Cape route to India, but the discovery of gold in the interior provided the more immediate backdrop to the rivalry with the Boers (settlers of Dutch origin) which erupted into a war for supremacy lasting from 1899 until 1902. Elsewhere, in Nigeria, Kenya, Uganda, the Rhodesias, Somaliland and Zanzibar, direct political authority was assumed, partly as a means of maintaining national prestige, but also to ensure that British traders were not excluded from possibly lucrative new markets and sources of raw materials by other European Powers operating tariff barriers. In fact, most of the tropical colonies seized in the 1880s and 1890s did not prove to be very profitable, but at the time British governments were anxious to secure a fair share of the territories which all the great Powers were scrambling for, and the potential value of which could not be predicted.

As we shall see in the remainder of this chapter, the theme of empire exercised a pervasive influence on many areas of social, intellectual and political life in Britain. Various issues were intimately connected with the wider and urgent question of Britain's character and destiny as an imperial power. Imperial considerations were crucial, for instance, in determining the shape of domestic party politics in the late Victorian and Edwardian eras.

THE IMPERIAL IDEA

It was Disraeli, in the 1870s, who placed the empire at the forefront of political debate, where it was to remain – directly or indirectly – for the rest of the century. But when he declared, in a public speech of June 1872, that the mission of the Conservative party was to 'uphold the empire', Disraeli did not simply mean that it was necessary to protect Britain's colonial possessions, important though this obviously was. The empire, for the somewhat mystically-minded Disraeli, was the supreme expression of the greatness of the British nation and the British people, and, in pledging to uphold it, he was identifying Conservative policy with a robust assertion of Britain's overseas interests generally. Imperial power brought with it national prestige, which was indispensable for maintaining Britain's standing in the eyes of the world. Disraeli had no preconceived programme for imperial expansion, and his government of 1874–80 merely responded to opportunities as they arose, but new acquisitions included the Fiji islands, the Gold Coast (Ghana) and Cyprus, while a financial stake was obtained in the vitally important Suez Canal Company. In the most flamboyant gesture of all, Queen Victoria was proclaimed Empress of India, in 1876, placing her on the same exalted footing as the other great European rulers.

Gladstone, it is true, returned as Liberal Prime Minister in 1880 on the basis of a melodramatic moral condemnation of Disraelian bombast, alleging that this had placed a crippling financial burden on the country and dragged it into unseemly and unnecessary conflicts with native peoples such as the Afghans and Zulus. This proved to be a temporarily compelling message, at a time of acute economic depression and unemployment, especially when there was considerable public dismay at the embarrassing setbacks initially suffered by British forces in these colonial wars. Ironically, Gladstone subsequently found himself undertaking far more

substantial colonial ventures than his hated rival had ever
envisaged. The anxiety to preserve British commercial and
financial interests in the Suez region propelled his ministry into
authorising the military occupation of Egypt in 1882, a move that
sparked off the 'scramble for Africa' among all the European
Powers. While there was always a sizeable element within late
Victorian Liberal opinion which shared the widespread public
enthusiasm for empire, Gladstone, all too clearly, was a reluctant
imperialist, and another section of his party consisted of 'little
Englanders' who were critical of the impulse driving the nation to
seize more overseas territory. Internal Liberal divisions on this
issue made it easy for Disraeli's Conservative successors to accuse
their opponents of lacking conviction, and of being unfit to lead a
great imperial nation. Such claims appeared to be substantiated
in 1885, when Gladstone's ministry failed to act quickly enough in
sending a relief expedition to save the lives of General Charles
Gordon and his beleaguered garrison at Khartoum, in the Sudan.

The imperial energy into which the Conservatives so effectively
tapped took on a number of forms. Practical politicians liked to
stress the economic opportunities afforded by Britain's overseas
possessions, which were sometimes likened to 'undeveloped
estates' requiring an injection of business enterprise. Such thinking
was undoubtedly reinforced by fashionable assumptions, derived
from Charles Darwin's theory of evolution, about the racial
inferiority of the peoples for whose government Britain had taken
responsibility, and these attitudes found an often crude expression
in the popular literature of the day. On the other hand, there were
also generous and humanitarian motives at work, which are
illustrated by the missionary activities undertaken by the main
Christian denominations. At the very least, their work reflected a
belief that native peoples could equally find salvation through faith
in the Christian God. In certain parts of Africa, Britain's 'civilising'
imperial presence was held to be justified for the purpose of
stamping out the evil practice of slavery. All of these perspectives
on Britain's imperial role were inspired by a sense of national
destiny, and the belief that Britain was fulfilling the obligations
assigned to it in the natural or divine order of things.[6]

An important distinction needs to be made between the tropical
empire and those regions where Britons themselves had settled in

considerable numbers, notably Canada, Australia, New Zealand and South Africa. With the great exception of India, it was to the 'white' colonies that most of Britain's imperial trade and investment flowed, and during the course of the nineteenth and early twentieth centuries these colonies were granted varying degrees of political autonomy. In an international climate where Britain faced competition, and possibly military danger, from geographically larger nations such as Germany, Russia and the USA, the question was raised whether links with the 'white' colonies ought to be strengthened in order to help the mother country maintain its position as a world leader. Britain's empire, dispersed around the globe, appeared to offer opportunities for the development of an economic, military and perhaps even political entity, capable of matching the great world Powers. This vision was promoted by the influential lectures of the Cambridge historian, J.R. Seeley, published as *The Expansion of England* (1883), and by the Imperial Federation League, a cross-party organisation founded in 1884.

Pride in Britain's imperial status proved to be a potent force for national cohesion in the late Victorian and Edwardian eras. This was inextricably linked with the resurgence of the monarchy as a symbol of national and imperial unity, after a brief period of popular dissatisfaction due to the widowed Queen Victoria's seclusion in the 1860s. Public affection and reverence for a woman widely – if by no means accurately – regarded as a model constitutional monarch, was further heightened by the splendid spectacle of her golden and diamond jubilees in 1887 and 1897. Victoria's jubilees were indeed great imperial occasions, drawing representatives from Britain's dependent territories in every part of the globe, and reinforcing the Queen's image as 'the mother of the empire'. Victoria ended her long reign as a glorious symbol of permanence in a changing world.

Her son, Edward VII, was particularly interested in the ceremonial side of his duties, and during his reign the State opening of Parliament was revamped, to include a grand public procession. When he died in 1910, Edward's body lay in State, a new innovation and a fitting way for the man to depart. Meantime, London's position at the heart of a vast empire was registered in the grand architectural designs of the period, including the War

Office, Admiralty Arch and other government buildings in Whitehall, while statues of national heroes populated Parliament Square. In many spheres of art, too, Britain's majestic empire found powerful and timely voices, for instance in the verse of Rudyard Kipling and (unintentionally) the music of Sir Edward Elgar.[7]

Popular enthusiasm for empire was expressed in many ways apart from the formal celebrations associated with events like the jubilees and Edward VII's coronation in 1902. The most important form of organised mass entertainment was the music hall, and a favourable presentation of the empire was commonly found in the acts and songs of this time, whether it was seen as a stage for feats of military valour or as a field of adventure and economic opportunity for ordinary working people. Undoubtedly, the most remarkable display of spontaneous emotion connected to an imperial episode came in May 1900, during the Boer war, when a British garrison besieged at Mafeking for seven months was finally relieved. According to the recently founded *Daily Mail*, on 19 May, the news of the relief of Mafeking reached London at about nine o'clock in the evening and, as if by magic, excited crowds suddenly appeared in the streets singing 'Rule Britannia' and 'Soldiers of the Queen'. Flags were hung everywhere and there was 'a very orgy of rejoiceful patriotism'. Nor was this phenomenon confined to the metropolis and its surrounding suburbs, for there was 'wild, unrestrained, irrepressible jubilation' in towns and cities all over Britain, as well as in Canada, Australia and New Zealand, which had sent troops to assist the British army. The hero of Mafeking, Robert Baden Powell, went on to establish the Boy Scout movement in 1907, which helped to instil the values of honesty, self-discipline and loyalty to King and Country in the minds of future generations of youngsters.[8]

UNIONISM ASCENDANT

The growing preoccupation in British political circles with issues relating to the empire developed into an obsession, during the 1880s, when Ireland returned to the forefront of debate. Although Ireland was not, constitutionally speaking, a colony, sending as it did 103 elected representatives to the Parliament in London, the

Catholic majority had never been happily reconciled to the Act of Union with Britain. Irish resentment at their country's subordinate relationship to a wealthier, more powerful, and above all Protestant British State, had periodically surfaced in various forms of agitation. In the early 1870s, the majority of Irish Liberal MPs formed themselves into a separate party demanding 'Home Rule', the precise meaning of which was originally unclear; but by 1880 the aggressively anti-British tone adopted by the new Irish leader, Charles Stewart Parnell, suggested that it meant complete independence. The challenge posed by Parnell's brand of Irish nationalism helped to destroy the Liberal ascendancy in Britain and establish a new political force, Unionism, with the Conservative party at its core, which was dedicated to maintaining the Union with Ireland in its existing form.

From a British point of view, control over Ireland was deemed indispensable for the sake of national security and international greatness. The fear that Catholic Powers such as France or Spain might seek to use Ireland as a platform for attack had traditionally influenced British policy, and in the later nineteenth century the USA, whose historic antagonism towards Britain had been reinforced by the presence of large numbers of Irish migrants fleeing the famine in the 1840s, was identified as another source of danger. Furthermore, so the argument went, if Britain was unable to prevent Ireland from breaking away and becoming independent, the consequences for imperial unity could be disastrous, as distant colonies might feel tempted to follow the Irish example. Disraeli tried to focus public attention on this issue in the 1880 general election campaign, seizing upon the fact that certain radical Liberals sympathised with the Home Rulers to substantiate his allegation that the Liberal party as a whole was involved in an unscrupulous alliance with Parnell. He went so far as to claim that the Liberals were hatching a sinister plot to 'enfeeble our colonies' by a 'policy of decomposition'. Disraeli's move did not pay off for the Conservatives immediately, but its political relevance to the party soon became clear.

Specific aspects of the Parnellite home rule campaign were highly offensive to British sensibilities. Beginning in 1877, militant Irish MPs adopted the strategy of deliberately obstructing parliamentary business at Westminster, through time-wasting procedural devices and endless speeches, in order to show that they could make it very difficult for the British to govern themselves until Ireland was allowed to govern itself. Such provocative behaviour was taken as an affront to a parliamentary system in which most Britons felt considerable pride. Further cause for concern came from the way that Parnell linked the home rule movement to agitation for land reform in Ireland: this gained considerable support from hard-pressed tenant farmers, who were feeling the effects of agricultural depression, and it was marked by widespread intimidation and violence. Gladstone's ministry conceded another Irish Land Act in 1881, establishing a land court with power to set rents and granting fixity of tenure to the farmers. This was an unprecedented invasion by the State of the contractual relations between landowners and their tenants, and many British politicians had grave misgivings about it. Terrorist outrages committed by extreme elements within the Irish nationalist movement included the murder of the Irish Chief Secretary, Lord Frederick Cavendish, and the senior civil servant T.H. Burke, in Phoenix Park, Dublin in May 1882. This, and several bomb attacks in London in 1884–5, only served to heighten British antagonism towards the idea of any change in the constitutional relations between the two countries. To those in Britain who were determined to resist Irish nationalist demands, it appeared that they were engaged in a struggle not only to save the empire, but to uphold law and order and protect the rights of property.

The defence of property became a matter of pressing concern in the mid-1880s, at a time when some radical Liberals, notably Joseph Chamberlain, were advocating controversial policies with an eye to the new electorate created by the third Reform Act. These proposals included a graduated income tax (meaning higher rates for those on higher incomes), the compulsory purchase of land to provide allotments and smallholdings for labourers, and the disestablishment and disendowment of the Church of England. Chamberlain's programme – dubbed as 'socialism' by his critics, both Liberal and Conservative – and the provocative manner of his platform oratory in the run-up to the 1885 general election, probably contributed to the striking gains made by the Conservatives in urban constituencies, particularly in London. Fears about the growth of 'socialist' influence within the Liberal party assisted the ongoing process by which important sections of the business and professional 'middle classes' drifted towards Conservatism. It is true that the Conservatives still lost in 1885, but a distinct geographical pattern of electoral strength was emerging, with concentrations of support in London, the home counties, and the suburban areas of the provincial towns, which was to become even more emphatic at succeeding elections and has persisted throughout the twentieth century.

However, the decisive breakthrough occurred in 1886 when Gladstone, convinced of the need to recognise that the Irish people as a *nation* were demanding political change, brought forward a Home Rule bill providing for the creation of a Parliament in Dublin responsible for purely Irish affairs. Gladstone argued that his plan would cement Irish allegiance to the union with Britain, but he met with fierce opposition from within his own party as well as from the Conservatives. Almost one hundred Liberal MPs, a broad cross-section of the party in terms of political ideology and social background, rebelled against their own leader and formed a separate organisation, the Liberal Unionist party. Acting together, the Conservatives and Liberal Unionists defeated Gladstone's bill in the House of Commons and subsequently scored a decisive general election victory. Their 'Unionist Alliance' proved to be the dominant force in British politics for the next twenty years, achieving further impressive electoral triumphs in 1895 and 1900.

Between 1886 and 1892 the Conservative government of Lord Salisbury, bolstered by independent support from the Liberal Unionists, pursued a policy of uncompromising resistance to home rule, equipping itself with emergency powers designed to stamp out unrest in Ireland. What was believed to be at stake here, as Salisbury reminded a public audience in Liverpool in January 1888, was the character of the British people and their reputation in the eyes of the world:

> I entreat you to give the lie to those who say that there can be no consistency of purpose, no tenacity of resolution, in a democratic government.... You are now on trial to see whether you have that tenacity and resolution. If you have not, you will be announcing to the world that the qualities by which your empire has been built up are no longer there to maintain it, and that it is at the mercy of the first accident that will throw it down.[9]

Gladstone and the Liberals returned to office after a narrow victory in the general election of 1892, fought mainly on non-Irish issues; but their second Home Rule bill, introduced the following year, was subjected to an at times almost frenzied attack in the House of Commons (fighting broke out on one occasion), and it was finally rejected by an overwhelming margin in the House of Lords. Gladstone retired shortly afterwards, and the divided and demoralised government led by his successor, Lord Rosebery, collapsed in June 1895, paving the way for Salisbury to become Prime Minister at the head of a Conservative–Liberal Unionist coalition ministry.

The most striking feature of late Victorian politics, therefore, is that in the increasingly democratic environment created by the third Reform Act of 1884, it was the Conservative party which prospered more than the Liberals. As the dominant partner in the Unionist Alliance, the Conservatives were at last able to portray themselves convincingly as a 'national party', appealing to all sections of society and transcending the interests of different classes. Firmly committed to the defence of property, the Union with Ireland and the integrity of the empire, the Conservatives and their allies won substantial support in urban and industrial constituencies in London, the West Midlands, Lancashire and the West of Scotland, as well as in many rural seats. The characteristic organisation of the age was the Primrose League, founded in memory of Disraeli in 1883, which achieved a membership of one million by 1891 and double that number by 1910. With its mock-medieval hierarchical structure of 'knights', 'esquires', 'dames' and so on (half of the members were female), the League inculcated a simple political doctrine of loyalty to the Crown, the empire and religion; but it promoted this message subtly within the context of social functions such as garden parties, fetes, dances, excursions and picnics. In London, meantime, the government of the country was entrusted to the reassuringly imposing figure of Lord Salisbury, the last peer Prime Minister, whose presence highlighted the fact that the political prestige of the old landowning elite had been shored up for a little longer, after 1886, thanks to the Conservative party's association with a popular cause.[10]

More incongruous, yet no less significant, was the role played by that most dynamic exponent of imperial ideas – Joseph

Chamberlain.[11] Chamberlain, as we have seen, had originally been a radical Liberal and the Conservatives' favourite *bête noire*. In 1886, however, he joined the Liberal Unionist revolt against Gladstone's Home Rule bill and went on to become securely integrated within the Unionist alliance. Asked to choose his office in Salisbury's coalition government of 1895, he opted for the Colonial Secretaryship, and successfully turned this into a key ministerial post. His finest hour arrived in the autumn of 1900 when, with the Boer war apparently all but over, he persuaded his colleagues to hold an early general election which registered a crushing triumph for the Unionists. Personally identified with the war, which he had certainly helped to provoke, Chamberlain dominated the campaigning in what came to be known as the 'Khaki election', showing few scruples about smearing his Liberal critics as enemies of their own nation.

Subsequent developments, on the other hand, removed much of the lustre from the Unionists' election victory. The war in South Africa dragged on until 1902, because of the Boers' obstinate use of guerrilla tactics long after they had been defeated in the conventional military sense. Quite apart from the enormous expense involved in maintaining a substantial expeditionary force overseas, totalling some £200 million, the policy of combating guerilla warfare by herding Boer civilians into concentration camps, where many thousands died of disease, earned Britain international opprobrium. Anxious to restore credibility both to his imperial vision and to the Unionist government, now headed by Salisbury's nephew, Arthur Balfour, Chamberlain embarked in 1903 upon a vigorous public campaign to promote what he euphemistically termed 'tariff reform'. Simply put, Chamberlain was proposing that Britain should abandon its venerable policy of free trade, enshrined in the great budgets of Peel and Gladstone, and instead impose tariffs on imported goods.

Tariff reform was presented as a bold solution to many of the most urgent problems confronting Britain at the dawn of the twentieth century. For domestic political purposes, the use of tariffs to exclude 'unfair' foreign competition seemed to offer a cure for unemployment, which was affecting certain sectors of the economy such as the metal trades of the West Midlands (Chamberlain's own backyard). In this way, socialist campaigners in trade unions and other organisations would hopefully be deprived of a means of winning converts to their cause from among the ranks of the working classes. Chamberlain went further and argued that taxes on foreign imports would raise the additional government revenue required to finance desirable welfare measures, including old-age pensions, the need for which had recently been highlighted by Booth's and Rowntree's investigations into the causes of poverty. But he also wanted to emphasise the direct relevance of the empire to the material prosperity of the British people, and he did this by suggesting that a system of 'imperial preference' should be introduced, so that the colonies were exempted from the tariffs applied to goods from foreign countries. The empire would obligingly supply cheap raw materials for British industry and provide markets for Britain's manufactured exports. Chamberlain thus aimed to strengthen economic ties with the colonies, which he believed to be essential for the nation's survival as a world Power. At a public meeting in Glasgow, in October 1903, he issued the dramatic warning that:

> all history is the history of States once powerful and then decaying. Is Britain to be numbered among the decaying States? Is all the glory of the past to be forgotten? Are we to prove ourselves unregenerate sons of the forefathers who left us so glorious an inheritance? ... Or are we to take up a new youth as members of a great empire, which will continue for generation after generation, the strength, the power, and the glory of the British race?[12]

In the event, Chamberlain's crusade had an ambiguous impact. He succeeded in plunging the Unionists into a period of internal ideological warfare, pitting zealous disciples of tariff reform against faithful adherents to free-trade orthodoxy. The real beneficiaries of this situation were the Liberals, who rallied to the defence of their sacred cow, free trade, and attacked Chamberlain's plan on its most vulnerable point – the taxation of imported foodstuffs ('dear bread'). A policy designed to transcend class interests succeeded in achieving precisely the opposite effect, by provoking criticism that it would burden poorer consumers while sparing wealthy income-tax payers from having to meet the cost of welfare reforms. At the general election of 1906 the Unionists suffered a devastating defeat, winning only 157 seats in the House of Commons: most of their remaining MPs, on the other hand, were committed to Chamberlain's policy. When his active career was ended shortly afterwards by a stroke, it appeared that Chamberlain had won over the Unionists to tariff reform, but at a terrible cost in terms of electoral weakness and removal from office. Not until the Great War of 1914–18 transformed the political landscape again would the Unionists fully recover from the effects of Chamberlain's tariff reform bombshell.[13]

LIBERAL REGENERATION

Although the Liberals were able to win a landslide victory (four hundred seats) at the 1906 general election by concentrating negatively on the defence of traditional free-trade principles, this ended a twenty-year spell in which the party had struggled to maintain its popular appeal. Gladstone's Irish Home Rule bill of 1886 had provoked the Liberal Unionist secession from the party, weakening it both in terms of lost personnel and diminished political credibility. Furthermore, the veteran leader's single-minded determination to keep home rule at the top of the Liberal agenda, despite the lack of sympathy for this cause amongst the British public, ensured that the party remained saddled with what some of Gladstone's colleagues privately regarded as an electoral albatross. After his retirement in 1894, home rule was effectively sidelined by Gladstone's successors, but personal animosities and political differences within the leadership prevented the Liberals from evolving a clear, alternative set of policies, and the 1895 general election resulted in a humiliating defeat. Internal divisions were further exacerbated by the Boer war, which left the party vulnerable to Chamberlain's accusations of 'unpatriotic' behaviour and contributed to another rebuff from the electorate in 1900.

Meantime, another important development was raising disturbing questions about the long-term prospects of the Liberal party. In February 1900 the Labour Representation Committee (LRC) was formed for the purpose of increasing the number of working men in the House of Commons. This was an umbrella organisation combining existing socialist groups, such as the Fabian Society (1884) and the Independent Labour Party (1893), with mainly non-socialist trade unions.[14] Elements of working-class consciousness in society had taken on what proved to be a permanent organisational form. The trade union movement was really galvanised into supporting and financing the LRC after a legal judgement of 1901, which left them open to civil action by employers for losses suffered during strikes. By 1903 the LRC posed a sufficiently convincing threat to the electoral hopes of the Liberals as to persuade the Liberal chief whip of the expediency of entering into a secret pact. The terms of the resulting arrangement allowed the LRC to contest some fifty specified seats, without Liberal opposition, in return for agreeing not to field candidates anywhere else in England and Wales. This made good tactical sense, in that it reduced the risk of Liberal and Labour candidates destroying each other's chances by splitting the anti-Unionist vote. Undoubtedly, the 'Lib-Lab pact' helped to maximise the Liberals' potential at the 1906 election, and they exploited to the full Unionist unpopularity and internal disarray, but this was achieved at an ominous price: namely, the election of twenty-nine LRC members, who proceeded to form themselves into the Parliamentary Labour party. It was a mark of the Liberals' insecurity in 1903, and, in particular, doubts about their ability to attract working men's votes in areas such as Lancashire, that they should have allowed the Labour cuckoo into their nest.[15]

If the Liberals faced a political dilemma presented by the emergence of a separate Labour party embodying, to some extent at least, socialist principles, this should not be interpreted as proof of a failure to adapt to changing circumstances. On the contrary, since the 1880s there had been a greater readiness by Liberals to deploy 'class' language against their opponents in order to establish their own political identity in relation to the working class portion of the electorate. But this was a distinctively Liberal version of class politics, in which the combatants were not capital and labour but the productive and unproductive classes. Gladstone had pointed the way in 1886 when he *claimed* that the opposition to his Home Rule bill came from 'the classes' – powerful vested interests such as landowners, the Church, the armed forces and the upper echelons of the legal profession – whereas 'the masses' virtuously supported his attempt to deliver 'justice to Ireland'. In other words, Gladstone was attributing an absence of class motive to the majority of the British people and alleging that the narrow pursuit of class interest was confined to the old ruling elite, which had opposed him. During the 1890s and early 1900s the implications of this Liberal analysis of the class-divide in British society were more fully worked out, leading to proposals for new forms of taxation specifically targeted at the very wealthy, and especially at landowners. David Lloyd George, the Chancellor of the Exchequer from 1908 until 1915, had been brought-up in rural North Wales and was the most prominent Liberal exponent of anti-landlordism. His provocative speeches depicted landowners as a parasitic minority feeding off the productive efforts of the vast majority of the people. Such an approach to class-based political action, asserting the common interests of businessmen and labourers against an idle and selfish elite, was the only one possible for a party whose own MPs were drawn, overwhelmingly, from business or professional backgrounds. However, there were obvious dangers involved in stoking up class antagonism for political purposes, as the Liberals risked being burned by their own fire if the forces of labour decided to turn against those of capital. For this reason, most Liberal leaders preferred in practice to hold back somewhat, treating class rhetoric as a useful weapon in their armoury at certain times rather than as a standard tool for all occasions.

Around the turn of the century, there was also evidence of a serious attempt to re-define Liberalism so that it addressed contemporary concerns about the condition of the people in a densely urbanised society. Classical Liberal theory, based on the general principle of laissez-faire and optimistic assumptions about social progress, patently failed to confront the pressing issues of the age, and Liberals were increasingly obliged to consider the need for more positive action by the State. There was greater understanding of the artificiality of a pure individualist creed, once it was recognised that individual identities were shaped by the society in which they existed and that without society the individual had no identity. This perception enabled Liberals to argue that individual liberty could only be secured *through* society, and that there was no reason why the State should not do more to help individuals fulfil their human potential.

In the writings of the journalist-academics, J.A. Hobson and L.T. Hobhouse, the case was made for welfare measures designed to liberate individuals from the fear of poverty and so provide a basic platform on which to build their lives. Property, according to these 'New Liberals', was similarly social in character, since it could not exist without the security provided by the State, and it was therefore deemed justifiable to introduce redistributive taxation in order to reclaim for society the social element in property. Redistributing wealth would also boost consumer demand for goods and services, making the capitalist economy operate more effectively. Hobson's diagnosis of 'under-consumption' as the root cause of the nation's economic and social problems fitted into a critique of imperial expansion, which he alleged was stimulated by capitalist interests in search of overseas outlets for their surplus investment funds. These financial resources, he concluded, could be much more usefully employed at home, provided there was sufficient consumer demand to be satisfied.

Equally influential, though, was the case for welfare reform put forward by the 'Liberal Imperialists', who included among their number the former Prime Minister, Rosebery, and the future premier, H.H. Asquith. Moved by contemporary fears about racial degeneration, which seemed to be borne out during the Boer war by the disturbing revelation that up to one-third of volunteers were unfit for active military service, the Liberal Imperialists called for State action to ensure that future generations of Britons were fit to serve a great empire. The need for 'national efficiency' became a popular watchword of the day, cutting across party-political boundaries. Both pro- and anti-imperial strands of Liberal thinking thus helped to expand the framework of political discussion, promoting a greater recognition of the legitimacy of State intervention to improve the welfare of the people.[16]

The Liberals in government were indeed responsible for a series of important welfare measures, beginning with medical inspections for schoolchildren and the provision of free school meals in the neediest cases. In 1908 old-age pensions were introduced for those over seventy, and this was followed by further legislation aimed at providing greater security for those in work. The Trade Boards Act of 1909 established machinery for fixing minimum wage rates in certain 'sweated' industries; employment exchanges came into being in 1910; and in 1911 two National Insurance Acts were passed, one providing sickness benefits and access to a doctor for most workers (not their families), the other providing unemployment benefits for workers occupied specifically in the building, shipbuilding and engineering industries, where trade fluctuations were particularly acute. No less significant was the way in which additional revenue was raised to finance these new social obligations assumed by the State. Lloyd George, in his 'People's Budget' of 1909, put up the rate of income tax for those on high earnings (over £2,000 per annum) and introduced a supertax for the very wealthiest of all (over £5,000 per annum), while the ground was prepared for future taxes on landowners. When the House of Lords rejected these proposals, the Liberals seized the opportunity to appeal to the country with the cry of 'the peers versus the people', and after their narrow election victory in January 1910 the budget was passed. Prior to the outbreak of war in 1914 plans were also being developed for legislation to improve the wages and housing conditions of rural labourers, a section of the community on whose future support the Liberals were pinning their electoral hopes, and the government was clearly edging towards the idea of a universal minimum wage.[17]

In strategic political terms, Liberal welfarism and tax changes were intended to achieve the simultaneous objects of discrediting the Unionists' tariff reform programme and containing the threat from Labour. By demonstrating that increased levels of direct taxation made it possible to finance welfare reforms within a traditional free-trade commercial framework, and by attacking the Unionists as heartless defenders of the interests of selfish wealth, the Liberals sought to keep their opponents on the 'right' of the political spectrum on the defensive. The general elections of January and December 1910 were at least a partial success, from this point of view, although the Liberals did lose many rural and suburban seats captured from the Unionists in the 1906 landslide. At the same time, the Liberal government was offering a non-socialist but radical alternative to the policy prescriptions put forward by 'extremist' elements within the Labour party, and in this way it was hoped that the 'left' of the spectrum would be obliged to co-operate with the broad Liberal 'left-centre'. Liberals such as Lloyd George were fond of talking about a 'progressive alliance' between their party and Labour, in which the latter was clearly expected to remain the junior partner. Certainly, Labour's electoral record before the Great War did not suggest that it was ready to go it alone and supplant the Liberals altogether. After the December 1910 election, with just forty-two seats in the House of Commons, few if any of which would have been won without the Lib-Lab pact, Labour looked to be essentially a trade-union and socialist pressure group rather than a party of government. In those by-elections between 1911 and 1914 where Lib-Lab co-operation broke down at the local level, Labour candidates invariably came bottom of the poll. Had the war not prevented a general election in 1915, it seems likely that the Labour leadership would have accepted an increased allocation of seats within a renewed Lib-Lab pact. The spectacularly rapid breakthrough made by Labour after the war, which will be discussed in chapter 6, did not look to be on the cards in 1914.[18]

AN EDWARDIAN CRISIS?

For all the Liberals' undeniable constructive achievements, doubts remain as to the party's future viability and, indeed, as to the survival of the fundamental values underpinning its approach to politics. The most enduringly influential book on the years preceding the outbreak of war is George Dangerfield's *The Strange Death of Liberal England*, first published in 1935 and still in print. Dangerfield pointed to the increasingly militant activities of certain specific groups – suffragettes, trade unionists and Ulster Protestants – between 1910 and 1914, which he argued were symptomatic of a general climate of revolt affecting society as a whole. According to this view, the nation was shedding its traditional Liberal values of rationalism, tolerance and commitment to working within a parliamentary and legal framework, preferring instead to resort to extremism and violence. It was an attitude that reflected the 'spirit of the age'. By 1914, so it is claimed, British society was rapidly descending into chaos, and a total collapse was only averted because the country was suddenly engulfed in a far greater European conflagration.

Dangerfield's melodramatic style and impressionistic approach fall a long way short of the standards set by modern historical scholarship; yet it is impossible to dismiss entirely the validity of his interpretation. Edwardian Britain, in its final phase,[19] undoubtedly witnessed some exceptionally turbulent times, and none of the problems highlighted by Dangerfield had been resolved before the Great War intervened. The crucial questions, though, are whether there really was a widespread repudiation of Liberal values by the Edwardian public, and whether the events of 1910–14 may have posed at least as great a dilemma for the Unionist opposition as for the Liberal government.

Since the formation of the Women's Social and Political Union by Emmeline Pankhurst and her daughters in 1903, the campaign for women's suffrage had taken on a new character. Impatient with the conventional pressure-group tactics pursued for many years by other organisations in the field, and frustrated by the unwillingness of the Liberals after 1906 to use their large parliamentary majority to force through legislation, Mrs Pankhurst and her followers resorted to ever more drastic methods of publicising their cause. Beginning with the disruption of political meetings, the Suffragettes (as they came to be known) graduated to chaining themselves to railings outside public buildings, smashing windows, setting fire to letter boxes and perpetrating direct physical attacks on Liberal ministers and their property. In the most dramatic episode of all, Emily Wilding Davison was killed when she ran in front of the King's horse at the 1913 Derby race. While the Suffragettes were clearly successful in drawing public attention to the question of votes for women, their activities were ultimately counterproductive, hardening the attitude of opponents such as the Prime Minister, Asquith, and alienating sympathetic politicians like Lloyd George. Confronted by numerous acts of vandalism and violence, Liberal ministers felt obliged to implement some decidedly illiberal measures in order to combat the Suffragette menace, including the force-feeding of women on hunger strike in prison, and the infamous 'Cat and Mouse Act' of 1913 which permitted hunger-strikers in declining health to be temporarily released and re-imprisoned later. It was difficult to see, in 1914, how the resulting stalemate between government and protesters might be broken, and it took the war, and the opportunities this provided for women to show their patriotism and responsibility, to create a new climate of feeling in which the women's suffrage issue could be settled as part of a wider measure of parliamentary reform.[20]

The irony of the Suffragette campaign – which, on the face of it, seems to support Dangerfield's argument about a general spirit of militancy, infecting women's minds as much as men's – is that their aim was the entirely constitutional one of obtaining for women the right to participate within the existing political system. Illiberal methods were being employed to secure an objective that was perfectly consistent with traditional Liberal values. Entrenched attitudes towards gender roles were obviously the main barrier to a solution of the problem, but it is important to recognise that gradual changes had been taking place. Victorian women always played some part, formally or informally, in the political process at various levels, and their opportunities expanded during the final decades of the nineteenth century through involvement in such organisations as the Primrose League, the Women's National Liberal Federation and the Independent Labour Party. Female householders also became eligible to vote and stand for election in areas of local government such as School Boards and Poor Law Boards.[21] The formation of Millicent Fawcett's umbrella organisation, the National Union of Women's Suffrage Societies, in 1897, was indicative of the fact that 'respectable' pressure for women's enfranchisement had been mounting for some years. In the Edwardian period, however, further progress was hampered by hard political realities: of a Liberal government, whose membership included a minority opposed to female suffrage, which was beset by other difficulties, and which could only conceivably have legislated for women as part of a comprehensive reform of the electoral system requiring more parliamentary time than it was able or willing to spare.[22]

One major distraction for Liberal ministers after 1910 was provided by the worsening state of industrial relations. Trade-union membership roughly doubled from two to four million between 1910 and 1914, and there was a wave of crippling strikes, some of them conducted on a nationwide scale, affecting the coal industry, the railways, the docks, shipbuilding and engineering. Whereas in 1909 there were 422 stoppages and about 2.7 million working days lost, in 1913 the figures were 1,459 stoppages and 9.8 million days lost. What seems to have been happening was that trade unionists who, it should be remembered, still only represented twenty per cent of the workforce in 1914, were exploiting the relatively full employment conditions of these years with a view to recovering the losses in real wages suffered as a result of recent price inflation. In 1913 the railwaymen, miners and dockers formed a 'triple alliance' designed to co-ordinate their wage bargaining with employers and so maximise their industrial muscle. Ominous though this seemed, it was certainly not intended as an instrument of industrial or political conquest: only a small minority of union activists, mainly concentrated in the South Wales coalfield, were 'Syndicalists', advocating industrial action as the best means of achieving a socialist reconstruction of society in which the workers (not the State) would take control of industry.[23] Nevertheless, Asquith's government resorted on several occasions to the deployment of troops to quell industrial disturbances in Tonypandy, Liverpool and elsewhere. Liberals were instinctively uncomfortable with the operation of trade unions, regarding them as sectional organisations trying to further their own interests at the expense of society as a whole. The government's welfare reforms reflected a preference for direct assistance to individuals by the State, but Asquith and his colleagues were reluctantly obliged at the same time to accustom themselves to the uncongenial role of mediators between combinations of employers and workmen.

The greatest distraction of all for the pre-war Liberal government arose from the imminent prospect of insurrection in Ireland, as the Protestants of Ulster prepared to resist forcibly their inclusion in a Home Rule bill for the whole of Ireland. How this situation came about can only be understood by setting it in the wider context of a British constitutional crisis, which, in its turn, illustrates the difficulties confronting the Edwardian Unionist party. Struggling to recover from their traumatic election defeat in 1906, the Unionists had wielded their overwhelming majority in the hereditary House of Lords to block carefully selected pieces of Liberal legislation. This culminated in the drastic decision to reject Lloyd George's 'People's Budget' of 1909, on the ground that old-age pensions ought to be financed through tariffs rather than income and land taxes. After two general elections, in January and December 1910, fought on the cry of 'the peers versus the people', the Liberals were able to force through a Parliament Act in 1911, which seriously curtailed the powers of the House of Lords.

The peers lost altogether their power over finance bills, and their hitherto unlimited right to veto legislation was replaced with a two-year delaying power. (At the same time, the maximum duration of Parliaments was reduced from seven years to five.) If this defeat for the Unionist opposition was not devastating enough, matters thereafter looked even more bleak because the Parliament Act cleared the path for an Irish Home Rule bill, which could not, as in the past, be blocked permanently by the Lords. In fact, having lost their overall majority after the 1910 elections, the Liberals were compelled to proceed with home rule as the price for Irish nationalist support in the House of Commons, which they needed in order to remain in office. Accordingly, in 1912 a bill was introduced to establish an Irish parliament in Dublin, and under the terms of the Parliament Act it was set to pass in 1914 regardless of the House of Lords.

With home rule at last becoming an immediate reality, the Unionist party had to determine the best way of opposing a measure that struck at the heart of their own political identity. Under the leadership of Andrew Bonar Law, the Unionists focused their efforts on the Ulster dimension to the Irish problem, since the Protestant community there was vehemently opposed to being subjected to a Catholic-dominated assembly in Dublin. Some of the language used by Bonar Law and his colleagues came perilously close to inciting the Ulster Protestants, led by Sir Edward Carson, to resist home-rule by force, although care was taken to clothe this opposition in constitutional forms by demanding a general election or a referendum on the issue. During the course of 1914, an increasingly dangerous state of affairs developed in Ireland, as Ulster Protestants imported weapons in preparation for armed resistance, Catholic nationalists took similar counter-measures, and the British government felt unsure of the army's loyalty if it was ordered to suppress a Protestant revolt. Asquith, who had recognised all along that a settlement might ultimately require the exclusion of Ulster from the home-rule arrangements, was guilty of misjudging the depth of Protestant sentiment, and his indolent mismanagement allowed matters to spiral out of control so that compromise was harder to obtain and bloodshed became a distinct possibility. Only the Great War was sufficient to break the deadlock, forcing a postponement of the whole issue until peace was restored to Europe.[24] By then, Catholic opinion in Ireland had hardened against the idea of mere devolution and in favour of complete independence, which was conceded in 1921 as part of a settlement involving the partition of the country to allow the six north-eastern counties to remain united with Britain.

It is extremely doubtful whether circumstances so specific to Ireland can be used to support Dangerfield's claims for a general psychology of violence in British society. Edwardian Britain, for all its problems, was in fact a comparatively orderly and law-abiding place: levels of recorded crime had fallen continuously since the 1860s, with those for homicide, wounding and non-violent offences against property down by more than half. In an important sense, the activities of the Suffragettes and trades unions represented the militancy of raised expectations in an increasingly prosperous and civilised society. What is true, all the same, is that the eruption of war on the continent of Europe, which took most people in Britain by surprise, extricated the country from a number of conflicts that had proved resistant to easy solution. Patterns of destructive behaviour were broken as the Unionist party in Parliament, Ulster Protestants, Suffragettes and trade unionists joined with the Liberal government in displaying their patriotic loyalty. For example, almost 2.5 million men *volunteered* for military service between August 1914 and December 1915, suggesting that the bonds of national unity were far stronger than any divisive influences. And when the war was over, Britain, its politicians and its people, found themselves in another world.

SIX

Wars and Depression, 1914–45

INTRODUCTION

The British nation was indelibly marked by the effects of its participation in the two greatest military conflicts of the twentieth century. Nowadays these are remembered as the First and Second World Wars, although contemporaries, unaware of further horrors to come, knew the first simply as the 'Great War'. Using the starkest form of measurement, the country lost about seven hundred and fifty thousand servicemen killed in the war of 1914–18, more than one and a half million suffered permanent injuries, including two hundred and fifty thousand who had limbs amputated, and unrecorded numbers were left mentally scarred. Such appalling casualty figures reflected the fact that Britain's military effort was concentrated on the Western Front, in Belgium and France, where the supremacy of artillery and machine guns meant that soldiers were trapped in a deadly and seemingly endless nightmare of trench warfare, in which neither side was able to gain much territorial advantage. The second war lasted longer, from 1939 until 1945, but tanks and aeroplanes now dictated the nature of military operations, making for a highly mobile form of combat; it was also a more truly global conflict, fought in several arenas outside Europe and in widely varying conditions. Direct military losses were considerably lower than in 1914–18, with around three hundred thousand servicemen killed and nearly four hundred and fifty thousand injured. On the other hand, civilian casualties were far higher in the second war, owing to the greater intensity of air attacks on targets in Britain itself, and the significance of this will become apparent later in the chapter.

If we look beyond the cost in terms of military and civilian casualties, it becomes clear that the experience of war affected the country in a number of other ways. Immense economic damage was inflicted, through the financial expense of fighting the wars and the permanent disruption they caused to old patterns of international trade, and this served to accelerate the process of decline relative to other nations, which was identified in chapter 5 as a problem facing Britain before 1914. In turn, the economic costs of war compounded the psychological effects as the nation suffered an erosion of confidence in its ability to maintain its position as a world-class Power. Both conflicts exerted creative as well as destructive influences on British society, however: the resulting changes have arguably been exaggerated in the case of 1914–18, but their significance in 1939–45 is unquestionable. On the face of things, the social impact of war was contradictory, in that class distinctions were heightened yet at the same time the bonds of national unity were reinforced, so that by 1945 they were probably stronger than ever before.

In the political sphere, dramatic changes occurred during and after the 1914–18 war. The Reform Act, carried shortly before the cessation of hostilities, gave voting rights to virtually all adult males and many females as well, with the result that the total electorate was massively increased from around seven million to twenty-one million. Within a few years, Labour had replaced the Liberals as the main party of the 'left', and intense debate still rages among historians about the connection between these two developments. Remarkably, though, the immediate beneficiaries of this process were the Conservatives, who lifted themselves out of their pre-war doldrums to dominate the political scene during the 1920s and 1930s, renewing their Disraelian claim to be the authentic 'national party'. It was not until the end of the Second World War that Labour broke through decisively, achieving an overall parliamentary majority for the first time. Before then, the crucial test of the resilience of Britain's inter-war political structure was its ability to withstand pressure from extremist movements, on the left and right of the political spectrum, of the kind that rose to power elsewhere in Europe in the context of a global economic crisis.

THE IMPACT OF WAR, 1914–18

Britain was not obliged to go to war in August 1914, and its intentions remained uncertain until the final moment. The crisis precipitated in the Balkans after the assassination of the Austrian Archduke, Franz Ferdinand, by a Serbian nationalist, provoked Austria-Hungary into taking military measures against Serbia with encouragement from her ally, Germany. This activated Russian support for their Serb client, which in turn drew Russia's ally, France, into the picture. Britain's decision to intervene alongside France and Russia, despite being only loosely tied to them by the ententes of 1904 and 1907, was ostensibly prompted by German violation of Belgium's neutrality, but in reality dictated by anxiety to preserve a 'balance of power' among the European States and prevent Germany from establishing a position of overwhelming superiority.[1] Memories of Napoleon Buonaparte and revolutionary France a century before still shaped British foreign policy perceptions. Contrary to expectation, the war was not over in a few months, and Britain found itself sending ever greater numbers of its young men to the slaughtering fields of Flanders. Once entered, the war seemed impossible to get out of without a humiliating loss of face. The enormous physical and financial strains on all the combatants finally proved too much for Russia, which withdrew after the Bolshevik Revolution of October 1917. Fortunately for Britain and France, this loss was compensated for by support from the USA, and the military balance was decisively shifted against Germany, which collapsed with surprising rapidity in the autumn of 1918.

Sadly, the one undisputed legacy of the First World War was its debilitating effect on Britain's economic power. In purely financial terms, the country spent approximately £9.5 billion on the war effort, and while some of this was covered by higher taxes, the bulk of it had to be raised through borrowing. As a result, the National Debt, which stood at £650 million in 1914, had risen to £8 billion by 1920, and debt interest payments at the later date consumed nearly one-quarter of all government expenditure. London's position as the financial capital of the world had also been surrendered to New York. Equally worrying was the fact that, after an immediate post-war boom in 1919–20, as pent-up consumer demand was satisfied and restocking occurred, there followed a dramatic slump in industrial output. Unemployment consequently passed the one million mark in 1921, and it never fell below that figure again until the Second World War. The problem persisted because the industries in which Britain had historically enjoyed international supremacy – textiles, coal, shipbuilding and iron and steel – experienced structural dislocation arising from the loss of valuable export markets. During the war, vital resources were diverted to meet immediate military production requirements, and maritime supply routes were also severely disrupted by German submarine attacks. In these circumstances, rivals such as the USA and Japan seized the opportunity to move into markets in Latin America and the Far East traditionally supplied by British manufacturers. To make matters even worse, hitherto reliable customers like Canada, India, Brazil and Argentina erected tariff barriers against imported goods, with a view to promoting their own industrial self-sufficiency. Lack of overseas demand after 1918 therefore meant that Britain's staple industries were confronted with the prospect of inexorable long-term decline.

There is far more controversy over the extent to which the 1914–18 war acted as an agent of social change. According to one school of thought, the impact of the war should be likened to a 'deluge', because it was a 'total war' in which the whole country was effectively mobilised, not just those engaged in combat at the front. To be more precise, it is argued that the war functioned as a catalyst, accelerating various changes that were already beginning to happen.[2] The need to organise the country into an efficient military machine obliged the government, for instance, to extend its role radically and assume wide-reaching powers over many areas of people's lives. Initial reliance on voluntary recruitment to the armed forces thus gave way in 1916 to the conscription of all adult males under the age of forty-one, something that would have been considered unacceptable before the war. As the conflict dragged on, more and more sectors of the economy were placed under government control or direction, including railways, shipping, mines, agriculture and munitions production, to ensure that the nation's resources were utilised to meet wartime requirements. At the same time, measures were implemented to protect the interests of the civilian workforce on whom the war effort depended so heavily: minimum wage rates were set in industries such as munitions; controls were imposed on food prices and rents; and rationing of some foodstuffs was eventually introduced in 1917. Steps were also taken to promote the welfare of mothers and their children, by expanding the provision of maternity clinics, so as to ensure a healthier adult population for the future. In other ways, too, not planned by the government, the war altered people's lives. Acute labour shortages, resulting from the absence of up to six million men on military service, brought improved living standards for many unskilled workers, who found new opportunities to move into better-paid jobs. Another significant development was the expansion of the female work-force, from 4.9 million in 1914 to 6.2 million in 1918, as women filled vacancies in factories and offices that had hitherto been the preserve of men. This contribution to the war effort helped bolster women's claim for the right to vote in parliamentary elections, which was finally conceded in 1918.

Persuasive as the 'war and social change' thesis may appear to be, some historians have questioned whether the changes wrought by the pressing demands of war survived for long beyond the return of peace in 1918, and whether these changes were capable of fundamentally re-shaping attitudes.[3] Indeed, the weight of contemporary evidence seems to indicate a widespread desire for the country to return to the 'normality' of pre-war days. This was most obviously true in the case of economic controls, and by the early 1920s most of the administrative apparatus constructed to regulate production, prices and wages had been dismantled. Political pressure, manifested in post-war by-elections, for the government to achieve economies in expenditure and put an end to 'waste', also meant that social programmes such as housing and education became victims of savage cuts. The improvised extensions of State power designed to cope with an emergency situation, which had especially benefited the poorest groups in society, therefore proved to be a largely temporary phenomenon.

For women, too, wartime developments had only limited long-term consequences. With the partial exceptions of clerical and secretarial occupations, no great shift took place in the structure of female employment, since those who had taken up jobs in traditionally male occupations were expected to make way for men returning from the war. Textile manufacturing and domestic service therefore continued to be the chief sources of female employment, and married women usually remained in the home. Nor does there seem to have been a widespread desire among women for things to be otherwise. In many ways, the psychological effect of the war had been to accentuate women's caring role, as nurses, and as anxious or grieving mothers, sisters, wives and sweethearts, and there was a natural yearning for the return of peacetime 'normality'. One of the great myths about the war is that of the 'lost generation' of young men, causing a shortage of suitable husbands, but in reality the decline of male emigration to the USA and the colonies (which had occurred at the rate of three hundred thousand per annum in the years immediately before the war), more than compensated for military fatalities. It is true that women did obtain the right to vote in 1918, but even this was initially confined to those over the age of thirty, on the assumption that political responsibility could best be entrusted to women who had reached the stage where they were likely to be married and with children. Another ten years elapsed before voting rights for women and men were equalised at the age of twenty-one. Women were also eligible to sit in the House of Commons, but the fact that by 1935 there were just nine female MPs supports the view that their absorption into the political system brought little in the way of significant change.

Any attempt to assess shifting attitudes among the millions of individual members of a society inevitably resorts to broad generalisation, but there are strong grounds for concluding that nostalgia for the pre-war era was a key element in popular thinking. Even memories of the glorious summer weather in the days immediately preceding the outbreak of war, trite as it may seem, coloured people's view of the pre-1914 era. These years had, after all, seen comparatively favourable employment conditions, which were then magnified for many civilian workers during the war itself. Expectations in 1918 that soldiers would return to 'a fit land for heroes to live in' (Lloyd George's famous phrase) did not therefore imply the repudiation of the past so much as a desire for its restoration and continuation. If a mood of disillusionment subsequently set in, it stemmed from the country's inability to sustain its economic buoyancy in a peacetime environment, and from the scourge of structural unemployment afflicting the traditional centres of industry.

Nevertheless, the war did have an enduring effect on society through its part in intensifying perceptions of class difference. This is not to deny the existence of patriotic responses to a national crisis, spanning all sections of the population, nor of a powerful sense of common purpose uniting the country. But it is to suggest that national solidarity, in the face of an external threat, did not entail the erosion of internal class barriers, and that if anything these psychological barriers were raised higher. For instance, organised labour had become increasingly assertive between 1910 and 1914, as we saw in chapter 5, and a new wave of militant industrial action occurred in the final year of the war and during the short-lived peacetime economic boom, as trade unions demanded wage rises to compensate for price inflation. Favourable wartime employment conditions were helpful for trade unions, whose membership expanded from 4.1 million in 1914 to a peak of over 8 million in 1920, when industrial relations deteriorated to their lowest point. Quite apart from the influence of union membership itself in promoting working-class consciousness, it appears that heavy wartime demand for unskilled labour squeezed the pay differentials between skilled and unskilled workers, eroding the hierarchical structures found in certain occupations and making for a somewhat greater sense of uniformity within the workforce. At the same time, those in the middle ranks of society became resentful of the heavy burden of wartime taxation imposed upon them – the standard rate of income tax rose from 1s. 2d. (6p.) to 6s. (30p.) in the pound – and fearful that a spirit of 'Bolshevikism' was infecting the unruly workers. These feelings combined to reinforce a defensive 'middle-class' identity amongst people who believed the country, and their place in it, to be in peril. As we shall now see, heightened class tensions in society are relevant for an understanding of developments in inter-war politics.

POLITICAL RECONSTRUCTION

The shockwaves from the First World War had their most devastating impact on the system of party politics, which, by 1924, had been restructured in such a way that Labour and the

Conservatives[4] were now the chief competitors for power, while the Liberals, the dominant force before the war, found themselves relegated to minor party status. So complex is the sequence of events, including four general elections in just six years, that clarity is best achieved with the help of the following table of post-war election results. This gives the number of seats won by each party and the percentage share of the total votes cast in parentheses.

	Conservatives	Liberals	Labour
1918	383 (38.7)	161 (25.6)	57 (22.2)
1922	345 (38.2)	116 (29.1)	142 (29.5)
1923	258 (38.1)	159 (29.6)	191 (30.5)
1924	419 (48.3)	40 (17.6)	151 (33.0)
1929	260 (38.2)	59 (23.4)	288 (37.1)

Although the Liberals were clearly in difficulties from the outset, their predicament was worse than the table at first sight indicates: for the fact was that in 1918 and 1922 they were divided into two mutually hostile groups under the rival leaderships of H.H. Asquith and David Lloyd George. Asquith had become Liberal Prime Minister in 1908 and was still in office when the war broke out. His reluctant response to the national emergency, once it became obvious that hostilities would not be concluded quickly, was to re-form his government as a coalition in May 1915. Several Conservatives, including the leader Andrew Bonar Law, and one Labour representative, Arthur Henderson, were thus brought into the Cabinet. However, by December 1916 there was growing impatience with Asquith's lethargic and uninspiring leadership, and he was forced to resign by his more dynamic Liberal colleague, Lloyd George, who, with backing from Conservative Cabinet members, claimed the premiership for himself. Lloyd George's 'treachery' provoked a bitter split in the Liberal ranks, as one section remained with him in the coalition, while the other, loyal to Asquith, stood aside from the government and gave independent support to the war effort. At the general election of December 1918, held immediately after the war ended, 133 Lloyd George Liberal MPs were returned, thanks to an agreement with the Conservatives, who did not run candidates against them, but only twenty-eight Asquithian Liberals survived. There were a number of constituencies where Lloyd George and Asquithian Liberals actually fought one another. With the party in acrimonious disarray at the national level, grass-roots Liberal organisation withered as activists and voters became demoralised and disillusioned. Lloyd George's coalition government lasted until October 1922, when the Conservatives finally abandoned him and formed their own government under Bonar Law. In spite of this, the Lloyd George and Asquithian Liberals still campaigned separately during the subsequent general election contest, from which only sixty-nine Asquithian and forty-seven Lloyd George Liberals emerged triumphant. Formal reconciliation did not occur until the autumn of 1923, and ill-feeling lingered on for many more years, beyond Asquith's own retirement in 1926. Tragically for the Liberals, by the time even a semblance of unity was restored, Labour had supplanted them as the main party of the 'left', and they were trapped in the unenviable position of being the 'third party' in an essentially two-party system.

Labour, which had been demonstrably the junior partner to the Liberals until 1914, dependent on an electoral pact for its existence, thereafter capitalised on the latter's self-inflicted injuries. In short, Labour eagerly filled the vacuum created by the shattering effect of wartime pressures on Liberal unity and self-confidence. Having reclaimed its independence from the coalition government in 1918, Labour sought to differentiate itself from the Liberals by inserting a clause in the party's constitution committing it, for the first time, to the socialist principle of public ownership of the means of production, distribution and exchange. Only modest gains were achieved at the 1918 general election, against the combined forces of the Lloyd George coalition, with Labour winning fifty-seven seats (compared to forty-two in December 1910), but the encouraging point was that the party had shown itself capable of winning seats in open competition with other parties. The decisive breakthrough came at the next election, in 1922, from which Labour emerged as the second largest party, making substantial gains from the Liberals in the industrial and mining areas of South Wales, Lancashire, the West Riding of Yorkshire, the north-east of England and central Scotland. Further gains were made at the election late in 1923, which paved the way for the formation of the first minority Labour government, in January 1924, headed by Ramsay Macdonald.

One of the most hotly disputed questions by historians of twentieth-century politics is whether the rise of Labour, to the point of becoming a viable party of government, was simply the product of fortuitous circumstances connected with the war and its aftermath, which had fatally damaged the Liberals, or whether it was the inevitable result of underlying social trends.[5] In other words, did the war alter the direction of events, or was the outcome pre-determined anyway? Undoubtedly there were important long-term developments from which Labour stood to benefit, notably the expansion of trade unionism and the accompanying growth of class-awareness, but it was also the case that the war artificially enhanced this phenomenon. Furthermore, the fact that Labour's breakthrough was only partially complete during the inter-war period, in the sense that the party never managed to win an overall parliamentary majority under a system of near-universal adult suffrage, suggests that there remained formidable barriers to its electoral progress. The advances that Labour did make may therefore have owed at least something to Liberal internal weakness. From this perspective, it is less than obvious that the demise of the Liberal party and the rise of Labour were historically 'inevitable'.

The crucial point is that Labour was never entirely what it purported to be: namely, *the* party of a unified 'working class'. If it had been, then it would have enjoyed a monopoly of government ever since 1918, whereas in reality its electoral performance throughout the twentieth century has been very patchy. Even before 1918, in the days of household suffrage, approximately two-thirds of voters were manual labourers, yet Labour was unable to break the old two-party mould. Recent research has cast further doubt on the claim that the party was held back in the pre-war era by the restricted franchise, showing that those who were excluded from the electoral register were mostly single men of all social classes, who had not yet set up their own households. It seems highly likely that a crucial generational shift in political attitudes occurred among younger people, during and after the war, although the operation of a secret ballot for elections and the absence of any kind of opinion polling before the late 1930s unfortunately makes this impossible to prove. If there is some substance to this idea, its causes were presumably not unrelated to the spectacle of internecine Liberal quarrelling, and this would reinforce the view that the war itself precipitated events that were not otherwise bound to occur.

Militant trade unionism also played a part in re-shaping attitudes, cultivating as it did a more powerful sense of class consciousness, or instinctive tribal allegiance, among key groups of workers like miners and railwaymen, who came to regard Labour as the party for working people. Trade unions and trade-union officials supplied much of the resources and personnel needed for extending Labour's organisational base in the constituencies, in the years immediately after the war. All of this helps to explain Labour's impressive electoral advances in some areas of the country between 1918 and 1923, where strongholds were established which have remained faithful to the party ever since. On the other hand, trade-union membership clearly received an enormous boost from favourable wartime conditions, and, after reaching a peak of eight million in 1920, numbers subsequently fell back because of the depression in many traditional industries, standing at 4.4 million in 1933. Moreover, the peak figure of eight million represented less than half of the workforce, which serves to emphasise the fact that the *organised* Labour movement did not encompass all working people. Indeed, it seems unlikely that Labour managed to obtain as much as fifty per cent of manual workers' votes nationally at any inter-war general election, despite the apparent advantage of universal suffrage.[6] Class identity cannot therefore provide a *complete* explanation of how and why working people voted as they did, and this makes it easier to understand Labour's difficulty in achieving domination of the political system.

If there was nothing inevitable about the sudden collapse of the Liberals and their displacement by Labour, it is nevertheless true that the Labour leader, Macdonald, was determined to exploit the opportunities he found to establish Labour as the main party of the 'left'. To this end, he refused to be drawn into any form of alliance with the Liberals, maintaining Labour's stance as an independent force and insisting that accommodation between the rival traditions was possible only if individual Liberals joined the Labour party (as some of them did during the course of the 1920s). His great chance came in January 1924 when Labour, now the second-largest party in Parliament, voted with the Liberals to turn out the Conservative government, enabling Macdonald to form a minority government. After taking office, Macdonald ostentatiously avoided doing any deal to secure Liberal support, being content instead to govern alone for a few months and give his party much-needed credibility. It was vital to reassure the public that the sky need not fall in because Labour was in charge of the nation's affairs. By the time Macdonald appealed to the country in a general election that autumn, the realignment of parties was complete and the Liberals were virtually squeezed out. Macdonald fully expected the Conservatives to win the election, as they did handsomely, but he regarded this as a price worth paying for eliminating the Liberal threat. In opposition between 1924 and 1929 he grew substantially in political stature, emerging as a figure with a national following who was a major asset to his party. He combined the appeal of one who had sprung from the common people himself (he was born in poverty in a remote Scottish fishing village), with a vague, unthreatening, ethical brand of socialism. In truth, he had no clear conception of the mechanics by which society might be transformed from a capitalist into a socialist mode. He also espoused an idealistic approach to international relations, which was reminiscent of Gladstone and had a natural attraction for a generation desperate to avoid another military conflagration. The general election of 1929 marked Macdonald's and Labour's high-water mark, demonstrating the party's ability to extend its electoral base beyond the industrial and mining heartlands. For the first time, Labour was the largest single party in Parliament, and, though still lacking an overall majority, Macdonald was able to form his second government.[7]

As support for the Liberals drained away to Labour on the 'left' of the political spectrum, so too was it mopped up by the Conservatives on the 'right'. The First World War had offered a welcome solution to the self-doubts and difficulties plaguing Edwardian Conservatism, allowing the party to reassert its patriotic credentials. After the Asquith–Lloyd George split in 1916, the Conservatives were the dominant partner in the coalition government, and they were naturally determined to bask in the reflected glory of ultimate military victory. Lloyd George, the charismatic and mercurial Prime Minister, was too great an asset to be discarded in 1918; but by the early 1920s, as the economic depression set in, his popularity waned and the feeling among Conservatives in favour of a return to conventional party politics gathered momentum. There was also concern and disgust at the premier's 'corrupting' influence on political life, which was highlighted by the scandal over the lax way he had allowed peerages and other honours to be awarded in exchange for contributions to his personal party fund.[8] Finally, in October 1922, the Conservatives repudiated the coalition, forcing Lloyd George to resign, and Bonar Law claimed his place. In the environment of the early 1920s, the Conservatives were presented with a perfect opportunity to position themselves as *the* party of property, stability and national and imperial cohesion, in opposition to the alleged menace of socialist confiscation and anarchy represented by Labour. This had a strong appeal to nervous electors of all classes, and the Conservative message was carefully pitched in a way calculated to attract female voters in their capacity as housewives and mothers. The party was rewarded with substantial gains from the Liberals in rural and suburban constituencies. By clothing a brand of politics inspired by 'class' anxieties into commitment to the welfare of the nation and the empire, the Conservatives succeeded in transcending social barriers and appealing to many ordinary working people, whose support in areas such as Greater London, the West Midlands and Lancashire, was clearly necessary for an aspiring party of government in the era of universal adult suffrage.[9]

Stanley Baldwin, who succeeded the dying Bonar Law as Conservative leader in 1923, admirably personified the supposed values and practices of the pre-war age which so much of the British public wished to see restored. He astutely conveyed the impression of being a simple, pipe-smoking, Worcestershire pig-farmer (this had some truth in it, although the family fortune was made in the iron industry), evoking the belief that here was a fundamentally decent, honest and straightforward man. Baldwin seemed to stand for everything that was best in the national character, tapping into powerful currents of rural nostalgia, which understandably flowed through a generation traumatised by the effects of war. His public persona is well illustrated by the titles of his speeches, published in book form, which included *On England* (1926), *Our Inheritance* (1928), *This Torch of Freedom* (1936) and *Service of our Lives* (1937). In practical terms, Baldwin's government of 1924–9 placed great emphasis on financial orthodoxy, jettisoning the pre-war commitment to tariff reform, and curbing expenditure for the sake of balancing the budget – like any prudent housekeeper. In 1925 the decision was taken to return the country to the gold standard. This meant that the value of sterling on the international money markets was fixed again at the 1914 rate in relation to gold (US\$4.86 to the pound), an apparently reassuring symbol of the country's return to 'normality' which absurdly over-valued the currency and exacerbated the problems facing Britain's export industries. The government's 'responsible' policies actually helped to create the conditions in which the trade union movement, already weakened by the loss of members due to rising unemployment, embarked in May 1926 on a General Strike designed to counter the demands for wage-cuts being made by employers struggling to compete in overseas markets. Baldwin and his colleagues were well prepared for the ensuing emergency, deploying troops to move food supplies, recruiting volunteers from the public to maintain other essential services, and carefully controlling the news media. The strike collapsed after just nine days, and though a legacy of bitterness was engendered within the diminished forces of organised Labour, the government was seen to have made a triumphant stand on behalf of the 'nation' against the 'selfish' sectional claims of the trade unions.[10]

NATIONAL CRISIS AND NATIONAL GOVERNMENTS

By 1929 the cautious, rather unimaginative policies pursued by Baldwin's government, famously expressed in the slogan 'safety first', no longer inspired such widespread public confidence, having patently failed to combat the deep-rooted problem of unemployment. At the general election held that autumn, Labour was able to capitalise on the mood for change and Macdonald secured a return to office. Labour itself was soon found wanting, however, when the country was engulfed by a crisis in the international economic system precipitated by the crash on New York's Wall Street stock market in October 1929. As the world plunged into depression, British exports were halved in less than two years, unemployment passed the two million mark in July 1930, and it rose relentlessly for another two years until it finally peaked at over three million. Faced with a projected budget deficit, and requiring an international loan to prop up the value of sterling, Macdonald's government in the summer of 1931 was in a state of total paralysis. Most Cabinet ministers instinctively felt unable to agree to the demand by the Chancellor of the Exchequer, Philip Snowden, for a ten per cent cut in unemployment benefits, yet they lacked any alternative prescription for the country's economic plight. The extraordinary outcome of this crisis was that Macdonald, encouraged by King George V, resigned, and immediately placed himself at the head of a new 'National government' in which he was joined by three former Cabinet colleagues (including Snowden), a handful of Labour back-benchers, sections of the Liberal party, and the whole of the Conservative party. By his decision to break with his own party and align with old opponents, Macdonald set the mould of domestic politics for the rest of the 1930s.[11]

Although Macdonald was still at the helm, the prime beneficiaries of the 1931 crisis were Baldwin and the Conservatives. The main body of the Labour party, embittered by what it regarded as Macdonald's gross act of betrayal, was temporarily discredited in the public's eyes as the party that had run away from the responsibilities of office in the country's hour of need. By contrast, the Conservatives, who supplied most of the parliamentary backing for the new government, reaffirmed their self-image as a force for national unity, and they were handsomely rewarded at the general election in the autumn of 1931 when 471 of their candidates were returned out of a landslide total of 554 National MPs. Labour was reduced to a rump of just fifty-two MPs. National governments were firmly in place for the remainder of the decade: the increasingly senile and isolated Macdonald finally departed in 1935, to be succeeded by Baldwin, and when he retired in 1937 Neville Chamberlain took over. These ministers presided over a painfully slow economic recovery, assisted by the unavoidable decision to abandon the gold standard and allow sterling to be devalued. This helped exporters by making British goods more competitive in overseas markets and also meant that domestic interest rates could be lowered. When the government received a fresh endorsement from the electorate in 1935, winning 435 seats (388 of them Conservatives), unemployment still stood at over two million, and it did not come down to 1.5 million until 1937. Nevertheless, the Conservatives and their National Liberal and Labour allies could claim credit for having provided political stability at a time of economic disaster, and for gradually restoring the nation's confidence in itself.[12]

The truly noteworthy feature of politics in the 1930s was the absence of any significant shift in voter allegiances away from the existing parties towards extreme organisations of the left and right offering drastic remedies for the country's problems. Unlike many of its European neighbours, Britain was not enticed by the promises of Communism or Fascism, and an exploration of the possible reasons for this can tell us much about the nature of inter-war society.[13]

It was essential to the preservation of the political structure, in a democratic age, that it included a non-revolutionary party of the left with a fairly broad electoral base. From its inception at the turn of the century, Labour's chosen strategy had been to obtain greater representation for working people in Parliament, in order to protect their interests, and the great strides forward taken by the party after 1918 ensured that it became firmly embedded in the nation's parliamentary culture. Of course, the debacle of 1931 was a terrible setback, but in spite of the heavy loss of seats there was some consolation in the fact that the party's share of the vote nationally was still 30.7% – virtually the same as in 1923, prior to the formation of Macdonald's first government. More promisingly still, Labour quickly showed signs of recovery at by-elections and in municipal contests from 1932 onwards, and at the 1935 general election it won 158 seats with thirty-eight per cent of the vote, its highest percentage share in the whole of the inter-war period.

Clearly, Labour still had a long way to go before it could hope to surmount the massive parliamentary legions behind the National government. On the other hand, with the independent Liberals winning just twenty-one seats and less than seven per cent of the vote in 1935, Labour unquestionably offered the only realistic alternative to the government, having reasserted its position in the industrial and mining heartlands. As things stood, there was never any serious prospect of Labour's leadership being tempted to endorse methods of 'direct action', by encouraging working people to take to the streets for the purpose of circumventing the parliamentary process.

In fact, Labour displayed an unrelenting hostility towards the Moscow-backed Communist party of Great Britain during the 1930s, rebuffing all overtures for co-operation. The Communists, led by Harry Pollitt, had no more than five thousand members in 1931. Their dismal performance at the general election of that year, when twenty-one out of twenty-six candidates lost their deposits (meaning that they obtained less than one-eighth of the votes cast in their respective constituencies), demonstrated the party's inability to be anything more than an irritant to Labour. Similarly, both Labour and the Trades Union Congress kept a frigid distance between themselves and the National Unemployed Workers Movement, a Communist-front organisation, whose hunger marches sometimes descended into violent clashes with the police. There is an instructive contrast here with the famous march to London from the destitute shipbuilding town of Jarrow, in 1936: this was carefully organised by the local Labour MP, Ellen Wilkinson, who was determined to emphasise its dignified and politically neutral character, and for this reason it received sympathetic receptions from the public and the authorities along its route.

On the intriguing psychological question of why mass unemployment should have bred far more apathy and fatalism than militancy among the unemployed, the key may well lie in the fact that those parts of the country worst affected in the 1930s had suffered from structural unemployment throughout the 1920s as well. In these areas, there was no sudden economic collapse in 1929–32, but rather, a marked deterioration in conditions that had already been bad for some years. As a matter of historical observation, prolonged unemployment appears to have a much less combustible effect on society than a period of inflationary economic boom, such as that which occurred in the years before and after the First World War, when trade union membership was high and demands for compensatory wage increases could be backed up with threats of strike action. At least the plight of the demoralised unemployed in the 1930s was partially alleviated by the wider availability of unemployment benefit, which had been extended to cover most categories of workers in 1920, so that they were spared the humiliation of entering a workhouse.

If Communism made little headway in 1930s Britain, the emergence of a Fascist movement under the charismatic leadership of Sir Oswald Mosley was certainly a more high profile and disturbing phenomenon.[14] Mosley's early political career had been characteristically wayward: beginning as a Conservative MP in 1918, he later switched to the Labour party and was appointed to junior office in Macdonald's government of 1929. However, he resigned in dramatic fashion the following year after the party conference narrowly rejected his ambitious plan for a public works programme designed to reduce unemployment. In March 1931 he and a handful of Labour MPs formed the 'New Party', but they were ill-prepared for the general election held that autumn, when all twenty-four New Party candidates were defeated (twenty-two losing their deposits). Mosley was in any case contemptuous of Parliament and the party system, considering them to be unsuitable instruments for carrying out bold policies, and he believed that strong leadership (his) was required to create a disciplined sense of national purpose and overcome Communist 'subversion'. Drawing inspiration from the Italian Fascist model developed by Benito Mussolini, Mosley advocated a 'Corporate State' in which the interests of capital and labour would be united, and the directive energy necessary to achieve economic reconstruction supplied.

He finally re-named his organisation the British Union of Fascists (BUF) in October 1932. For a time, the BUF attracted some wealthy and influential backers, including the press magnate Lord Rothermere, owner of the *Daily Mail*, but the ugly scenes which occurred during a disorderly rally at Olympia in June 1934 tarnished Mosley's reputation and frightened off many Conservative sympathisers. From this point, the BUF became more openly anti-Semitic and focused its activities on the East End of London, where a sizeable Jewish immigrant community lived, and this forced the government to pass a Public Order Act in 1936 banning uniformed processions. BUF membership peaked at around forty thousand in 1934, but plummeted to just five thousand by the time of the 1935 general election, recovering slightly later in the decade. It never came close to gaining a parliamentary foothold, having been pre-empted at the outset by the formation of the National government, whose existence offered reassurance, to the middle classes especially, that there was no danger of the country being subjected to a left-wing takeover. In this way, the National government proved to be an invaluable bulwark against right-wing extremism.

The search for explanations of Britain's relative immunity from political extremism may become easier once it is appreciated that unrelieved depression and misery was never the experience of most of the population. Historians have often dwelt exclusively on the evidence of stagnation and hardship, and overlooked the alternative and equally valid picture of improved employment opportunities, rising living standards and greater leisure time.[15] Some areas of the country, notably London and the south-east of England, did not suffer the mass unemployment levels found in parts of Wales, Scotland and the north of England, and for the majority of people fortunate enough to be in work this was undoubtedly a time of modestly increased prosperity. Falling prices during the economic troughs of the early 1920s and early 1930s, coupled with fairly stable wage rates, meant that *real* earnings (measured in terms of what money could buy) were rising. When this is taken in conjunction with the continuing trend towards smaller families, traceable from late Victorian times, it emerges that average real *family* incomes roughly doubled between 1914 and 1939. (As always, the very poorest groups in society were the exception to the rule.)

The resulting boom in consumer demand helped to stimulate newer industries such as light electrical goods, chemicals and processed foods, and the spread of electric power supplies enabled factories to set up closer to the markets they were supplying – for instance, along London's arterial roads, the Great West Road and the South Circular Road. Oxford and Birmingham, meantime, established themselves as the main centres of motor-vehicle production, turning out motorcycles, buses, coaches, lorries and vans, as well as private cars (of which two million were on the road by 1939) for the more affluent. The retail sector was also boosted by increased consumer expenditure, and chain stores such as Sainsbury's, Woolworth's and Marks and Spencer expanded their networks of branches. One aspect of the general economic recovery of the mid to late 1930s was a boom in housing construction, and it is a telling sign that in 1939 thirty-one per cent of homes were owner-occupied, compared to ten per cent in 1914. With increased purchasing power, and the widespread adoption of the forty-eight-hour working week in place of the old fifty-four-hour norm, many people were able to take advantage of commercial forms of recreation. Indeed, the 1930s were the heyday of the cinema and dance halls, and of spectator sports such as football, speedway and greyhound racing. More gradually, the practice of providing paid holidays for employees was taking hold, allowing more people to enjoy the benefits of a trip to the seaside, and the first holiday camps were opened in the late 1930s. In numerous ways, therefore, the economic and social climate in inter-war Britain was not naturally receptive to messages from extreme political ideologies.

BRITAIN AT WAR, 1939–45

When Britain declared war on Nazi Germany, on 3 September 1939, a National government was still in charge of the country's affairs, but in these dramatically altered circumstances it seemed less than credible as a government of national unity. Neville Chamberlain, the Prime Minister since 1937, had always antagonised the Labour opposition by his stiff manner and intellectual arrogance, which was in marked contrast to Baldwin's conciliatory style. More fundamentally, the decision to go to war marked the failure of Chamberlain's policy of 'appeasement', by which he had hoped to satisfy German grievances stemming from the Versailles peace settlement at the end of the First World War. Acquiescence in Adolf Hitler's absorption of Austria into the German Reich, and the subsequent endorsement, by the notorious Munich agreement of September 1938, of Germany's annexation of the Sudetenland (an area of Czechoslovakia populated largely by German speakers), merely encouraged the dictator to press his territorial ambitions further. This led to the seizure of another large slice of Czechoslovakia in the spring of 1939, and, finally, to the invasion of Poland, which prompted Britain and France's exasperated engagement in war.[16] Chamberlain remained at his post through the so-called 'phoney war' of late 1939 and early 1940; but as Nazi forces proceeded to sweep through north-western Europe, backbench Conservative unrest over the failure of military operations in Norway, coupled with the Premier's inability to secure Labour's participation in a remodelled National government, obliged him to resign in May 1940. He was replaced by the foremost Conservative critic of appeasement, Winston Churchill, who committed the country to a principled and defiant stand against Nazi aggression, despite the fact that within weeks of his appointment Britain's army was driven into a humiliating retreat and evacuation from Dunkirk, while France fell to the enemy.

Bereft of military allies in Europe, Britain could do little more than fight for its existence as an independent nation. Churchill's inspirational radio broadcasts, in which he promised the British people 'blood, toil, tears and sweat', but declared that this would also be the nation's 'finest hour', set the tone for a spirited, if hopelessly mismatched, resistance to Nazi domination of Europe. The heroic success of the Royal Air Force against the German Luftwaffe in the 'Battle of Britain', during the summer and autumn of 1940, averted for the time being a threatened invasion. It was not until the end of 1941, however, after Hitler's ill-fated attack on the Soviet Union and the USA's entry into the war on Britain's side, that there was a realistic prospect of eventual victory. Operations in the North African desert against Germany and its ally, Italy, later spread to Italy itself. Then, on 6 June 1944, 'D-Day', Britain and its allies launched the invasion of Normandy, which signalled the beginning of the end for Germany's occupation of Western Europe. Britain and America were simultaneously occupied in an exhausting struggle against Germany's Far Eastern ally, Japan, which captured Singapore and Hong Kong in 1942 and threatened India, before its defeat in August 1945, three months after the collapse of Hitler's regime.

The Second World War, far more emphatically than the First, became a 'people's war', touching the lives of civilians as well as military personnel.[17] With the advantage of past experience, the government moved quickly in September 1939 to mobilise the economy on to a wartime footing, carrying an Emergency Powers Act which established six new ministries to deal with supply, economic warfare, information (i.e. propaganda), food, shipping and home security. Conscription of men into the armed forces was introduced at once, and in 1941 it was extended to single women aged between twenty and thirty. Many women were assigned to work in agriculture, the civil service, and munitions and engineering factories, while half a million joined the auxiliary branches of the armed services. National financial stringency, together with the effects of enemy submarine action against mercantile shipping in the Atlantic, meant that rationing of some foods was introduced as early as January 1940, and it was gradually extended to cover a wider range of foodstuffs and other items such as clothing, footwear and furniture.

Of the utmost psychological significance was the way that the civilian population experienced direct physical danger, through Luftwaffe bombing campaigns – which were at their height in the 'blitz' of 1940–1 – and the terror of V1 and V2 rocket attacks in the final year of the conflict. Anticipating an aerial bombardment, the authorities had arranged at the commencement of hostilities for the evacuation of 1.5 million mothers and children from urban target areas to safer parts of the country, where they were often billeted on local families. No absolutely reliable statistics are available for civilian casualties in air raids, but it is likely that at least sixty thousand were killed (compared with 1,400 as a result of Zeppelin airship attacks in 1914–18), a further eighty-six thousand suffered serious injuries and over a hundred and fifty thousand were slightly injured. The government established an emergency medical service, co-ordinating the existing patchwork of hospital facilities, in order to cope with this situation. Large numbers of workers spent their nights on fire-watch duty, or served in the Home Guard. In material terms, much of the country's basic infrastructure, including roads, gas and water supplies, and sewerage systems, were badly damaged, and many public and private buildings were devastated. Some 220,000 homes were totally destroyed and around four million (one-third of the total housing stock) suffered damage to a greater or lesser extent. London was the main casualty, particularly the docklands area in the East End, but provincial centres like Coventry, Exeter and York were not safe either, and many of the country's ports, including Dover, Portsmouth, Plymouth, Bristol, Cardiff, Liverpool, Glasgow and Hull, were badly hit.

Britain's desperate fight to ensure its own survival, the direct impact of the conflict on the civilian population, the enormous sacrifices demanded of the public in everyday matters, and the obvious need to reconstruct the country once hostilities had ceased, all help to explain why the events of 1939–45 produced a decisive shift in popular attitudes of a kind that was not seen in 1914–18.[18] If the government was capable of harnessing the nation's resources for military purposes, and had restored full employment as a result, then the natural question in many people's minds was why could this not be carried on in peacetime so as to build a better world to live in? This is not to suggest that the majority of Britons were suddenly converted to socialism, in an ideological sense, but many aspects of people's ordinary lives, such as jobs and housing, were politicised to an unprecedented degree.[19] Indeed, Churchill's government was fully aware of the importance of holding out hope for a brighter future, in order to secure the public's co-operation and forbearance for the present.

It would be naive, though, to suppose that what emerged in the early 1940s was simply a spontaneous demand for change generated 'from below', by the people. On the contrary, it reflected changing perceptions on the part of many politicians, bureaucrats, intellectuals and other opinion-formers, as to what could be achieved through State intervention, which had been gradually developing in the years before the war. For instance, the economist John Maynard Keynes, in his *General Theory of Employment, Interest and Money* (1936), had demonstrated how government taxation and expenditure policies could be used to regulate consumer demand at a level sufficient to maintain full employment, and his theories steadily attracted converts in political and administrative circles during the war. Consequently, there was a growing conviction that it would be both morally wrong and quite unnecessary to allow the economy to slip back into its inter-war mode, and by 1944 Churchill's government had committed itself in a white paper to sustaining full employment in peacetime by means of Keynesian techniques.

In various quarters, there was exploitation of the opportunity provided by the war to encourage people to expect and demand improvements in many areas of their lives. J.B. Priestley, the socialist playwright and novelist, used a series of immensely popular BBC radio broadcasts in 1940 to convey the message that there could be no going back to the conditions of the 1930s, and that the war effort demonstrated the benefits of collective action and a strong sense of communal interdependence. In January 1941 the leading weekly magazine, *Picture Post*, devoted an entire edition to the subject of post-war reconstruction, and its 'Plan for Britain' covered employment, social security, housing, town and country planning, education, health, farming and recreation. The virtues of 'planning', and the cult of the 'expert' who knew what was best, were rapidly acquiring intellectual respectability at this time. In the most momentous development of all, the government set up an inquiry into social insurance, chaired by the academic and former civil servant Sir William Beveridge, which reported in December 1942 in favour of a comprehensive welfare system, providing security 'from the cradle to the grave'. Beveridge's report helped to crystallise many existing ideas in this field, and it received extensive publicity, including full front-page coverage in the mass-circulation *Daily Mirror*. The popularity of Army Education Corps courses, and the weekly discussion groups organised by the Army Bureau of Current Affairs, testified to the extent to which interest in the long-term social purpose of the war was also prevalent among the troops.

The experience of 'total war' on an unprecedented scale, and the new climate of public opinion generated by it, radically transformed the position of the Labour party, which was increasingly perceived as the party best suited to the task of peacetime reconstruction.[20] By agreeing to serve in Churchill's coalition government in 1940, Labour leaders such as Clement Attlee (appointed Deputy Prime Minister), Herbert Morrison and Ernest Bevin gained valuable administrative experience connected mainly with the home front, thereby erasing the party's traumatic memories of 1931 and its lingering reputation for incompetence. Significantly, Labour was consistently ahead of the Conservatives in opinion polls from 1943 onwards – the figures for December of that year showing Labour at forty per cent, Conservatives at twenty-seven per cent and Liberals at ten per cent. Opinion polls were still in their infancy and politicians paid little attention to them, but they were in fact a reliable pointer to the stunning general election victory achieved by Labour in 1945, when the war in Europe was over and the adversarial system of party politics had been restored. Despite Churchill's colossal personal status as a war leader, it seems that the Conservatives as a whole were tarnished by their association with the appeasement policy of the 1930s, which was widely blamed for allowing the war to happen in the first place, and by the retrospective impression that they had complacently presided over an era of mass unemployment. Labour duly reaped all the political benefits, and was perfectly entitled to present itself as a 'patriotic' party; but it was conveniently forgotten that in the 1930s it had not supported expenditure on rearmament. As the party re-built its credibility and expanded its electoral appeal, the exigencies of war also strengthened its traditional power base by providing an artificial stimulus to industries such as shipbuilding and engineering, located in Labour's heartlands, and creating conditions of full employment which boosted trade-union membership from around six million to eight million. Between 1939 and 1945, as in the earlier war, class awareness grew up alongside feelings of national solidarity.

Clearly, the war had disastrous consequences for Britain's economic, military and imperial standing. Total military expenditure in this period amounted to some £23 billion, and the government was forced to resort to massive borrowing, with the result that the National Debt trebled from £7.1 billion to £21.3 billion. It has been estimated that the nation's wealth shrank by about one-quarter because of the effects of the war.[21] Before the end of 1940, the country was already fighting beyond its financial means, and it depended heavily on generous credit arrangements, particularly with the USA and Canada, to obtain the necessary supplies for prosecuting the war. As in the 1914–18 conflict, export industries suffered from the disruption to international trade, and there was bound to be a long struggle ahead to regain lost markets. More ominously still, the liquidation of a large portion of the nation's overseas assets to raise money for the war effort meant that in future there would be less investment income with which to cover the traditional trade deficit in 'visible' goods. Militarily speaking, Britain was subordinated to the USA after that country's entry into the war in December 1941, a fact underlined by the appointment of General Eisenhower as supreme allied commander in charge of the Normandy landings. The humiliating early setbacks suffered against Japan also diminished Britain's prestige in the eyes of its subject peoples, and this foreshadowed the dismantling of much of the Asian empire soon after the war, beginning with India in 1947. In fighting to release Europe from Nazi thraldom, and to combat Japan's bid for regional supremacy, Britain's own status as a great military and imperial power was fatally undermined.

Some historians have recently questioned whether the war against Nazi Germany was worth the sacrifice involved, arguing that Britain would have done better to accept the peace terms which Hitler seemed prepared to offer in the summer of 1940.[22] Given the country's total isolation at that point, it is understandable that certain government ministers were attracted by the idea of a peace deal, but Churchill's presence ensured that Britain fought on regardless. The obvious objection to the notion of reaching an accommodation with Germany is that it would have served Hitler's purposes admirably, leaving him free to throw everything into an onslaught against the Soviet Union, which might well have succumbed if the operation had been launched early in 1941. As it was, Britain in the early 1940s managed to tie up German forces in North Africa and the Mediterranean, and Germany itself had to contend with bombing raids on its cities. British neutrality would, moreover, have precluded any hope of American intervention to liberate Europe, since this required the use of Britain as a platform for operations on the continent. To stand aside risked allowing Hitler to establish a hegemonic position over the whole of Europe, placing Britain in a situation where its continued existence rested on German sufferance. At the very best, Britain would have been reduced to the status of a satellite, obliged to allow the use of its ports so that Germany could establish control of the Atlantic, but there is no reason to think that in the long term an aggressive, expansionary Nazi regime could have resisted the temptation offered by Britain's own commercial, financial and colonial resources.

In the event, the country drew enormous emotional strength from the gallant way in which it had resisted a vicious and genocidal regime, at immense cost to itself. This belief entered into the collective memory of the British people, where it remains to this day. Although the Second World War undoubtedly weakened the country physically, its psychological effect was quite the opposite, promoting as it did a robust sense of unity and common purpose. The 'Dunkirk spirit', manifested in the miraculous, improvised evacuation of one third of a million troops from France in 1940, when military disaster was transformed into morale-boosting triumph, was celebrated by Priestley in his radio broadcasts and became a source of national pride. So too, popular notions of the stoicism displayed by the civilian victims of German bombing, and the cheerful willingness of all sections of society to accept their fair share of sacrifice and suffering (even the King and Queen were bombed at Buckingham Palace), had a powerful myth-making potential. Like most myths, of course, it contained a substantial grain of truth but concealed plenty of examples of individual selfishness and cowardice.[23] Above all, this was a national myth which elevated in esteem the virtues and rights of the 'common people', whose material well-being would occupy much of the attention of governments in the post-war world.

SEVEN

Affluence and Decline: Britain since 1945

INTRODUCTION

For the overwhelming majority of the British people, the post-war era has been one of unprecedented improvement in material prosperity. In these years, the economy has undergone a remarkable process of 'democratisation', gearing itself to supplying the wants of the whole population and even coming to depend on an ever-expanding domestic market to sustain growth and profitability. What were luxuries for the privileged few in the 1940s are now necessities for almost everyone: washing machines, refrigerators, vacuum cleaners, televisions, telephones, motor cars and foreign holidays. Technological developments have made available new consumer goods undreamt of fifty years ago, including microwave cookers, stereo music systems, video machines and personal computers. Home ownership has become the norm, expanding from roughly one-third of occupiers in 1945 to two-thirds at the present time. Average real earnings (allowing for inflation) more than doubled between 1945 and 1990, while working hours have been reduced by around a quarter for many occupational groups, but even this does not give a complete picture. The trend since the 1960s for married women to remain at work has supplemented the earnings of many households, for whom two incomes are commonly regarded as essential for maintaining the high living standards to which they have become accustomed. Further shrinkage in the average size of families, which presently stands at less than two children per family unit, has also contributed to their increasing disposable wealth. By the 1960s commentators were already referring to the emergence of an 'affluent society', and serious misgivings were expressed by some about the social and moral effects of unrestrained material acquisitiveness.

Paradoxical as it might seem, the same period has also witnessed a dispiriting slump in Britain's status as a world power. Of course, *relative* economic decline had been a familiar experience since the late nineteenth century (see chapters 5–6), but this now reached the point where Britain was no longer simply being caught up by its industrial competitors but was falling a long way behind in many areas.[1] If the economy managed to expand at a healthy rate of 2.8 per cent per annum between 1951 and 1973, this was still substantially lower than the growth achieved by many other countries, notably the vanquished wartime enemies, Germany and Japan. Consequently, Britain's twenty-five per cent share of total world manufactured exports in 1950 fell to less than ten per cent by 1975. Limits to the economy's capacity for growth were worryingly apparent even in the 1950s and 1960s, as the propensity to import more than was exported led to periodic balance of payments crises. Inflation was kept under reasonable control until the late 1960s, but thereafter it too became a major cause for concern, while high unemployment has been a persistent feature of economic life since the 1970s. Chronically low levels of productivity (output per worker, a measure of efficiency), and the dismal state of industrial relations in key sectors like coal-mining and car manufacturing, earned the country the unenviable reputation of being the 'sick man of Europe', suffering from the 'British disease'. Only in the 1980s were measures taken, with some degree of success, to tackle these deep-seated problems. While living standards have in fact continued to rise up to the present day – at least, for those in regular employment – it remains the case that post-war governments have been haunted by recurring doubts about the economy's ability to go on delivering the prosperity that people felt they were entitled to expect.

Britain's diminished international stature is more transparently obvious in respect to its military capability. The war effort between 1939 and 1945 virtually bankrupted the country, and in a post-war world dominated by the rivalry between the two new superpowers, the USA and the USSR, it was only possible for Britain to act as a junior partner to the Americans.[2] It is true that certain modern trappings of a world-class power were obtained, including a small arsenal of nuclear weapons and a permanent seat on the Security Council of the United Nations (set up in 1945 as a forum to promote international peace and co-operation), which conferred the right to veto any resolution put forward. It is also true that Britain assumed an important role in the defence of Western Europe in the 1950s, stationing a permanent army in West Germany and thus helping to persuade the USA to maintain a presence on the continent as well. However, Britain could not act in any significant way against American wishes. This reality was brutally exposed during the Suez crisis of 1956, when a joint military operation with France, to gain control of a vital waterway, nationalised by Egypt, had to be halted due to American economic pressure.

In the humiliating aftermath of Suez, the nation's military commitments were reviewed, leading to substantial cutbacks in expenditure. The Suez fiasco probably also helped, in the longer term, to accelerate the decolonisation of Africa, which was carried out with irresponsible (but perhaps unavoidable) haste during the 1960s. Britain has since seemed to suffer from a multiple identity crisis, struggling to find an entirely plausible role for itself in the modern world. Simultaneously, links have been retained with most of the former colonies, through the organisation of the Commonwealth, although this has seldom been an effective player in world politics and its value for trading purposes has gradually declined; great emphasis has been placed on the 'special relationship' with the USA, and Britain's unique ability to act as a broker between America and Europe, although this relationship has inevitably been one-sided and not always very intimate; and hesitant steps have been taken to integrate Britain with its Western European neighbours, although this has proved to be a deeply divisive issue in domestic politics and has failed to inspire popular enthusiasm.

It is often said that post-war politicians have attempted a discreet management of national decline, concealing the full truth from the public and, perhaps, from themselves. Domestically speaking, national self-deception was aided by the existence, for roughly a generation, of a consensus between the main parties as to the legitimate scope and functions of government, which apparently confirmed that the proud British tradition of political stability was as strong as ever. This consensus broke down in the 1970s, however, under the pressure of worsening economic circumstances, and it was followed by a period of dangerous polarisation before a new consensus (arguably) emerged in the 1990s. Similarly, post-war society, impressively cohesive as it seemed at first, later displayed symptoms of disintegration, but in this case the 1990s have brought no reversal of the trend. Indeed, serious questions are currently being asked about what, if anything, really binds the British people together.

THE POLITICS OF CONSENSUS, 1945–70

The exceptional demands made upon the country's resources in wartime, and the measures adopted to cope with them, helped to effect a major shift in the political and intellectual centre of gravity, enhancing the credibility of those collectivist principles espoused by the Labour party. Paul Addison has advanced the thesis that changing wartime attitudes produced a broad consensus between the rival political parties, resting on an acceptance of the policies implemented by Clement Attlee's Labour administration of 1945–51. In other words, the Conservatives were obliged to acclimatise themselves to a post-war environment in which governments took on greater responsibility for promoting the well-being of their citizens. Contrary to the assumption apparently made by some critics of Addison's view, it did not follow that Labour and Conservative politicians were in total agreement on each and every area of public policy, merely that a general framework was established within which all post-war governments were expected to operate. Accordingly, it was acknowledged that the government had a responsibility to regulate the economy so as to achieve a high and stable level of employment, and that a comprehensive system of State welfare should be provided. Both of these policy objectives were already gaining adherents during the war itself, as we saw in chapter 6. On the other hand, it would be wrong to suppose that the so-called 'Attlee consensus' was completely in place in 1945, or that its shared values ever went entirely unchallenged.[3]

In July 1945 Labour scored a stunning victory at the polls, winning 393 seats and forty-eight per cent of the votes, in defiance of the general belief that Winston Churchill would carry the day for the Conservatives. Labour now possessed an overall parliamentary majority for the first time in its history, and with it the authority to embark on an extensive legislative programme attuned to the public's proven desire for permanent change.[4] Conscious of the mistakes made during the transition to a peacetime economy after 1918, Labour ministers were resolved to keep in place the emergency controls exercised by the recent coalition government, including the power to allocate raw materials for industry, and the rationing of food, fuel, clothing and furniture. Their immediate aim was to encourage an export drive in order to pay off overseas debts incurred as a result of the war. Certain vital industries, mostly those exhibiting monopoly tendencies and in desperate financial straits, were taken under formal State control. Thus, the railways and coalmines, and the gas, electricity, iron and steel and road haulage industries were all nationalised, along with the Bank of England.

Important steps were taken to improve the quality of life for ordinary people, offering them security against the consequences of unemployment and ill health. The system of national insurance, which had been gradually extended since its introduction in 1911, finally became comprehensive in 1946, so that everyone was entitled to a subsistence-level unemployment benefit in return for weekly contributions made while in work (the scheme's financial calculations rested on the assumption of virtually full employment). In July 1948 the National Health Service was established, drawing the existing hospitals and general practices into a publicly-controlled network providing free medical treatment for all at the point of delivery. These benefit and health measures were the cornerstones of what came to be known as the 'Welfare State', which operated on the principle of 'universality', seeking to cover every section of society in the hope of perpetuating the feelings of communal solidarity nurtured by the war effort. In a very different field, Attlee's government laid the foundations of Britain's post-war defence strategy, helping in 1949 to create the North Atlantic Treaty Organisation (NATO), designed to protect Western Europe from the menace of Soviet Communism, and secretly embarking on a programme to acquire a nuclear deterrent force.

By the end of the 1940s, the broad outlooks of the Labour and Conservative leaderships had converged to a far greater extent than they would have wished the electorate to realise. As public frustration with bureaucratic restrictions and consumer goods shortages grew,[5] the Labour government began to relinquish economic controls that could no longer be justified, and items such as clothing and furniture were de-rationed. Attlee and his colleagues showed themselves to be pragmatic socialists, whose practical ambition was to create not a Soviet-style command economy but a 'mixed economy', combining elements of public ownership with those of private enterprise. Reformed capitalism, it was hoped, would function more equitably for the benefit of the whole community. Consequently, Labour's budgets, towards the end of the party's term of office, relied increasingly on manipulation of the level of consumer demand, through taxes and interest rates, as a means of steering the economy towards desired goals (above all, full employment), and much less on centralised planning controls. The evolving consensus of the post-war years was thus a two-way process, involving the abandonment or modification of certain socialist principles on the part of many Labour politicians.

For its part, the Conservative opposition naturally exploited popular discontent with rationing and austerity as a means of highlighting its own credentials as the party of free enterprise. But it had nevertheless absorbed into its thinking the fundamental principles behind Labour policies. Whatever the reluctance felt by Churchill and some of his colleagues, there was little serious Conservative resistance to the creation of the Welfare State or even to most of the nationalisation programme. Moreover, Conservatives of the younger generation, like R.A. Butler, were positively enthusiastic in the way they embraced the new ideas, and this resulted in the publication of the *Industrial Charter* in 1947, affirming the party's commitment to exercising a guiding control over the economy so as to ensure efficiency, full employment and the resources for social welfare.

When the Conservatives returned to office after the general election of October 1951, Labour's post-war legacy was therefore left substantially intact, apart from the decisions to privatise road haulage and iron and steel – the nationalisations of which had always been controversial. Such was the continuity between the policies of the new Chancellor of the Exchequer, Butler, and his Labour predecessor, Hugh Gaitskell, that in 1953 the *Economist* magazine coined the term 'Butskellism' to describe this phenomenon. The Conservatives even managed to outdo their rivals in the area of housing, where they achieved a construction rate of three hundred thousand new homes per annum between 1953 and 1957, many of them council properties for letting to the poorest groups in society. Iain Macleod, another of the 'one-nation Tories' self-consciously acting in the tradition of Disraeli, paved the way as Health minister for a major programme of hospital building, while Sir Edward Boyle pushed for the expansion of State education. Undoubtedly, Conservative ministers had the immense good fortune to preside over the nation's affairs at a time when the economy was finally stepping out of the wartime shadows, thanks largely to the expansion of international trade generated by the mighty American economy and by recovery in Western Europe. In these auspicious conditions, almost all forms of rationing were soon abandoned, and Butler was able to deliver tax cuts in his budgets, fuelling an economic boom in 1953–5 that saw the first flowering of 'affluence'. A remark by Harold Macmillan, shortly after he became Prime Minister in 1957, that the British people had 'never had it so good' (in a public speech actually warning about the dangers of inflation), has always been remembered as epitomising the buoyant mood of the time. Happily for the Conservatives, while they accepted a greater role for the State, they were also able to promote free enterprise in a number of other ways: for example, by permitting the creation of the Independent Television Company in 1955 to break the BBC's monopoly, and by the cautious relaxation of controls on private rents in 1957. Winning three general elections in a row, the Conservatives remained in power until 1964, led by a succession of patrician figures – Churchill, Sir Anthony Eden, Macmillan and Sir Alec Douglas Home – who recognised the expediency of State interventionism for the sake of national cohesion and stability.[6]

It is a remarkable fact that, at a time when the organised Labour movement, in the country and in Parliament, had apparently come into its own, the forces of Conservatism regrouped with sufficient rapidity to ensure that the party flourished during the 1950s. From this perspective, it may be said that the worst consequences of a system of party politics representing 'class' interests – of capital versus labour – were largely avoided, as the Conservatives accommodated themselves to the requirements of government in the post-war world and attracted support from voters across the social spectrum. The drawback to having a relatively quiet political life, however, was that it entailed resorting to a form of economic appeasement, whereby successive governments failed to tackle the problems arising from a destructive pattern of industrial relations. Insofar as a muted version of class warfare was waged in post-war Britain, it occurred at the workplace rather than the election platform or in Parliament, and it reached a point where matters were getting seriously out of hand by the 1970s. Trade unions pressed for wage rises which could not be justified by improvements in productivity, while they clung to outdated restrictive practices in defiance of an often obtuse management. Governments, for their part, shrank from confrontation with workers in the public sector, where over-manning and inefficiency were endemic. Conservative ministers aggravated the situation with unscrupulous pre-election tax giveaways, in 1955, 1959 and 1964, which, by artificially boosting consumer spending, stoked up inflationary pressures which in turn prompted trade unionists to demand compensatory wage increases. Ultimately, it can be argued, political stability and comfortable living standards were obtained at the price of economic stagnation in the longer term, especially by comparison with the gains achieved in other Western countries.

The overall impression of a political system shaped by a substantial convergence of views concerning the aims and responsibilities of government, valid as it is in many ways, does need to be qualified. Consensus was always more noticeable at the front-bench level than it was among rank-and-file MPs or grass-roots party activists. There certainly were critics of government policy on the 'right' of the Conservative party, who condemned 'excessive' public expenditure and the reluctance to allow unfettered scope for the free market; but such dissidents were mostly kept out of high office, and the main forum for expressing their doubts was the annual party conference rather than

Parliament. Nevertheless, their arguments foreshadowed the dramatic sea change in attitudes that swept over the party in the 1970s.

Of more immediate significance was the evidence of deep and bitter divisions within the Labour opposition over its future programme. On the one hand, there were 'moderates' clustered around Hugh Gaitskell, Attlee's successor as party leader in 1955, who were essentially consolidators, believing that the right balance between public and private ownership had already been struck. Anthony Crosland, whose influential book *The Future of Socialism* was published in 1956, looked to continued economic growth, instead of further redistribution of existing wealth, as the best means towards attaining greater social equality. By contrast, those on the 'left' of the Labour spectrum, whose idol was Aneurin Bevan, advocated wholesale nationalisation of major industries and of the banking sector, and they successfully blocked Gaitskell's attempt in 1959 to drop the commitment to public ownership from the party's constitution. A second – partially intertwined – strand of left-wing thinking challenged the Attlee government's legacy in the field of national defence, by deploring Britain's pro-American and anti-Soviet stance as a participant in NATO. The emergence of the Campaign for Nuclear Disarmament in the late 1950s also strengthened opinion within the party in favour of abandoning nuclear weapons, to Gaitskell's dismay.

By the early 1960s persistent signs of the country's inability to achieve sustained economic growth, without creating inflation and balance-of-payments problems, prompted a major reassessment of governmental strategy designed to bring this into line with the harsh reality of Britain's reduced circumstances in the modern world. Macmillan and his colleagues had already implemented cuts in defence expenditure, following the Suez debacle, and the decolonisation of Africa was now proceeding at a rapid pace. Meantime, the government entered into exploratory negotiations with a view to applying for membership of the European Economic Community (EEC), which Britain had declined to join at its inception in 1957, but which was proving alarmingly successful in spreading prosperity behind its tariff walls. This decision reflected the new perception that Britain's long-term future lay in developing its trade links with industrialised and wealthy neighbours in Western Europe, rather than relying on the mostly poorer markets of its former colonies.

To exploit the full potential of EEC membership, Macmillan recognised that the economy must first be put into better shape. Borrowing from France the concept of 'indicative planning', his government therefore adopted a more interventionist approach, seeking to direct economic development along desired paths. In 1961 a temporary pay freeze was imposed on public sector workers, and voluntary pay restraint urged upon the private sector, while a National Economic Development Council (NEDC) was set up to provide a consultative forum in which government, employers and trade unions could set growth targets for various parts of the economy. The aim was to create a stable environment conducive to long-term industrial investment projects, which would lead to greater efficiency. However, the government's incomes policy met with considerable resentment and resistance, and in 1963 the cornerstone of Macmillan's 'new approach' came crashing down when France vetoed Britain's application to join the EEC.

Ironically, a government that had self-consciously embarked upon a programme to 'modernise' the nation's economy and its relations with the wider world, was increasingly regarded by the public as tired and uninspiring. It fell victim to a relentless campaign of ridicule from a new generation of satirists, associated with the Cambridge Footlights review, *Beyond the Fringe* (which enjoyed a long run in the West End), the magazine *Private Eye* and the television programme *That was the week that was* (or TW3). The press in general was openly hostile, and Macmillan's reputation was badly mauled during the Profumo scandal of 1963, when it was revealed that the Secretary for War had lied to the House of Commons about his involvement with call-girls connected to personnel at the Soviet embassy. Macmillan retired that autumn, but his successor, Sir Alec Douglas Home, who renounced his Earldom in order to become Prime Minister, appeared to be yet another representative of a patrician class hopelessly out of touch with the popular mood.

By contrast, the Labour party in 1963 had elected as its new leader the forty-six-year-old Harold Wilson, a seemingly down-to-earth grammar-school-boy-made-good from the North of England, who cleverly tapped into the prevailing sense of listless discontent and vague desire for national rejuvenation. Wilson helped his party to broaden its appeal among a younger, idealistic and questioning generation, which had grown up during the years of post-war affluence with heightened expectations of its political leaders. Above all, Wilson's talk of forging a modern nation out of 'the white heat of a second industrial revolution', by harnessing science and technology, projected a dynamic, forward-looking image, which generated sufficient enthusiasm to carry Labour to a narrow general election victory in October 1964, ending thirteen years of Conservative rule. Early in 1966 an appeal to the electorate to give Wilson's government a working parliamentary majority was answered resoundingly in the affirmative.[7]

Labour entered office pledged to breaking out of the 'stop-go' syndrome of the Conservative years – temporary periods of inflationary economic expansion followed by deflationary tax and interest-rate rises to bring things back under control – which was held to be harming the country's long-term development. In practice, Labour's policies were an extension of the 'indicative planning' model tentatively adopted by Macmillan's government. A Department of Economic Affairs (DEA) was established, with the task of co-ordinating policies to promote stable, long-term growth, using the existing NEDC as an advisory body. Its ambitious 'national plan', published in September 1965, looked forward to twenty-five per cent aggregate growth by 1970. The DEA, in turn, set up a Prices and Incomes Board, to keep wage and price rises under control, while the new Ministry of Technology was supposed to disseminate ideas and information to industry, and the Industrial Re-organisation Corporation was meant to encourage company mergers, in the belief that large-scale enterprises could achieve greater efficiency. Centralised planning of economic growth, carried out in a 'scientific' spirit, was very much the intellectual fashion of the day. Unfortunately for Wilson's government, these new organisations never achieved whatever potential they might have had, and the DEA in particular was virtually suffocated at birth by departmental rivalries in Whitehall. In any case ministers were soon compelled by the worsening state of the economy to resort to the same 'stop-go' policies as their Conservative predecessors, and the DEA's national plan was scrapped in 1966 (as was the DEA itself in 1969). There followed a politically damaging devaluation of the pound,[8] in November 1967, which was intended to ease the country's balance of payments crisis by making exports more competitive. By this stage, Wilson had been converted to Macmillan's conclusion that Britain's future lay in membership of the EEC, but the renewed application made in 1967 was again vetoed by France. Wilson, like Macmillan, was essentially trying to keep alive the values behind the post-war 'consensus', adapting his methods to fit the realities of the modern international context; but his government's failure to fulfil the high expectations raised in 1964 merely contributed to the cynicism and disillusionment with politicians that was spreading among the British people.[9]

DIVERGENCE AND RE-CONVERGENCE: POLITICS SINCE 1970

During the 1970s, the unceasing pressure on the pillars of the post-war consensus finally became unsupportable. Long-standing weaknesses in the country's economic performance, shown up in worsening balance-of-payments deficits, a depreciating currency and disturbingly high levels of inflation, were exacerbated by the OPEC (oil-producing) countries' decision in 1973 to quadruple the price of their vital commodity. This resulted in a serious disruption to international economic growth. Britain's extraordinary achievement, in this context, was to manage to combine both rising unemployment and rampant inflation – two problems hitherto regarded as alternatives – in what was described as 'stagflation'. Attempts to prop up the edifice of consensus through wage-restraint policies met with obstinate resistance from the vested interests involved, especially trade unions in the State sector, and this was taken to the point where it posed a serious challenge to the authority of democratically-elected governments. Towards the end of the decade, even Labour ministers were compelled to abandon some of the sacred policy cows of the previous generation, notably the commitment to full employment, and among Conservative politicians there was a more fundamental questioning of the principles behind the post-war economic settlement. In short, the way was being prepared for the so-called 'Thatcher revolution' of the 1980s, the repercussions of which are still with us.

The Conservative government of Edward Heath, which came into office after a rather unexpected general election victory in June 1970, initially appeared to mark a new departure from the State interventionism of the past and towards a more 'free-market' approach.[10] Tax and spending cuts were delivered in the 1971 budget, while the unloved Prices and Incomes Board was abolished. In its place, the Industrial Relations Act of 1971 was supposed to provide a framework for 'responsible' trade-union activity, including a requirement that ballots must be held before strikes were called. Heath was an ardent moderniser and enthusiastic Europeanist: indeed, his vision for Britain's future success and prosperity focused on membership of the EEC, which was at last achieved on 1 January 1973.[11]

By this stage, however, the government's overall strategy was already in serious difficulty, as the first giveaway budget had intensified the inflationary spiral, encouraging the unions (most of which boycotted the Industrial Relations Act) to press for compensatory wage rises. With the economy deteriorating, ministers were forced into a series of embarrassing policy 'U-turns'. Large subsidies were handed out to inefficient State industries like steel and shipbuilding, to avoid job losses; the ailing Rolls Royce car- and engine-making company was nationalised for the same reason; and in 1972 the government resorted to a statutory prices-and-incomes policy in a bid to curb inflation. At heart, and in spite of what his aloof and arrogant manner suggested, Heath was really a politician of the consensus school, trying to keep the post-war settlement alive in ever-more desperate circumstances.

In 1972, twenty-three million working days were lost through industrial action, the highest figure since the year of the General Strike (1926), and strikes by the miners and electricity workers resulted in power cuts for homes and businesses. The winter of 1973–4 saw the declaration of a state of emergency and a three-day week for industry, as the miners tried to exploit the international oil crisis to extract another substantial pay rise. A frustrated Heath decided to appeal directly to the country, by going to the polls in February 1974 and putting the question: 'Who governs Britain?' The voters' reply, a hung Parliament with Labour as the largest single party, suggested that they were not entirely sure, but thought that perhaps Harold Wilson ought to be allowed another try.

Wilson returned to office with a fragile base of parliamentary support, which was only slightly strengthened by a second general election in October 1974. His sole policy instrument was a rather nebulous 'social contract', agreed with the trade-union movement while in opposition. This held out some hope that Labour might handle industrial relations issues more effectively than the Conservatives, because of the presumed mutual goodwill and desire for co-operation between Labour and the unions. In fact, the social contract was quite useless as a means of promoting voluntary wage restraint, and inflation, which averaged sixteen per cent per annum over the period 1973–80, peaked at around twenty-eight per cent in 1974. Ministers were compelled to introduce a formal prices and incomes policy, and, in a momentous step, cuts in government expenditure were implemented. This latter move reflected the increasingly widespread conclusion among politicians that post-war demand-management techniques were no longer working. The policy of simply increasing the amount of money in circulation, in order to keep consumer demand high enough for full employment to be maintained, was now identified as the underlying cause of the nation's inflationary ills. In retrospect, the failure of Wilson's social contract can be seen as the painful last gasp of the post-war consensus.

The full implications were spelt out with unusual clarity by James Callaghan, Wilson's successor as Labour Prime Minister in 1976, who informed his party conference that autumn that the historic commitment to full employment had ceased to be a feasible objective. Worse news quickly followed, as the drain on the nation's reserves from trying to prop up the value of sterling on the currency markets placed the government in the humiliating position of having to ask the International Monetary Fund for a bridging loan. Financial assistance came with strings attached, in the form of a requirement that expenditure be cut further. The stringent policies enforced by Labour ministers were successful in gradually reducing inflation over the next couple of years, while the flow of oil from the North Sea, a valuable new national asset, helped to ease the balance-of-payments worries; but unemployment, which already exceeded one million in 1976, stood at around 1.5 million by 1978 – a hitherto intolerable level. Callaghan's determination to persist with a strict pay policy ultimately discredited his government during the 'winter of discontent', in 1978–9, when strikes by public-sector workers led to the depressing spectacle of uncollected refuse piling up in the streets and even (so it was alleged) dead bodies being left unburied.[12]

Margaret Thatcher, who had replaced Heath as Conservative leader in 1975, was the beneficiary of Labour's troubles at the general election of May 1979, and this inaugurated a remarkable term of office lasting for eleven-and-a-half years and including further election victories in 1983 and 1987.[13] The new Prime Minister openly repudiated the policies of past administrations, Conservative as well as Labour, which she held to be responsible for the nation's economic weakness. In place of the discredited consensual approach, Thatcher offered 'conviction politics' and uncompromising leadership, and she was determined to shake the country out of its old habits and revitalise it. Her government pursued with ideological fervour the 'monetarist' discipline regretfully adopted by Labour after 1975. However the recipe of spending cuts and high interest rates coincided with another sharp downturn in the international economy, caused by a second sudden jump in oil prices, and greatly exacerbated the unemployment situation. The number out of work was over three million (nearly twelve per cent of the workforce) by 1981, but ministers were unapologetic in treating this as a necessary price to pay for eliminating the scourge of inflation. There was an incidental advantage, from the Conservatives' point of view, in that mass unemployment weakened the trade-union movement and forced it on to the defensive, with the result that wage demands had to be moderated.

As the economy recovered in the mid-1980s, there was evidence that the government's shock therapy had compelled businesses to streamline their operations, bringing with it significant improvements in productivity and higher living standards for those who had jobs. On the other hand, many manufacturing companies succumbed to the effects of the monetarist medicine and unemployment throughout the decade was permanently stuck at a level (never below 1.5 million) that would have been considered politically and socially unacceptable before the 1970s. Furthermore, the frenetic boom of the late 1980s, and the prolonged depression that followed in the early 1990s, raised a question mark as to whether Thatcherite solutions had really transformed the workings of the British economy in the way that was often boasted.

The essence of 'Thatcherism', as it evolved with increasing confidence during the 1980s, was an attempt to galvanise the economy by tackling 'supply-side' problems. In other words, whereas the thrust of post-war policy had been to achieve economic growth by controlling the level of consumer demand, it was now deemed necessary to concentrate on improving the processes by which demand was met by suppliers of goods and services. This was as much to do with re-shaping cultural attitudes as it was with exhorting businesses to become more efficient. Many over-manned State industries, including gas, electricity, steel and telecommunications, were privatised, in the belief that the icy breeze of competition in an open market would compel them to adopt new working practices and offer a better deal to their customers, while the public were encouraged to buy shares in them on generous terms, giving millions of citizens an interest in their profitable running. Similar thinking lay behind the policy of allowing council-house tenants to buy their homes, as it was hoped that giving such people a property-stake in society would make them more responsible, resourceful and independent. Incentives for people to work harder were provided by the drastic reduction of the top rate of income tax from eighty-three to forty per cent, and of the standard rate from thirty-three to twenty-five per cent, while a substantially larger share of the fiscal burden fell on taxes on expenditure – primarily Value Added Tax.

The government's boldest move was its legislation to regulate and restrict the activities of trade unions: secret ballots were required for the election of officials and before strike action could be taken; the 'closed shop' (compulsory union membership) and 'secondary picketing' (of businesses not directly involved in a dispute) were outlawed; and the unions' immunity from civil action for damages was removed. In 1984–5, the long-anticipated confrontation with the coal miners ended in defeat for the union and its emasculation as a political force. Trade-union membership as a whole declined from its historic peak of fifty-three per cent of the workforce in 1979 to under forty per cent by the 1990s. The overall effect of the government's economic policies and trade-union reforms was to shift the balance of power in the workplace decisively towards employers, who found it easier to impose pay deals linked to productivity, and to demand greater flexibility from their employees.

'Thatcherism' sought to emphasise people's individual identities as consumers, shareholders and homeowners, at the expense of their collective identity as producers. It represented a bid to modernise British society by 'Americanising' it, instilling faith in the virtues of the free market, admiration for entrepreneurial dynamism and the striving for personal betterment, and disdain for bureaucracy. Partly for this reason, Thatcher became increasingly hostile to the EEC, which seemed to embody precisely the kind of regulatory instincts that she was anxious to suppress. Another problem arose from her suspicion of the drive towards centralising power in Europe, with the ultimate goal of creating some form of federal state. Friction with senior Cabinet colleagues over the best strategy for dealing with Britain's European partners dogged the final years of Thatcher's premiership, and this issue provided the sub-text to her downfall, after a Conservative leadership contest in November 1990,[14] although the immediate cause was the unpopularity of an ill-considered scheme for replacing the system of local rates with an individual 'poll tax'.

John Major, who succeeded Thatcher as Prime Minister, pulled off a rather surprising general election victory in April 1992, the fourth in a row for the Conservatives. However, his government always suffered from the lack of any clear sense of policy direction, and Major failed to establish himself convincingly either as a surrogate for Thatcher or as someone significantly different. The problems he faced were undoubtedly symptomatic of the ideological divisions within the Conservative party, which were particularly acute on the question of Europe.

Britain's disastrous experiment with membership of a European system of fixed exchange rates ended abruptly, in September 1992, when sterling was forced out of the system by the money markets and substantially devalued, while ministers were obliged to raise taxes and interest rates. This episode totally destroyed the Conservatives' reputation as the party of competent economic management. The story of the remaining years of Major's government can only be described as the longest death-rattle in modern political history, marked as it was by mounting public disillusionment and eventual disgust, amid revelations of 'sleaze' involving Conservative politicians who had grown too accustomed to the privileges of power.[15] And yet, while the Conservatives were in a sorry state of disarray, and were finally put out of their misery at the general election of 1997, Thatcher's legacy to Britain has also to be judged by reference to the extraordinary political metamorphosis undergone by the Labour party during its eighteen-year exile in opposition.

In the 1980s, as in the 1950s, Conservative dominance was assisted by a damaging ideological conflict fought within Labour's ranks. Early in the decade, a dramatic shift towards the 'left' was registered by Michael Foot's triumph in the leadership contest to succeed Callaghan, and by the near-election of Tony Benn as his deputy. Benn was the foremost advocate of a radical socialist programme involving extensive nationalisation, unilateral nuclear disarmament and withdrawal from the EEC (regarded by many socialists as a capitalist club), which were soon adopted as official party policy. Alarmed at the direction in which the party was moving, a group of former Cabinet ministers, Roy Jenkins, David Owen, William Rodgers and Shirley Williams, known as the 'gang of four', formed the Social Democratic Party (SDP) in 1981 with the support of some two-dozen backbench Labour MPs. The SDP entered into an 'Alliance' with the Liberals, who had survived as a small third force since 1945 and shown signs of expanding their electoral base in the 1960s and 1970s. With the anti-Conservative forces thus obligingly split, Thatcher's government secured substantial majorities in the 1983 and 1987 general elections.

Neil Kinnock became Foot's successor as Labour leader in 1983. Though originally on the left of the party himself, he gradually began to restructure its policy-making apparatus and procedures for selecting parliamentary candidates, concentrating greater power in his own hands and marginalising those 'militant' elements which had infiltrated at the grass-roots level. After

Labour's defeat in 1987, Kinnock embarked on a systematic 'policy review', by which means he gently jettisoned the Bennite programme in the hope of making the party electable again. Labour's crab-like movement towards the centre ground, over the next few years, was made easier by the acrimonious demise of the Liberal–SDP Alliance, whose high hopes of 'breaking the mould' of two-party politics had been disappointed.[16] The Conservatives' fourth consecutive election victory in 1992 indicated that there were lingering voter apprehensions about a 'tax and spend' Labour government, and the subsequent change of leader from Kinnock to John Smith was meant to overcome this psychological obstacle to Labour's regaining power.

Following Smith's sudden death in 1994, his youthful replacement, Tony Blair, resolved to go further and faster in distancing Labour from its image as the party of State control. Blair and his advisors re-branded the party, rather like a soap powder, as 'New Labour', and even persuaded the membership to drop the clause in the party's constitution committing it to public ownership. Shorn of all potentially embarrassing economic-policy obligations, Labour focused its energies on exploiting public dissatisfaction with Major's government, and was rewarded with a landslide majority at the polls in May 1997.

In the 1990s, therefore, despite Thatcher's own political demise, it appeared that the Labour party was absorbing the central tenets of Conservative economic philosophy in much the same way as the Conservatives had come to terms with Labour thinking after the Second World War. Future historians may well write about the 'Thatcher consensus' as well as the 'Attlee consensus'. This fundamental shift in attitudes was facilitated, and rationalised in the minds of Labour's leadership, by a fashionable emphasis on the implications of 'globalisation' – the perception that, in a world dominated by multi-national conglomerates and instant computerised financial transactions, the power of national governments to control or direct events was inevitably limited. In addition, Blair and his colleagues preached the need for the country to equip itself for survival in this intensely competitive international environment by 'modernising' its ways of doing things. Vague talk of 'modernisation', indeed, was invoked like some magical incantation, offering a panacea for every problem.

As a result of Labour's conversion – that of its frontbench, at least – the Blair government was determined at the outset to operate within broadly the same parameters of economic policy as its Conservative predecessors. Strict control of inflation was accorded top priority, the public expenditure limits bequeathed by the Conservatives were faithfully adhered to, the benefits of the free market openly acknowledged, and no attempt made to reverse the privatisation programme or dismantle the trade-union reforms of the 1980s. Some of Labour's high-profile policies, such as those designed to end the culture of welfare dependency, and to promote education and training for the young, are entirely in keeping with the supply-side approach advocated by Thatcher. Of course, it is hazardous to judge a government's record before its term of office has ended, but Labour's radicalism has been visible to date chiefly in the area of constitutional reform, where its 'modernising' impulse has been directed at the House of Lords, and at devolution for Scotland, Wales and London.

POST-WAR SOCIETY: COHESION AND FRAGMENTATION

The Second World War powerfully reinforced the bonds of social solidarity, and memories of this period have continued ever since to define the British people's sense of themselves as a nation. At the beginning of the twenty-first century, British attitudes towards the rest of the world are still shaped, albeit less consciously than a generation ago, by what happened between 1939 and 1945. Inevitably, though, the long passage of time has gradually dissolved the internally adhesive effects of wartime experiences. Furthermore, there are many signs to suggest that other, pre-existing forms of social identity, are coming increasingly to the forefront and assuming greater *political* significance. These are not necessarily incompatible with the survival of British national feeling, but they reflect the growing complexity of modern society and its resulting tendency towards fragmentation. Meantime, the traditional focal points for expressions of 'Britishness' have struggled to maintain their credibility and inspire unified responses from the people. By the year 2000, it was therefore much harder to identify the forces capable of holding the country together in the long term.

It is true – and important – to say that most of the competing social identities discussed below have manifested themselves in other Western countries, and probably the nearest thing to a common denominator is the spread of affluence, with all its ramifications. At one level, affluence has obviously tended to promote the atomisation of society, elevating the fulfilment by individuals of their own needs and wants to the point where this seems to be regarded as the primary purpose of human endeavour. Enlarged incomes, personal transportation by means of the motor car, impersonal shopping by means of the supermarket (or Internet), home ownership (preferably away from city centres), and domestic technology such as televisions and computers for entertainment, have all helped to create a society founded on the desire for privacy. Individuals and families are nowadays more likely to lead somewhat isolated, self-contained existences, in which communal action has less of a part to play. But affluence has also helped to fragment society into groups, deriving their identities from considerations of age, gender or ethnicity, rather than from nationality.

The 1950s witnessed the emergence of a distinct 'youth culture', made possible, in the final analysis, by the increased earnings and plentiful employment opportunities which accompanied the onset of affluence. For the first time, teenagers were recognised as a separate consumer group with their own interests and tastes, expressed in the dramatic rise of rock and roll and other styles of popular music, the adulation of film icons such as James Dean and Marlon Brando, and the desire to dress fashionably in jeans or in 'teddy boy' outfits. Often, teenagers' demand for personal freedom led them to adopt rebellious attitudes towards their parents and the authorities. The full flowering of British youth culture appeared in the 1960s, when, for a brief moment, London was the swinging place to be and Liverpool produced a string of successful pop groups, including The Beatles. Ironically, a phenomenon that owed so much of its existence to the commercialisation of leisure contained within it elements hostile to capitalist values. This was instanced by the idealism of the 'hippies' in the late 1960s, and, in more recent times, by campaigns over environmental issues. To make matters even more bewildering, there has always been a tendency for youth culture to divide into sub-cultures, connected with a particular style of dress or allegiance to a particular style of music. It is now taken for granted that acute generational tensions will be found in society, and, while the culture of one generation permeates the mainstream as that generation grows older, so another comes along to take up youth's self-appointed task of upsetting its elders.

For increasing numbers of women since the 1970s, an emphasis on gender has suggested a more meaningful category than any other for defining themselves in relation to society.[17] This is a remarkable illustration of the way that a form of social identity that obviously has always existed can quite suddenly take on a new political significance. Again, it is due in no small part to the spread of affluence that many women have been able to widen their personal horizons. Improved educational provision, especially readier access to places at universities, has produced cohorts of well-qualified young women ambitious to enter professions like medicine, the law and teaching, or to embark on careers in business and management generally. In a 'mature' economy requiring more people to work in offices, service industries and light manufacturing, and relying far less on heavy manual labour, new employment opportunities are available where women can compete on equal terms with men. Post-war advances in nutrition and medical care have benefited women's health generally, while the introduction of the contraceptive pill in the early 1960s, together with the legalisation of abortion in 1967, have allowed women to take greater control of their reproductive function. With dramatically heightened expectations of what life can offer women, many have rejected the conventional path towards marriage, housewifery and child rearing, and sought instead to renegotiate their relationships with men or even avoid them entirely. As part of this process, an organised feminist movement has emerged pushing a broad agenda of specifically 'women's issues' into the public domain, such as equal pay, marital and divorce entitlements, childcare provision for working mothers, and attitudes towards rape and domestic violence.

At the beginning of the twenty-first century, approximately three million out of the fifty-five million inhabitants of Britain are non-whites, whose family roots lie mainly in the former colonies of the Caribbean and the Indian subcontinent. These newcomers and their descendants are heavily concentrated in parts of London, and in provincial centres like Birmingham, Bradford, Leicester and Luton. The peak of immigration occurred in the 1950s and 1960s as people, acting usually on their own initiative, sought better lives in a prosperous 'mother' country offering greater economic opportunities.[18] Generally speaking, relations between the new arrivals and the indigenous population were characterised by mutual ambivalence. Indigenous white Britons often resented the intrusion of what they regarded as 'alien' cultures, and such feelings were manifested in overt and covert discrimination, harassment, and sometimes outright violence. For their part, the immigrants were in the rather strange position of having come to live among their former colonial masters, and, while some enthusiastically embraced the values of their new homeland, not all wished to become totally 'assimilated' into another society. Resistance to the dilution of their own religions and cultures has been very strong among certain immigrant communities, while resentment at their sense of inferior status in Britain has prompted a defiant assertion of cultural separateness on the part of some of the younger generation born in this country.

Ethnic identities therefore have the potential to override any sense of national identity shared with the white population. Slowly and painfully, British society has managed to evolve – and is still doing so – into what appears on balance to be a viable new form, through the interaction between white and coloured people, and it is fortunate that blatantly racist political parties have failed to gain an electoral foothold. There are many encouraging signs of individuals from the immigrant communities making valuable contributions to society, in such areas as sport, popular music, retailing, restaurants and the medical profession, and they are beginning to have an impact on the political system as well. Nevertheless, the relevant point for our purpose is that significant numbers of citizens of contemporary Britain may have different personal perceptions of what it is to be 'British' from those of the white majority. Multi-racialism has added a further dimension to the complex structure of modern society.

Even among indigenous Britons, the absence of complete homogeneity has been highlighted by the resurgence of Celtic nationalism in Scotland and Wales.[19] Once more, this is a case of identities that had never ceased to exist returning to the fore and assuming vital added relevance to the lives of many people. It is difficult to determine whether this phenomenon is a cause or effect (probably both) of Britain's decline as a major power; nor is it entirely obvious why it should have gathered momentum at precisely the time that it did.

The Scottish National Party (SNP) and its Welsh counterpart, Plaid Cymru, were founded in the inter-war period, but it was only in the late 1960s that they emerged as potentially significant political forces.[20] Both movements exploited a prevailing sense of deprivation, relative to affluent England, arising from the structural decline of heavy industries and rising unemployment, and this was combined with a subjective belief that central government in London was remote and indifferent to their needs. Welsh nationalism has achieved its greatest impact by voicing demands for official recognition of the Welsh language, and tends to be rather insular in character. Scottish nationalism, by contrast, is a more overtly self-confident phenomenon, and it acquired added plausibility in the 1980s when the SNP shed its original hostility to Britain's membership of the EEC and developed the idea of independence from England within a federal European framework. This has allowed the Scots to revive memories of their independent nationhood before 1707, and of historic relationships with other States like France.

Popular support for the nationalist parties since the 1960s fluctuated wildly, but by the 1990s they seemed capable of posing a serious threat to the Labour party's electoral supremacy in Scotland and Wales. Consequently, Labour was compelled to embrace the idea of devolution, and referendums finally paved the way for the creation of assemblies in Edinburgh and Cardiff in 1999. Devolution is clearly a dangerous gamble, intended by its authors to reconcile Scotland and Wales to the English connection and so draw the sting from nationalism; but there is a real possibility that it may have the contrary effect and validate support for full independence, while simultaneously provoking an English nationalist counter-reaction. As the new millennium proceeds, the future political cohesion of Britain seems far from guaranteed.

In such an endlessly variegated society, authentic displays of *British* national unity are increasingly hard to find. Many historic sources of strength and pride seem unlikely to exercise such a creative influence in the future. It is so long since Britain was the 'workshop of the world', and its commercial arm dominated trade around the globe, that the people have grown accustomed to their country's relative economic mediocrity. The empire, too, is very much a thing of the past, and Britain's closer ties with Europe have rendered the Commonwealth of less economic value, so that it operates nowadays as little more than a vaguely articulated community of sentiment. Britain's military prowess continues to give it a disproportionate influence in international affairs, but even here it has been obliged to moderate its pretensions since the 1950s and accept a firmly subsidiary role to the USA. The collapse of Communism in Eastern Europe in the late 1980s, and the consequent removal of any direct threat to national security, has further reduced Britain's sense of military purpose, and drastic cut-backs in expenditure on the armed forces were imposed in the 1990s. In the nation's finest hour of recent times, the Falklands War of 1982, a task-force was sent to recover a group of islands in the South Atlantic invaded by Argentina. This was undoubtedly a great military success, and stimulated intense patriotic feelings, but it is difficult to imagine such circumstances arising again or Britain's diminished armed forces being capable of a similar response. Britain's future part seems destined to be no more than that of a useful international trouble-shooter, providing specialist support for operations such as the United Nations peace-keeping forces in the Balkans.

Traditional institutions have experienced difficulty in maintaining their claims to relevance in a country whose people are at once so diverse and demanding, yet often so contrary in their attitudes. The Protestant Churches, which in earlier times played a crucial role in shaping British national identity (see chapter 1), long ago ceased to exercise much of a hold over the popular imagination, as society became ever more urbanised and materialistic. Parliament, which until the 1950s commanded widespread respect and was often regarded as an ideal model for the rest of the world, has similarly lost a great deal of its prestige, the victim of governmental failure to arrest the country's relative economic decline and the resulting infection of the national mind with creeping self-doubt. The decision to broadcast Parliament's proceedings has apparently done nothing to restore its old authority, and, if anything, has served to highlight its ineffectiveness as a check on the actions of ministers.

Most dramatic of all has been the fluctuating reputation of the monarchy, an historically resilient institution which has usually commanded considerable public affection and reverence. For a time, the strategic decision taken in the 1960s to make the royal family less remote and bring it closer to the people, for example through public walkabouts and television documentaries, seemed on balance to be vindicated, given the notable success of Queen Elizabeth's silver jubilee celebrations in 1977 and the worldwide fascination with the Prince of Wales's marriage to Lady Diana Spencer in 1981.

However, the corrosive effects of relentless exposure to a sensationalist and prurient news media, which turned royalty into actors in an increasingly sordid and ridiculous soap opera, gradually weakened the pillars of respect upholding the monarchy. The near-hysterical reaction to the tragic death of Diana, Princess of Wales, in a car accident in 1997, exemplifies the ambiguous situation in which modern royalty finds itself: at one level, the remarkable display of grief at the loss of the 'People's Princess' pointed to the monarchy's continued ability to serve as a focus for national sentiment, for which many people clearly have an emotional need; but it was manifested in a way that was intended as a rebuke to a royal family perceived as being the heartless villains in the saga of a wronged heroine. It may still be possible for the monarchy to retrieve some of its lost popularity, but the business of royalty in the twenty-first century is unlikely to become any easier, and one may doubt whether the institution will ever again feel entirely secure in its position.

Nothing better illustrates the predicament of modern Britain than its fraught relationship with Europe.[21] Discreet changes in the name of the body joined by Britain in 1973 – from European Economic Community to European Community and then to European Union – reflect an aspiration for 'ever-closer union', economic, political and military, apparently shared by many member States, but which the majority in this country are profoundly uneasy with. The British people, far more than their continental neighbours, have failed to evolve a European identity to coexist with their national one, and the two are usually treated as mutually exclusive. British politicians, on the whole, have found it more profitable to act up to voter antipathy towards Europe than to project a positive vision of what Britain in Europe might achieve.

Whether it was advisable, in the first place, for Britain to join an organisation oriented towards fulfilling the economic and strategic interests of France and Germany is certainly debatable, but somewhat beside the point after more than a quarter of a century. What is clear is that Britain has contrived to get the worst of both worlds, retaining its European membership, with the loss of sovereignty that this entails, yet being unwilling to participate wholeheartedly in the 'club' and constantly grumbling about the rules. Such ambivalent behaviour can partly be attributed to the increasing fragility, for internal reasons, of Britain's national identity, to a habit of dwelling on remembrance of former glories, and to an enduring belief – not entirely misplaced – in the uniqueness of Britain as an island state.

Curiously enough, while Europe is generally supposed to present the greatest threat to British independence, the dissolving effects of American cultural domination tend to be overlooked. It is an inescapable fact that, for most of the twentieth century, and particularly since 1945, all aspects of the behaviour and lifestyles of people in Britain were imperceptibly transformed by influences emanating from across the Atlantic. In films, television programmes and popular music, America has projected an image which has done more than anything else to erode characteristically British habits and ways of doing things; and these are in danger of being submerged into a bland, globally uniform style, affecting choice of dress, expressions of speech, mannerisms and gestures, and tastes in food and drink. The shared language and historical links between the two countries go far towards explaining why American cultural hegemony has been found less obtrusive by the British than by, for example, the French. Paradoxically, Britain's welcoming embrace of the American way of life has helped to preserve its sense of separateness from European neighbours.

BRITAIN AT THE MILLENNIUM

Inevitably, any book of this kind, attempting to survey the creation and subsequent history of a nation over the course of many centuries, must end with a sense of incompleteness. It is quite conceivable that Britain's existence as a unified political entity is drawing to a close, and that in the near future it will fragment into its English, Welsh and Scottish components. In a more extreme scenario, England itself could disintegrate into several regions. There is no intrinsic reason why recognition, through devolved assemblies, of Scottish and Welsh identities, and other regional ones for that matter, should be incompatible with the preservation of allegiance to Britain as an overall political structure, and a federal arrangement could indeed help to strengthen British national unity. People, as this book has sought to emphasise, can possess many identities pertaining in different contexts. But there is a real prospect that the simultaneous transfer of powers to European institutions may have the effect of pulling Britain apart. Even if it does manage to survive, it may come increasingly to resemble a rather tattered umbrella, with too many sentimental associations to be discarded, perhaps, but of limited practical utility nonetheless.

Unpredictable circumstances could still arise which serve to reinvigorate belief in British nationhood, and the most likely cause of this is the external one of fear of absorption into a federal Europe. Alternatively, Britons may learn to restrain their distrust of foreigners and reconcile themselves to expressing their national values through participation in a variety of international structures, including the European Union and NATO. In this respect, Britain possesses immense natural advantages arising from its remarkable historical traditions and the fact that it is the home of a major international language. For the moment, though, it appears rather more likely that the psychological legacy of this unusually long, continuous history, reinforced as always by geographical isolation, will prevent the people of Britain from fully coming to terms with the reality that they no longer reside in a powerful and self-sufficient nation-state.

Appendices

1. BRITISH MONARCHS

Although the political creation of Great Britain by the Anglo-Scottish Act of Union did not take place until 1707, it should be noted that the English and Scottish Crowns had been combined under the same monarchs since the Stuart succession to the English throne in 1603. Queen Anne was the last reigning member of the Stuart dynasty; George I (also Elector of Hanover) was the first of the Hanoverian rulers. The link with Hanover was broken when Queen Victoria came to the throne, in 1837, as the Hanoverian Crown could not be inherited by a female: it passed instead to her uncle, the Duke of Cumberland. On Victoria's marriage to Prince Albert in 1840, the royal family surname became Saxe-Coburg-Gotha, which was changed to Windsor in 1917 in deference to wartime anti-German feeling.

1702–14	Anne
1714–27	George I
1727–60	George II
1760–1820	George III
1820–30	George IV (acted as Prince Regent from 1811)
1830–37	William IV
1837–1901	Victoria
1901–10	Edward VII
1910–36	George V
1936	Edward VIII (abdicated on 11 December)

1936–52	George VI
1952–	Elizabeth II

2. PRIME MINISTERS

Since the time of Walpole, the holder of the office of First Lord of the Treasury has usually been the acknowledged head of the government, and it is these persons who are listed below. However, there were some cases where the position was unclear (e.g. Wilmington) and others where power was shared with another senior minister. Many eighteenth- and early nineteenth-century governments contained some admixture of rival groupings, making a rigid classification by party misleading. All of the Prime Ministers listed below were personally Whigs, apart from Bute, until 1770, and most of those in power between 1770 and 1830 were regarded, or came to be regarded, as Tories (with the few exceptions noted). Party labels are supplied for the post-1830 period: 'Conservative' replaced Tory in the 1830s, and 'Liberal' gradually superseded Whig in the 1840s and 1850s.

1721–42	(Sir) Robert Walpole
1742–43	Earl of Wilmington
1743–54	Henry Pelham
1754–56	Duke of Newcastle
1756–57	Duke of Devonshire (jointly with William Pitt)
1757–62	Duke of Newcastle (jointly with Pitt until 1761)
1762–63	Earl of Bute
1763–65	George Grenville
1765–66	Marquess of Rockingham
1766–70	Duke of Grafton (Pitt, now Earl of Chatham, the supposed head until 1768)
1770–82	Lord North
1782	Marquess of Rockingham (Whig)
1782–83	Earl of Shelburne (Whig)
1783	Duke of Portland (nominal head of the Fox–North coalition)
1783–1801	William Pitt (the Younger)
1801–04	Henry Addington
1804–06	William Pitt (the Younger)

1806–07	Earl Grenville (Whig-dominated coalition)
1807–09	Duke of Portland
1809–12	Spencer Perceval
1812–27	Earl of Liverpool
1827	George Canning (Tory-dominated coalition)
1827–28	Viscount Goderich (same)
1828–30	Duke of Wellington
1830–34	Earl Grey (Whig)
1834	Viscount Melbourne (Whig)
1834–35	Sir Robert Peel (Conservative)
1835–41	Viscount Melbourne (Whig)
1841–46	Sir Robert Peel (Conservative)
1846–52	Lord John Russell (Whig)
1852	Earl of Derby (Conservative)
1852–55	Earl of Aberdeen (Peelite–Whig coalition)
1855–58	Lord Palmerston (Whig)
1858–59	Earl of Derby (Conservative)
1859–65	Lord Palmerston (Liberal)
1865–66	Earl (formerly Lord John) Russell (Liberal)
1866–68	Earl of Derby (Conservative)
1868	Benjamin Disraeli (Conservative)
1868–74	William Ewart Gladstone (Liberal)
1874–80	Benjamin Disraeli (cr. Earl of Beaconsfield 1876) (Conservative)
1880–85	William Ewart Gladstone (Liberal)
1885–86	Marquess of Salisbury (Conservative)
1886	William Ewart Gladstone (Liberal)
1886–92	Marquess of Salisbury (Conservative)
1892–94	William Ewart Gladstone (Liberal)
1894–95	Earl of Rosebery (Liberal)
1895–1902	Marquess of Salisbury (Conservative–Liberal Unionist coalition)
1902–05	Arthur James Balfour (same)
1905–08	Sir Henry Campbell-Bannerman (Liberal)
1908–15	Herbert Henry Asquith (Liberal)
1915–16	Herbert Henry Asquith (all-party coalition)
1916–22	David Lloyd George (Conservative-dominated coalition)
1922–23	Andrew Bonar Law (Conservative)

1923–24	Stanley Baldwin (Conservative)
1924	Ramsay Macdonald (Labour)
1924–29	Stanley Baldwin (Conservative)
1929–31	Ramsay Macdonald (Labour)
1931–35	Ramsay Macdonald (Conservative-dominated coalition)
1935–37	Stanley Baldwin (same)
1937–40	Neville Chamberlain (same)
1940–45	Winston Churchill (all-party coalition)
1945–51	Clement Attlee (Labour)
1951–55	(Sir) Winston Churchill (Conservative)
1955–57	Sir Anthony Eden (Conservative)
1957–63	Harold Macmillan (Conservative)
1963–64	Sir Alec Douglas Home (Conservative)
1964–70	Harold Wilson (Labour)
1970–74	Edward Heath (Conservative)
1974–76	Harold Wilson (Labour)
1976–79	James Callaghan (Labour)
1979–90	Margaret Thatcher (Conservative)
1990–97	John Major (Conservative)
1997–	Tony Blair (Labour)

3. MAJOR WARS INVOLVING BRITAIN

It is impractical to include all of the numerous colonial conflicts in which Britain has been engaged.

1702–13	War of the Spanish Succession (alliance of several European Powers formed to curb French expansionism)
1718–20	War of the Quadruple Alliance (designed to curb Spanish ambitions in the Mediterranean)
1739–	War of Jenkins's Ear (trade war with Spain, merging into the next conflict)
1740–48	War of the Austrian Succession (to protect Austria from Prussia and France)
1756–63	Seven Years War (allied with Prussia against France, Spain and Russia)
1775–83	War of American independence (loss of American colonies)

1793–1815 French Revolutionary and Napoleonic Wars
(series of alliances to curb French expansionism; brief
peace in 1802–3)

1854–56 Crimean War (acting with France to protect Turkey
from Russia)

1899–1902 Boer War (to achieve colonial supremacy in South
Africa)

1914–18 First World War (alliance against Germany, Austria-
Hungary and Turkey)

1939–45 Second World War (alliance against Germany, Italy
and Japan)

1950–53 Korean War (United Nations force defending South
Korea from North Korea and China)

1982 Falklands War (to recover South Atlantic islands
invaded by Argentina)

1990–91 Gulf War (United Nations force to liberate Kuwait
from Iraqi occupation)

Notes

CHAPTER ONE

1. D.J.V. Fisher, *The Anglo-Saxon Age, c. 400–1042* (London: Longman, 1973); H.P.R. Finberg, *The Formation of England, 550–1042* (London: Paladin, 1974).
2. The Normans were themselves of Viking origin, having settled in France early in the tenth century.
3. M.T. Clanchy, *England and its Rulers, 1066–1272* (London: Fontana, 1983); Anthony Tuck, *Crown and Nobility, 1272–1461* (London: Fontana, 1985).
4. Arthur first appeared in Geoffrey of Monmouth's Latin *History of the Kings of Britain* (*c.*1138). The great irony is that if Arthur existed, he must have been a Celtic Briton of the fifth or sixth centuries fighting the Saxon invaders whose eventual triumph led to the formation of the English Kingdom!
5. For the role of Protestantism in shaping the national consciousness, see Patrick Collinson, *The Birthpangs of Protestant England* (London: Macmillan, 1988). Some Catholic historians, on the other hand, have argued for the strength of popular allegiance to the old religion: Eamonn Duffy, *The Stripping of the Altars: Traditional Religion in England, c. 1400–1580* (New Haven, CN, and London: Yale University Press, 1992).
6. John Guy, *Tudor England* (Oxford: Oxford University Press, 1988); Penry Williams, *The Later Tudors: England, 1547–1603* (Oxford: Clarendon Press, 1995); Alan G.R. Smith, *The Emergence of a Nation State, 1529–1660* (London: Longman, 1995).
7. Principally, *On the Laws and Customs of England* (in Latin).
8. R.G. Davies and J.H. Denton (eds), *The English Parliament in the Middle Ages* (Manchester: Manchester University Press, 1981).
9. The anniversary of Elizabeth I's accession to the throne (17 November) also remained an important date in the calendar of national celebrations well into the eighteenth century.

10. It should be noted that English attempts to gain control over Ireland were also taking place from the twelfth century onwards.
11. John Davies, *A History of Wales* (London: Penguin, 1994).
12. Gaelic, from which Irish and Scottish is derived, is a separate branch of the Celtic language from British, out of which the Welsh, Cornish and Breton languages evolved.
13. J.D. Mackie, *A History of Scotland* (London: Penguin, rev. edn., 1991).
14. Margaret, who married James IV of Scotland in 1503.
15. Barry Coward, *The Stuart Age* (London: Longman, 1994); Mark Kishlansky, *A Monarchy Transformed: Britain 1603–1714* (London: Penguin, 1996).
16. Keith M. Brown, *Kingdom or Province? Scotland and the Regal Union, 1603–1715* (London: Macmillan, 1993).
17. Derek Hirst, *Authority and Conflict: England 1603–1658* (London: Arnold, 1986); Ann Hughes, *The Causes of the English Civil War* (London: Macmillan, 2nd edn., 1998).
18. J.G.A. Pocock, *The Ancient Constitution and the Feudal Law* (Cambridge: Cambridge University Press, 2nd edn., 1987); R.J. Smith, *The Gothic Bequest: Medieval Institutions in British Thought, 1688–1863* (Cambridge: Cambridge University Press, 1987).
19. Charles had no children from his marriage to Catherine of Braganza, although he had numerous illegitimate offspring.
20. Tim Harris, *Politics under the later Stuarts* (London: Longman, 1993); J.R. Jones, *Country and Court: England 1658–1714* (London: Arnold, 1978).
21. Whig was a Scottish term for an insurgent, Tory an Irish name for an outlaw.
22. These were radical Protestant groups, emerging in the seventeenth century, which dissented from the organisation and forms of worship of the Church of England. They included Quakers, Baptists, Independents and Unitarians.

CHAPTER TWO

1. There are obvious similarities here with the situation in the reign of William III.
2. J.H. Plumb, *The Growth of Political Stability, 1675–1725* (London: Penguin, 1969); Jeremy Black (ed.), *Britain in the Age of Walpole* (London: Macmillan, 1984); Jeremy Black, *Robert Walpole and the Nature of Politics in Early Eighteenth-Century Britain* (London: Macmillan, 1990).
3. Nicholas Rogers, *Whigs and Cities: Popular Politics in the Age of Walpole and Pitt* (Oxford: Clarendon Press, 1989), deals with the very large constituencies.
4. Notably Paul Monod, *Jacobitism and the English People, 1688–1788* (Cambridge: Cambridge University Press, 1989). For a general survey of the phenomenon, see Murray Pittock, *Jacobitism* (London: Macmillan, 1998).

5. Kathleen Wilson, *The Sense of the People: Politics, Culture and Imperialism in England, 1715–1785* (Cambridge: Cambridge University Press, 1995).

6. Marie Peters, *Pitt and Popularity: The Patriot Minister and London Opinion during the Seven Years War* (Oxford: Clarendon Press, 1980), and *The Elder Pitt* (London: Longman, 1998).

7. Peter Thomas, *John Wilkes: A Friend to Liberty* (Oxford: Clarendon Press, 1996). Wilkes sought the reform of abuses, not the overthrow of the constitution, and he was later to deplore the French Revolution.

8. Linda Colley, *Britons: Forging the Nation, 1707–1837* is of seminal importance for this point and for the remainder of this chapter.

9. J.V. Beckett, *The Aristocracy in England, 1660–1914* (Oxford: Blackwell, 1986).

10. John Brooke, *King George III* (London: Constable, 1972).

11. Peter Thomas, *Lord North* (London: Allen Lane, 1976). North's was a courtesy title held by virtue of the fact that he was the heir to an earldom. He sat in the House of Commons throughout the period of his premiership.

12. H.T. Dickinson (ed.), *Britain and the American Revolution* (London: Longman, 1998).

13. Thanks to a cynical alliance between the Whig leader, Charles James Fox, and his old adversary, North, which shocked many contemporaries. For what follows, see John Derry, *Politics in the Age of Fox, Pitt and Liverpool* (London: Macmillan, 1990).

14. H.T. Dickinson (ed.), *Britain and the French Revolution, 1789–1815* (London: Macmillan, 1989).

15. Notably by Colley, *Britons*, chapters 5–7.

16. J.C.D. Clark, *English Society, 1688–1832* (Cambridge: Cambridge University Press, 1985). Such anglocentricity is apparent in other titles referred to in this section.

17. See the exchange between Clark and Joanna Innes in *Past and Present* (1987), cxv, pp. 165–200, cxvii, pp. 195–207.

18. A.D. Gilbert, *Religion and Society in Industrial England, 1740–1914* (London: Longman, 1976); William Gibson, *Church, State and Society, 1760–1850* (London: Macmillan, 1994).

19. John Cannon, *Aristocratic Century: The Peerage of Eighteenth-Century England* (Cambridge: Cambridge University Press, 1984). Presumably Cannon's argument would be equally applicable to Scotland.

20. For a classic statement of this view, see Harold Perkin, *The Rise of Modern English Society, 1780–1880* (London: Routledge and Kegan Paul, 1969), pp. 61–2.

21. John Brewer, *The Sinews of Power: War, Money and the English State, 1688–1783* (London: Unwin Hyman, 1989).

22. Paul Langford, *A Polite and Commercial People: England, 1727–1783* (Oxford: Clarendon Press, 1989), and *Public Life and the Propertied Englishman, 1689–1798* (Oxford: Clarendon Press, 1991).

23. Frank O'Gorman, *Voters, Patrons and Parties: The Unreformed Electorate of Hanoverian England, 1734–1832* (Oxford: Clarendon Press, 1989).
24. See Ian R. Christie, *Stress and Stability in Late Eighteenth-Century Britain: Reflections on the British Avoidance of Revolution* (Oxford: Clarendon Press, 1984).

CHAPTER THREE

1. M.W. Flinn, *The Origins of the Industrial Revolution* (London: Longman, 1966), is a good starting-point. Textbook accounts relevant for the whole of this section include: Peter Mathias, *The First Industrial Nation, 1700–1914* (London: Methuen, 2nd edn., 1983); Maxine Berg, *The Age of Manufactures, 1700–1820* (London: Routledge, 1994); John Rule, *The Vital Century, 1714–1815* (London: Longman, 1992), and M.J. Daunton, *Progress and Poverty, 1700–1850* (Oxford: Oxford University Press, 1995).
2. M.W. Flinn, *British Population Growth 1700–1850* (Macmillan: London, 1970); E.A. Wrigley and R.S. Schofield, *The Population History of England, 1541–1871* (London: Arnold, 1981).
3. Joan Thirsk (ed.), *The Agrarian History of England and Wales, Vol. V, 1640–1750 Vol. VI, 1750–1850* (Cambridge: Cambridge University Press, 1985, 1989).
4. B.R. Mitchell and Phyllis Deane, *Abstract of British Historical Statistics* (Cambridge: Cambridge University Press, 2nd edn., 1971).
5. N. McKendrick, J. Brewer and J.H. Plumb, *The Birth of a Consumer Society: The Commercialisation of Eighteenth Century England* (London: Europa, 1982).
6. R.G. Wilson and J.T. Ward (eds), *Land and Industry* (Newton Abbot: David and Charles, 1971).
7. R. Floud, K. Wachter and A. Gregory, *Height, Health and History: Nutritional Status in the United Kingdom, 1750–1980* (Cambridge: Cambridge University Press, 1990).
8. E.N. Williams (ed.), *The Eighteenth Century Constitution* (Cambridge: Cambridge University Press, 1960); Richard Pares, *King George III and the Politicians* (Oxford: Clarendon Press, 1953); Michael J. Turner, *British Politics in an Age of Reform* (Manchester: Manchester University Press, 1999).
9. Brian Hill, *The Early Parties and Politics in Britain, 1688–1832* (London: Macmillan, 1996).
10. Dror Wahrman, *Imagining the Middle Class: The Political Representation of Class in Britain, c. 1780–1840* (Cambridge: Cambridge University Press, 1995).
11. Frank O'Gorman, *Voters, Patrons and Parties: The Unreformed Electorate of Hanoverian England, 1734–1832* (Oxford: Clarendon Press, 1989), emphasises the continuity between the pre- and post-1832 electoral systems, whereas John A. Philips, *The Great Reform Bill in the Boroughs: English Electoral Behaviour 1818–1841*

(Oxford: Clarendon Press, 1992), based on eight case studies, presents a more varied picture, in which some constituencies were always fiercely partisan but others were only galvanised during the reform crisis of the early 1830s.

12. Hannah Barker, *Newspapers, Politics and English Society, 1695–1855* (London: Longman, 2000); Peter Jupp, *British Politics on the Eve of Reform* (London: Macmillan, 1998), pp. 331–57. Newspapers and journals were part of a much wider print culture including cartoons, squibs and almanacks.

13. J.R. Oldfield, *Popular Politics and British Anti-Slavery, 1787–1807* (Manchester: Manchester University Press, 1995); Clare Midgley, *Women against Slavery, 1780–1870* (London: Routledge, 1992).

14. Philip Harling, *The Waning of 'Old Corruption': The Politics of Economical Reform in Britain 1779–1846* (Oxford: Clarendon Press, 1996).

15. William Thomas, *The Philosophical Radicals* (Oxford: Clarendon Press, 1979).

16. Albert Goodwin, *The Friends of Liberty: The English Democratic Movement in the Age of the French Revolution* (London: Hutchinson, 1979); J. Ann Hone, *For the Cause of Truth: Radicalism in London, 1796–1821* (Oxford: Clarendon Press, 1982).

17. However, the main criticism of E.P. Thompson's *The Making of the English Working Class, 1760–1832* (London: Penguin, 1968), is that it relies heavily on evidence of militancy among artisan groups like handloom weavers and framework knitters, who were being driven to the wall by factory-based production methods. They represented a slowly dying force, acting out of desperation, rather than a dynamic new social class.

18. J.E. Cookson, *Lord Liverpool's Administration, 1815–22* (Edinburgh: Scottish Academic Press, 1975).

19. John Cannon, *Parliamentary Reform 1640–1832* (Cambridge: Cambridge University Press, 1973).

20. Norman Gash, *Politics in the Age of Peel* (Brighton: Harvester Press, 2nd edn., 1977); T.A. Jenkins, *Parliament, Party and Politics in Victorian Britain* (Manchester: Manchester University Press, 1996).

21. This observation has led to some tendentious claims about the detrimental effects on Britain's long-term economic development, notably by Martin J. Wiener, *English Culture and the Decline of the Industrial Spirit, 1850–1980* (Cambridge: Cambridge University Press, 1981). For an effective critique, see James Raven, 'British History and the Enterprise Culture', *Past and Present*, cxxiii (1989), pp. 178–204.

CHAPTER FOUR

1. Geoffrey Best, *Mid-Victorian Britain, 1851–75* (London: Fontana, 1979); Asa Briggs, *Victorian People: a Reassessment of Persons and Themes, 1851–67* (London: Penguin, 1965).

2. Edward Royle, *Chartism* (London: Longman, 3rd edn., 1996), provides an excellent introduction to the vast literature on this subject.

3. Norman McCord, *The Anti-Corn Law League* (London: Allen and Unwin, 1968).

4. Norman Gash, *Sir Robert Peel* (London: Longman, 2 vols, 1961–72); T.A. Jenkins, *Sir Robert Peel* (London: Macmillan, 1999).

5. Dating back to Adam Smith's *Inquiry into the Nature and Causes of the Wealth of Nations* (1776). Peel's Tory predecessors, Pitt and Liverpool, had both experimented with free-trade policies.

6. In fact, it is impossible to *prove* that free-trade policies brought about economic prosperity.

7. As in Leone Levi's *History of British Commerce* (1872). It should not be supposed from this that contemporaries were untroubled by some of the social consequences of 'progress', or unaware of the tension between capitalist practices and Christian values: see G.R. Searle, *Morality and the Market in Victorian Britain* (Oxford: Clarendon Press, 1998).

8. Owen Dudley Edwards, *Macaulay* (London: Weidenfeld and Nicholson, 1988); David Cannadine, *G.M. Trevelyan: A Life in History* (London: HarperCollins, 1992).

9. Owen Chadwick, *The Victorian Church* (London: A. & C. Black, 2 vols, 1966–70); Hugh Macleod, *Religion and the Working Classes in Nineteenth Century England* (London: Macmillan, 1984).

10. F.M.L. Thompson, *English Landed Society in the Nineteenth Century* (London: Routledge, 1963).

11. Hippolyte Taine, *Notes on England* (London: Caliban Books, 1995 edn., trans. E. Hyams).

12. G.R. Searle, *Entrepreneurial Politics in Mid-Victorian Britain* (Oxford: Oxford University Press, 1993).

13. W.D. Rubinstein, *Elites and the Wealthy in Modern Britain* (Brighton: Harvester, 1987).

14. F.M.L. Thompson, *The Rise of Respectable Society, 1830–1900*.

15. Sotheron's diary, 28–30 June 1838 with memorandum, Gloucestershire Record Office, D1571/F388.

16. This is not to deny that later generations of Labour leaders drew inspiration from Chartism.

17. Somerset Record Office, DD/SAS/TN 162/1. Taunton was one of many constituencies where corrupt practices continued to blight the electoral process, however.

18. Jonathan Parry, *The Rise and Fall of Liberal Government in Victorian Britain* (New Haven, CN, and London: Yale University Press, 1993); T.A. Jenkins, *The Liberal Ascendancy, 1830–1886* (London: Macmillan, 1994).

19. Mill's thinking had grown out of the utilitarian tradition of Jeremy Bentham. It is important to stress the extent to which the individualist creed in the nineteenth century represented a *radical* impulse.

20. Kingsley Martin, *The Triumph of Lord Palmerston* (London: Hutchinson, 2nd edn., 1963); E.D. Steele, *Palmerston and Liberalism, 1855–1865* (Cambridge: Cambridge University Press, 1991).

21. He was condemned for having bowed to French pressure to legislate against foreign revolutionaries living in exile in Britain, after an assassination attempt on the Emperor Napoleon III. On this occasion, Palmerston's fault was that he was not belligerent enough!

22. Recent biographies include H.C.G. Matthew, *Gladstone, 1809–98* (Oxford: Oxford University Press, 1998), and Richard Shannon, *Gladstone* (London: Penguin, 2 vols., 1999).

23. Robert Blake, *Disraeli* (London: Eyre and Spottiswoode, 1966); Robert Stewart, *The Foundation of the Conservative Party, 1830–67* (London: Longman, 1978); Richard Shannon, *The Age of Disraeli, 1868–1881* (London: Longman, 1992); T.A. Jenkins, *Disraeli and Victorian Conservatism* (London: Macmillan, 1996).

24. This was opposed by a group of dissident Liberals known as the Adullamites, of whom Robert Lowe was the most prominent, on the ground that working men were too ignorant or venal to be entrusted with the franchise. Nevertheless, the Adullamites later returned to the Liberal fold and Lowe held high office in Gladstone's first ministry.

CHAPTER FIVE

1. B.R. Mitchell and Phyllis Deane, *Abstract of British Historical Statistics* (Cambridge: Cambridge University Press, 2nd edn., 1971).

2. Food accounted for over fifty per cent of average household expenditure at this time, making the decline in prices especially significant.

3. David Cannadine, *The Decline and Fall of the British Aristocracy* (New Haven, CN, and London: Yale University Press, 1990).

4. Paul Kennedy, *The Rise of the Anglo-German Antagonism, 1860–1914* (London: Allen and Unwin, 1980).

5. R.A. Hyam, *Britain's Imperial Century, 1815–1914* (London: Macmillan, 2nd edn., 1992); Bernard Porter, *The Lion's Share: A Short History of British Imperialism, 1850–1995* (London: Longman, 3rd edn., 1996); Ronald Robinson and J.A. Gallagher, *Africa and the Victorians* (London: Macmillan, 1961), remains the classic study of the scramble for Africa.

6. A.P. Thornton, *The Imperial Idea and its Enemies* (London: Macmillan, 2nd edn., 1985).

7. David Cannadine, 'The Context, Performance and Meaning of Ritual: the British Monarchy and "the invention of tradition"', in E.J. Hobsbawm and T. Ranger (eds), *The Invention of Tradition* (Cambridge: Cambridge University Press, 1983).

8. J.M. Mackenzie, *Propaganda and Empire: The Manipulation of British Public Opinion, 1880–1960* (Manchester: Manchester University Press, 1984).

9. Lady Gwendolen Cecil, *Life of Robert, Marquess of Salisbury* (London: Hodder and Stoughton, 1921–32), iv, pp. 165–6.

10. Martin Pugh, *The Tories and the People, 1880–1935* (Oxford: Blackwell, 1985); Richard Shannon, *The Age of Salisbury, 1881–1902* (London: Longman, 1996).

11. Peter Marsh, *Joseph Chamberlain: Entrepreneur in Politics* (New Haven, CN, and London: Yale University Press, 1994).
12. J.L. Garvin and Julian Amery, *The Life of Joseph Chamberlain* (London: Macmillan 1932–69), vi, p. 472.
13. E.H.H. Green, *The Crisis of Conservatism, 1880–1914* (London: Routledge, 1995), is mainly concerned with economic issues in the Edwardian period.
14. Henry Pelling, *The Origins of the Labour Party, 1880–1900* (Oxford: Oxford University Press, 1965).
15. G.R. Searle, *The Liberal Party: Triumph and Disintegration, 1886–1929* (London: Macmillan, 1992).
16. Michael Freeden, *The New Liberalism* (Oxford: Clarendon Press, 1978); H.C.G. Matthew, *The Liberal Imperialists* (Oxford: Oxford University Press, 1973); G.R. Searle, *The Quest for National Efficiency* (Oxford: Blackwell, 1971).
17. Derek Fraser, *The Evolution of the British Welfare State* (London: Macmillan, 2nd edn., 1984); Bruce K. Murray, *The People's Budget 1909–10: Lloyd George and Liberal Politics* (Oxford: Clarendon Press, 1980).
18. Duncan Tanner, *Political Change and the Labour Party, 1900–1918* (Cambridge: Cambridge University Press, 1990).
19. The term 'Edwardian' is commonly extended to cover the early years of the reign of George V, 1910–14. Books on the period as a whole include Alan O'Day (ed.), *The Edwardian Age: Conflict and Stability, 1900–1914* (London: Macmillan, 1979); David Brooks, *The Age of Upheaval* (Manchester: Manchester University Press, 1995); and David Powell, *The Edwardian Crisis* (London: Macmillan, 1996).
20. Andrew Rosen, *Rise up Women!* (London: Routledge and Kegan Paul, 1974); David Morgan, *Suffragists and Liberals* (Oxford: Blackwell, 1975); Sandra Holton, *Feminism and Democracy, 1900–1918* (Cambridge: Cambridge University Press, 1987); Cheryl Law, *Suffrage and Power: The Women's Movement, 1918–1928* (London: Tauris, 1997).
21. Jane Lewis, *Women in England, 1870–1950* (Brighton: Harvester, 1984); Patricia Hollis, *Ladies Elect: Women in English Local Government, 1865–1914* (Oxford: Clarendon Press, 1987).
22. The point here is that if the Liberals had simply extended the franchise to women on the same terms as currently existed for men, i.e. votes for women *householders*, they risked advantaging their Unionist opponents since most of the new voters would have been widows and other women of independent property.
23. John Lovell, *British Trade Unions, 1875–1933* (London: Macmillan, 1977).
24. Patricia Jalland, *The Liberals and Ireland* (Brighton: Harvester Press, 1980).

CHAPTER SIX

1. Michael Howard, *The Continental Commitment* (London: Penguin, 1974); Zara Steiner, *Britain and the Origins of the First World War* (London: Macmillan, 1977).
2. Arthur Marwick, *The Deluge: British Society and the First World War* (London: Macmillan, 2nd edn., 1991).
3. Gerard J. DeGroot, *Blighty: British Society in the era of the Great War* (London: Longman, 1996). John Turner (ed.), *Britain and the First World War* (London: Unwin Hyman, 1988), is a useful collection of essays on various aspects of the war.
4. By this stage, they had reverted to their old name of Conservatives, Lloyd George's Irish settlement of 1921 having removed the Unionist issue from British politics.
5. G.R. Searle, *The Liberal Party: Triumph and Disintegration, 1886–1929* (London: Macmillan, 1992), provides an excellent introduction to the controversy. Notable contributions on different sides of the debate are Ross McKibbin, *The Evolution of the Labour Party, 1910–1924* (Oxford: Oxford University Press, 1974), and Duncan Tanner, *Political Change and the Labour Party, 1900–1918* (Cambridge: Cambridge University Press, 1990).
6. Martin Pugh, *The Making of Modern British Politics, 1867–1939* (Oxford: Blackwell, 2nd edn., 1993), p. 253.
7. David Marquand, *Ramsay MacDonald* (London: Jonathan Cape, 1977).
8. K.O. Morgan, *Consensus and Disunity: the Lloyd George Coalition Government, 1918–1922* (Oxford: Clarendon Press, 1979); G.R. Searle, *Corruption in British Politics, 1895–1930* (Oxford: Clarendon Press, 1987).
9. John Ramsden, *The Age of Balfour and Baldwin, 1902–1940* (London: Longman, 1978); Philip Williamson, *Stanley Baldwin: Conservative Leadership and National Values* (Cambridge: Cambridge University Press, 1999).
10. H.A. Clegg, *A History of British Trade Unions, 1911–1933* (Oxford: Clarendon Press, 1985).
11. Robert Skidelsky, *Politicians and the Slump* (London: Macmillan, 1967); Philip Williamson, *National Crisis and National Government, 1926–32* (Cambridge: Cambridge University Press, 1992).
12. Nick Smart, *The National Government, 1931–40* (London: Macmillan, 1999).
13. Andrew Thorpe (ed.), *The Failure of Political Extremism in inter-war Britain* (Exeter: Exeter University Press, 1989).
14. Robert Skidelsky, *Oswald Mosley* (London: Macmillan, 2nd edn., 1990).
15. For the revisionist view, see Chris Cook and John Stevenson, *Britain in the Depression: Society and Politics, 1929–39* (London: Longman, 1994), and Peter Dewey, *War and Progress: Britain 1914–1945*. Keith Laybourn, *Britain on the Breadline, 1918–1939* (London: Sutton, 1998), re-states the pessimist case.

16. Estimates of Chamberlain's policy vary considerably: John Charmley, *Chamberlain and the Lost Peace* (London: Hodder and Stoughton, 1989), is decidedly more sympathetic than R.A.C. Parker, *Chamberlain and Appeasement: British Policy and the Coming of the Second World War* (London: Macmillan, 1993).
17. Angus Calder, *The People's War* (London: Pimlico, 1992).
18. Paul Addison, *The Road to 1945: British Politics and the Second World War* (London: Pimlico, 1994); Harold L. Smith (ed.), *War and Social Change: British Society in the Second World War* (Manchester: Manchester University Press, 1986).
19. Nevertheless, S. Fielding, P. Thompson and N. Tiratsoo, *England Arise! The Labour Party and Popular Politics in the 1940s* (Manchester: Manchester University Press, 1995), find considerable evidence of apathy and indifference among working people.
20. Stephen Brooke, *Labour's War: The Labour Party and the Second World War* (Oxford: Clarendon Press, 1992); Kevin Jeffreys, *The Churchill Coalition and Wartime Politics, 1940–1945* (Manchester: Manchester University Press, 1991).
21. Dewey, *War and Progress*, p. 295.
22. John Charmley, *Churchill: End of Glory* (London: Hodder, 1993).
23. Angus Calder, *The Myth of the Blitz* (London: Pimlico, 1991).

CHAPTER SEVEN

1. B.W.E. Alford, *Britain in the World Economy Since 1880* (London: Longman, 1996), provides a long-term perspective.
2. David Reynolds, *Britannia Overruled: British Policy and World Power in the Twentieth Century* (London: Longman, 1991).
3. Paul Addison, *The Road to 1945: British Politics and the Second World War* (London: Pimlico, 1994); Harriet Jones and Michael Kandiah (eds), *The Myth of Consensus* (London: Macmillan, 1996).
4. K.O. Morgan, *Labour in Power, 1945–1951* (Oxford: Clarendon Press, 1984); Henry Pelling, *The Labour Governments, 1945–1951* (London: Macmillan, 1984).
5. Memorably depicted in the Ealing comedy film, *Passport to Pimlico* (1949), in which an area of London declares its independence from the rest of Britain and discards all of its bureaucratic restrictions.
6. John Ramsden, *The Age of Churchill and Eden, 1940–1957* (London: Longman, 1995), and *The Winds of Change: Macmillan to Heath, 1957–1975* (London: Longman, 1996).
7. Ben Pimlott, *Harold Wilson* (London: HarperCollins, 1992); R. Coopey, S. Fielding and N. Tiratsoo (eds), *The Wilson Governments, 1964–1970* (London: Pinter, 1993).
8. It was particularly damaging because the previous Labour government, in 1949, had also been forced to devalue the pound.
9. Among Labour activists, there was also much anger at the government's determination to retain nuclear weapons and the diplomatic support given to the USA over the war in Vietnam.

10. John Campbell, *Edward Heath* (London: Jonathan Cape, 1993); Stuart Ball and Anthony Seldon (eds), *The Heath Government, 1970–74* (London: Longman, 1996).
11. Belatedly confirmed by a referendum in 1975, which produced a two-to-one majority for remaining in the EEC.
12. K.O. Morgan, *Callaghan* (Oxford: Oxford University Press, 1997).
13. To date, the best studies of the Thatcher era are products of the 'higher journalism': Peter Jenkins, *Mrs Thatcher's Revolution* (London: Cape, 1987); Peter Riddell, *The Thatcher Era* (Oxford: Blackwell, 1991); Hugo Young, *One of Us* (London: Pan, 1993).
14. Thatcher defeated Michael Heseltine in the first ballot, but narrowly failed to achieve the majority required by the party rules for outright victory. She did not stand in the second ballot.
15. Anthony Seldon, *Major: A Political Life* (London: Weidenfeld and Nicholson, 1997).
16. The parties eventually amalgamated and adopted the name Liberal Democrats.
17. Jane Lewis, *Women in Britain since 1945* (Oxford: Blackwell, 1991).
18. This was by no means a new phenomenon: many Irish people and Eastern European Jews settled in Britain before 1945 and provoked similar hostile reactions from the indigenous population. Colin Holmes, *John Bull's Island: Immigration and British Society, 1871–1971* (London: Macmillan, 1988).
19. Set in context by K.O. Morgan, *Rebirth of a Nation: Wales 1880–1980* (Oxford: Oxford University Press, 1981), and Richard J. Finlay, *A Partnership for Good? Scottish Politics and the Union since 1880* (Edinburgh: John Donald, 1997).
20. Possibly there is a connection with the eruption of Catholic nationalism in Northern Ireland at around the same time.
21. John W. Young, *Britain and European Unity, 1945–92* (London: Macmillan, 1993).

Bibliography

See the chapter endnotes for specialist reading. Some of the books cited below obviously overlap slightly between centuries.

GENERAL AND REFERENCE

Cannon, J. (ed.) *The Oxford Companion to British History*. Oxford, Oxford University Press, 1997

Cook, C. and Stevenson, J. *The Longman Handbook of Modern British History, 1714–1995*. London, Longman, 1996

Gardiner, J. and Wenborn, N. *The History Today Companion to British History*. London, Collins and Brown, 1995

Morgan, K.O. (ed.) *The Oxford History of Britain*. Oxford, Oxford University Press, 1999

Palmer, A. and V. *The Chronology of British History*. London, Century Ltd, 1992

Ramsden, J. and Williams, G. *Ruling Britannia: A Political History of Britain 1688–1988*. London, Longman, 1990

Royle, E. *Modern Britain: A Social History 1750–1997*. London, Arnold, 1997

Thompson, F.M.L. (ed.) *The Cambridge Social History of Britain 1750–1950*. Cambridge, Cambridge University Press, 3 vols, 1990

EIGHTEENTH CENTURY

Black, J. *The Politics of Britain 1688–1800*. Manchester, Manchester University Press, 1993

Christie, I.R. *Wars and Revolutions: Britain 1760–1815*. London, Arnold, 1982

Colley, L. *Britons: Forging the Nation, 1707–1837*. New Haven, CN, and London, Yale University Press, 1992

Holmes, G. *The Making of a Great Power, 1660–1722*. London, Longman, 1993

Holmes, G. and Szechi, D. *The Age of Oligarchy, 1722–1783*. London, Longman, 1993

Hoppit, J. *A Land of Liberty? England 1689–1727*. Oxford, Clarendon Press, 2000

Jarrett, D. *England in the Age of Hogarth*. New Haven, CN, and London, Yale University Press, 1986

Langford, P. *A Polite and Commercial People: England 1727–1783*. Oxford, Clarendon Press, 1989

Murdoch, A. *British History 1660–1832: National Identity and Local Culture*. London, Macmillan, 1998

O'Gorman, F. *The Long Eighteenth Century: British Political and Social History 1688–1832*. London, Arnold, 1997

Porter, R. *English Society in the Eighteenth Century*. London, Penguin, 2nd edn., 1990

Prest, W. *Albion Ascendant: English History 1660–1815*. Oxford, Oxford University Press, 1998

Rule, J. *Albion's People: English Society 1714–1815*. London, Longman, 1992

Speck, W.A. *Stability and Strife: England 1714–1760*. London, Arnold, 1977

NINETEENTH CENTURY

Bentley, M. *Politics without Democracy 1815–1914*. Oxford, Blackwell, 2nd edn., 1996

Briggs, A. *The Age of Improvement 1783–1867*. London, Longman, 2nd edn., 2000

Evans, E.J. *The Forging of the Modern State, 1783–1870*. London, Longman, 2nd edn., 1996

Feuchtwanger, E.J. *Democracy and Empire: Britain 1865–1914*. London, Arnold, 1985

Gash, N. *Aristocracy and People: Britain 1815–1865*. London, Arnold, 1979

Harris, J. *Private Lives, Public Spirit: A Social History of Britain 1870–1914*. Oxford, Oxford University Press, 1993.

Hoppen, K.T. *The Mid-Victorian Generation 1846–1886*. Oxford, Clarendon Press, 1998

Matthew, H.C.G. (ed.) *Nineteenth Century Britain 1815–1901*. Oxford, Oxford University Press, 2000

McCord, N. *British History 1815–1906*. Oxford, Oxford University Press, 1991

Read, D. *The Age of Urban Democracy: England 1868–1914*. London, Longman, 2nd edn., 1994

Robbins, K. *Nineteenth-Century Britain: Integration and Diversity*. Oxford, Clarendon Press, 1988

Rubinstein, W.D. *Britain's Century: A Political and Social History 1815–1905*. London, Arnold, 1998

Thompson, F.M.L. *The Rise of Respectable Society, 1830–1900*. London, Fontana, 1988

TWENTIETH CENTURY

Beloff, M. *Wars and Welfare: Britain 1914–1945.* London, Arnold, 1984

Childs, D. *Britain since 1939: Progress and Decline.* London, Macmillan, 1995

Clarke, P. *Hope and Glory: Britain 1900–1990.* London, Penguin, 1996

Dewey, P. *War and Progress: Britain 1914–1945.* London, Longman, 1997

Johnson, P. (ed.), *Twentieth-Century Britain: Economic, Social and Cultural Change.* London, Longman, 1994

Lloyd, T.O. *Empire, Welfare State, Europe: English History 1906–1992.* Oxford, Oxford University Press, 1993

Marwick, A. *British Society since 1945.* London, Penguin, 3rd edn., 1996

McKibbin, R. *Classes and Cultures: England 1918–1951.* Oxford, Oxford University Press, 1998

Morgan, K.O. *The People's Peace: British History 1945–1989.* Oxford, Oxford University Press, 1990

Perkin, H. *The Rise of Professional Society: England since 1880.* London, Routledge, 1989

Pugh, M. *State and Society: British Political and Social History 1870–1997.* London, Arnold, 1999

Robbins, K. *The Eclipse of a Great Power, 1870–1992.* London, Longman, 1994

Sked, A. and Cook, C. *Post-War Britain 1945–1992.* London, Penguin, 1993

Stevenson, J. *British Society 1914–1945.* London, Penguin, 1984

Index